THE GROWTH OF A SUPERPOWER

America from 1945 to Today

DOCUMENTING AMERICA
THE PRIMARY SOURCE DOCUMENTS OF A NATION

THE GROWTH OF A SUPERPOWER

America from 1945 to Today

EDITED BY JEFF WALLENFELDT, MANAGER, GEOGRAPHY AND HISTORY

Educational Publishing

IN ASSOCIATION WITH

EDUCATIONAL SERVICES

Published in 2013 by Britannica Educational Publishing
(a trademark of Encyclopædia Britannica, Inc.)
in association with Rosen Educational Services, LLC
29 East 21st Street, New York, NY 10010.

Distributed exclusively by Rosen Educational Services.
For a listing of additional Britannica Educational Publishing titles, call toll free (800) 237-9932.

First Edition

Britannica Educational Publishing
J.E. Luebering, Senior Manager
Adam Augustyn, Assistant Manager
Marilyn L. Barton: Senior Coordinator, Production Control
Steven Bosco: Director, Editorial Technologies
Lisa S. Braucher: Senior Producer and Data Editor
Yvette Charboneau: Senior Copy Editor
Kathy Nakamura: Manager, Media Acquisition
Jeff Wallenfeldt: Manager, Geography and History

Rosen Educational Services
Shalini Saxena: Editor
Nelson Sá: Art Director
Cindy Reiman: Photography Manager
Brian Garvey: Designer, Cover Design
Introduction by Jeff Wallenfeldt

Library of Congress Cataloging-in-Publication Data

The growth of a superpower: America from 1945 to today/edited by Jeff Wallenfeldt.—1st ed.
    p. cm.—(Documenting america: the primary source documents of a nation)
Includes bibliographical references and index.
ISBN 978-1-61530-699-2 (library binding)
1. United States—History—1945–Sources. 2. United States—Foreign relations—1945-1989—
Sources. 3. United States—Foreign relations—1989—Sources. I. Wallenfeldt, Jeffrey H.
E838.3.G76 2013
973.91—dc23

2012008498

Manufactured in the United States of America

On the cover: (main): An MQ-9 Reaper lands at Joint Base in Balad, Iraq, in 2008. The
MQ-9 Reaper is one of the unmanned aerial vehicles (UAVs) used by the U.S. Air Force and
other divisions of the armed forces for its hunt-and-kill capabilities as well as its usefulness in
intelligence gathering. *U.S. Air Force photo/Tech. Sgt. Erik Gudmundson*

On the cover (document): Detail of the Marshall Plan. *U.S. National Archives and Records
Administration*

On page x: U.S. Pres. Richard Nixon *(left)* meeting with Communist Party leader Leonid
Brezhnev in 1972 during his historic visit to Moscow. The trip signalled a slight relaxation
of Cold War tensions between the United States and the Soviet Union, which had coloured
international relations since the end of WWII, and was a foreign policy triumph for the
president. © *AP Images*

On pages 1, 12, 21, 37, 45, 53, 65, 74, 83: A flower rests on a panel at the National
September 11 Memorial in New York City, which honours over 3,000 individuals whose lives
were tragically lost as a result of the terrorist attacks on the World Trade Center and the
Pentagon as well as those who perished after the crash of a hijacked plane in Pennsylvania.
Getty Images

CONTENTS

7

13

15

46

50

5

CHAPTER 7: "IT'S THE ECONOMY, STUPID": THE BILL CLINTON ADMINISTRATION 65

CHAPTER 8: AMERICA AFTER 9-11: THE GEORGE W. BUSH ADMINISTRATION 74

CHAPTER 9: "YES WE CAN": THE BARACK OBAMA ADMINISTRATION 83

81

92

Hero or villain? Profile in courage or scandal? Often virtue is in the eye of the beholder, and how we see history's actors and actions depends on our perspective. For most Americans the name Benedict Arnold is synonymous with *traitor*. Yet sequestered in the Saratoga National Historical Park in upstate New York is a marble-slab monument adorned with a bas-relief cannon, boot, wreath, and epaulet on one side and these words on the other:

In memory of
the "most brilliant soldier" of the
Continental Army,
who was desperately wounded
on this spot, the sally port of
BURGOYNES "GREAT
(WESTERN) REDOUBT"
7th October 1777,
winning for his countrymen
the Decisive Battle of the
American Revolution
and for himself the rank of
Major General

Before he sold out his country, Benedict Arnold was one of its greatest heroes, and, nameless, this memorial celebrates his valour without losing sight of his perfidy, or his humanity—depending upon how you look at it and how well you know his story.

It is a matter of perspective.

Like Benedict Arnold, the name Richard Nixon provokes, and has always provoked, strong associations and responses. For the millions of Americans who elected him president in 1968 and again in 1972, his "silent majority," Nixon was a champion of law and order. For liberals and leftists, he was "Tricky Dick," whose penchant for deceit and dishonour was as boundless as his ambition. Few individuals were more central to the drama of American history in the second half of the 20th century than Nixon. Before serving as Dwight D. Eisenhower's vice president, Nixon, as a congressman and senator from California, came to national prominence as a militant anticommunist who doggedly pursued Alger Hiss as a member of the House Un-American Activities Committee. As president, he continued America's ill-fated war in Vietnam against the communist Viet Cong and North Vietnamese. Ironically, it was through Nixon's policy of détente, or engagement, with the America's two great Cold War communist nemeses, China and the Soviet Union, that he arguably had his greatest impact on world history. Returning from a triumphant summit in Moscow in 1972, Nixon, a Republican, told a joint session of Congress that the Basic Principles of Mutual Relations between the United States and the U.S.S.R that he had signed were predicated on "the recognition that two nuclear nations, each of which has the power to destroy humanity, have no alternative but to coexist peacefully, because in a nuclear war there would be no winners, only losers."

But if Nixon's greatest contribution to international affairs was his efforts to diffuse tensions between the United States, the Soviet Union, and "Red" China, his lasting impact on American history was the infamy of the Watergate scandal, which nearly brought about his impeachment, led to his resignation of the presidency in disgrace, and resulted in a crisis in confidence that cast a shadow over the American political system for decades. Yet it was at the nadir of his political fortunes—with the misdeeds of all the president's men exposed and his complicity no longer in doubt—that Nixon may have been at his most sympathetic and eloquent as he said good-bye to the White House staff:

We want you to be proud of what you have done. We want you to continue to serve in Government, if that is your wish. Always give your best, never get discouraged, never be petty; always remember others may hate you, but those who hate you don't win unless you hate them, and then you destroy yourself.

American history is often more complex than it first appears. Good and evil are frequently intertwined. Truth is illusive. There is no better way to try to comprehend the complexity of American history than through the unadulterated words—written or spoken—of those who lived and shaped it. This volume offers both a selection of primary source documents and a narrative historical survey that describes the events, issues, individuals, and groups that were central to the period between the middle of the 20th century and the

present. When the primary source documents are short, they are presented whole with the running text of the narrative; more often, excerpts are provided that give a flavour of the document, which is presented more fully in the Appendix. Specific introductions for each document provide additional context, but it remains for the reader to make sense of the ideas and opinions contained in the documents and to draw his or her own conclusions regarding the post–World War II history of the United States.

The story begins not in the United States but in Europe, where, in the wake of the war, the clash of ideology between capitalism and communism left Turkey threatened by Soviet expansionist goals and Greece engulfed in civil war. Weakened by World War II and struggling economically, the British were no longer able to defend the Greek government against the communist rebellion aided by Albania, Bulgaria, and Yugoslavia. In 1947 U.S. Pres. Harry Truman, a Democrat, reacted by outlining what became known as the Truman Doctrine, promising economic and financial aid to Greece and Turkey and establishing the policy of the United States "to support free peoples who are resisting attempted subjugation by armed minorities or by outside pressures." In articulating this policy of "containment" of Soviet geopolitical ambitions, Truman said, "The seeds of totalitarian regimes are nurtured by misery and want....They reach their full growth when the hope of a people for a better life has died. We must keep that hope alive." Toward this end and recognizing the precarious nature of western Europe's war-ravaged economy, the United States extended economic aid through the European Recovery Program (better known as the Marshall Plan), a policy that Secretary of State George C. Mashall said was "directed not against any country or doctrine but against hunger, poverty, desperation, and chaos. Its purpose...the revival of a working economy in the world so as to permit the emergence of political and social conditions in which free institutions can exist."

In the United States the fear of communist infiltration of American life resulted in a growing "Red Scare," the flames of which were fanned principally by Sen. Joseph McCarthy, a Republican from Wisconsin, who conducted hearings to root out communists that he claimed had infested the State Department. The paranoid era of McCarthyism began in 1950 with a speech in which McCarthy announced the beginning of "a moral uprising" that would end "only when the whole sorry mess of twisted, warped thinkers are swept from the national scene so that we may have a new birth of national honesty and decency in government." In fact it ended with a Senate censure of McCarthy.

In general the 1950s in the United States was a prosperous period presided over for two presidential terms by Republican Eisenhower, who oversaw the termination of hostilities in another Cold War conflict, the Korean War (1950-53), prevented the Soviet invasion of Hungary from exploding into a wider war,

and helped bring about the withdrawal of British, French, and Israeli forces from Egypt to bring to an end the Suez Crisis. "Should a nation which attacks and occupies foreign territory in the face of United Nations disapproval be allowed to impose conditions on its withdrawal?" Eisenhower asked before answering, "If we agree that armed attack can properly achieve the purposes of the assailant, then I fear we will have turned back the clock of international order." Eisenhower's America is often characterized as a place of great conformity and complacency, but it was anything but that for African Americans engaged in the burgeoning civil rights struggle or for the bohemian Beat refugees from middle-class comfort. Even Eisenhower in his farewell address in 1961 warned against "the acquisition of unwarranted influence...by the military-industrial complex," cautioning that "Only an alert and knowledgeable citizenry can compel the proper meshing of the huge industrial and military machinery of defense with our peaceful methods and goals so that security and liberty may prosper together."

John F. Kennedy, the charismatic Democrat from Massachusetts who succeeded Eisenhower, invigorated many, especially the young, with his promise to lead the country to a New Frontier. In his inaugural address he famously challenged Americans to "ask not what your country can do for you—ask what you can do for your country." Kennedy had written (though probably not alone) the Pulitzer Prize–winning *Profiles in Courage* (1956) and while he was in the White House, the film *P.T. 109* (1963), depicting his own heroism during World War II, was released. But perhaps a more telling profile of the young president's courage was the Cuban Missile Crisis in 1962, when he demanded the withdrawal of Soviet missiles from Cuba, calling upon Soviet leader Nikita Khrushchev to "halt and eliminate this clandestine, reckless, and provocative threat to world peace" and "to move the world back from the abyss of destruction."

When Kennedy was assassinated in November 1963, suffusing the nation with sorrow, Vice Pres. Lyndon B. Johnson assumed the presidency. As the civil rights movement, led most prominently by the Rev. Martin Luther King, Jr., pushed issues of access and equity to the top of the national agenda, Johnson dramatically extended Kennedy's efforts at social reform. He oversaw the enactment of the Civil Rights (1964) and Voting Rights (1965) acts, declared a War on Poverty, and employed "creative federalism" to undertake programs in the cities, countryside, and classrooms aimed at building a "Great Society" in which "the demands of morality and the needs of spirit" could be "realized in the life of the nation." Johnson, however, also greatly expanded Kennedy's commitment to support South Vietnam, and the growing unpopularity of the Vietnam War ultimately undid his presidency. On the same night that he declared a cessation of bombing of North Vietnam in the hope of hastening the war's end, he also announced, "I shall not seek and I will not accept the nomination of my party for another term as your President."

America in the 1960s and '70s was in tumult. A huge gap in values and understanding had opened between the "Greatest Generation" of World War II and their "Baby Boom" children, who were as engaged in a social and sexual revolution as they were in the civil rights and antiwar movements. It was against this backdrop that the Watergate scandal unfolded, in which the break-in at the Democratic National Committee's office and subsequent cover-up efforts brought about the downfall of Nixon.

Democrat Jimmy Carter, the little-known former governor of Georgia who defeated Nixon's replacement as president, Gerald Ford, in the 1976 presidential election, came into office hoping to restore trust in government. Although he masterfully negotiated the Camp David peace accords between Israel and Egypt, his one-term presidency was widely considered a failure, undermined by the taking of American hostages in Iran and by inflation and unemployment at home. But what some saw as weakness and defeatism in Carter, others came to believe was foresight, with his so-called Malaise Speech the ultimate litmus test.

In 1980 Republican Ronald Reagan swept Carter out of—and neoconservatism into—the White House, deeply altering the political culture of the country in the process. A committed supply-side free marketeer and staunch anticommunist who wore sunny optimism on his sleeve, Reagan sought to make government smaller and the military more powerful. "Death and taxes may be inevitable, but unjust taxes are not," Reagan said in 1985, pointing to the "gathering force" of what he called a second American revolution "born of popular resentment against a tax system that is unwise, unwanted, and unfair." Reagan's massive military buildup is given credit by many for having brought concessions from reformist Soviet leader Mikhail Gorbachev at the nuclear-arms negotiating table. But regardless of whether Reagan's policies or the implosion of its own was more responsible for the demise of the Soviet Union and bloc, there is no denying the force of Reagan's words at the Brandenburg Gate in 1987, when he called on Gorbachev to prove his commitment to liberalization by tearing down the Berlin Wall. The Reagan administration was less successful in its efforts to undermine leftist regimes in Central America, but if the Iran-Contra affair tarnished the reputation of the "Great Communicator" (so-named because of his tremendous ability to convey his vision), it failed to prevent Reagan from becoming the enduring guiding spirit of American conservatism.

Less adept at the "vision thing" was George H.W. Bush, Reagan's vice president and successor. As president, Bush oversaw the successful multinational effort to expel Iraq from Kuwait in the Persian Gulf War in 1991, which he characterized as an historic opportunity "to forge for ourselves and for future generations a new world order—a world where the rule of law, not the rule of the jungle, governs the conduct of nations." Bush, however, was bedeviled by a sluggish economy and lost the 1992 election to Bill Clinton, the Democratic governor of Arkansas, who came into office promising himself and his accomplished wife, Hillary, as a two-for-one package. Indeed, he gave her responsibility for spearheading his administration's efforts to reform health care. The first lady sought an "American solution for an American problem by creating an American health care system that works for America" by providing quality and choice. Lacking the necessary support for enactment, however, the plan died on the vine without ever coming to vote. The 1994 mid-term elections brought a Republican majority to the House with a promise to fulfill their Contract with America, but Clinton skillfully rallied to win reelection in 1996. His second term, however, fell victim to a scandal arising from his affair with a White House intern that was at the centre of a report authored by independent counsel Ken Starr. Clinton was impeached by the House but acquitted by the Senate. Under Clinton's watch the economy had maintained one of the longest periods of continuous growth in American history, and the national deficit had become a surplus.

Clinton's vice president, Al Gore, the Democratic presidential candidate in 2000, won the national popular vote by some 500,000 votes but lost the controversial election to Republican Texas Gov. George W. Bush (son of George H.W. Bush) as a consequence of a U.S. Supreme Court decision regarding the electoral results in Florida. Bush found himself president of a deeply politically divided country that was shocked by the Sept. 11, 2001, terrorist attacks by Islamist radicals that left some 3,000 dead in New York City, Washington, D.C., and Pennsylvania. "Tonight we are a country awakened to danger and called to defend freedom. Our grief has turned to anger, and anger to resolution. Whether we bring our enemies to justice, or bring justice to our enemies, justice will be done," Bush pledged in an address to a joint session of Congress that became known as the Declaration of War on Terrorism.

The United States and Britain (aided later by other NATO allies) invaded Afghanistan, where the Taliban government provided sanctuary for the al-Qaeda terrorist network that was responsible for the September 11 attacks. The Afghanistan War was still in full swing when the Bush administration shifted its focus to Iraq, which Bush officials claimed possessed weapons of mass destruction and inferred was connected with the September 11 attacks (though neither claim was ultimately substantiated). The United States, supported primarily by Britain, invaded Iraq and deposed its longtime despotic ruler Saddam Hussein but became embroiled in a long-running

war with insurgents. That conflict grew unpopular enough at home to be criticized even by some of those who had been strong supporters of the initial incursion, such as Conservative Democratic Rep. John Murtha of Pennsylvania, though Bush maintained enough support to be re-elected in 2004.

Four years later the story was different, as Sen. Barack Obama, a Democrat, became the first African American to be elected president, riding into office on a pledge to change Washington. Even before he took office, he faced the challenge of the financial and economic collapse that became known as the Great Recession. Having proclaimed "an end to the petty grievances and false promises, the recriminations and worn-out dogmas, that for far too long have strangled our politics," Obama concluded his inaugural address by saying "With hope and virtue, let us brave once more the icy currents, and endure what storms may come. Let it be said by our children's children that when we were tested we refused to let this journey end, that we did not turn back nor did we falter; and with eyes fixed on the horizon and God's grace upon us, we carried forth that great gift of freedom and delivered it safely to future generations."

CHAPTER 1

"THE BUCK STOPS HERE!": THE HARRY TRUMAN ADMINISTRATION

U.S. Pres. Franklin D. Roosevelt died suddenly of a cerebral hemorrhage on April 12, 1945, shocking both the public and Harry S. Truman, who had replaced Roosevelt's previous vice president, Henry A. Wallace, on the victorious 1944 Democratic ticket. Truman's term as vice president had lasted just 82 days, during which time he met with the president only twice. Roosevelt, who apparently did not realize how ill he was, made little effort to inform Truman about the administration's programs and plans, nor did he prepare Truman for dealing with the heavy responsibilities that were about to devolve upon him. The day after taking the presidential oath of office, Truman told reporters that he felt as if "the moon, the stars, and all the planets had fallen" on him and asked them to pray for him. He was hardly, however, as scholars have noted, a political naïf. History would remember him as man thrust into leadership at a critical time in the life of his country who fully embraced his responsibility (as a sign on his desk read, "The Buck Stops Here!").

THE TRUMAN DOCTRINE AND CONTAINMENT

Nevertheless, Truman had been chosen as vice president for domestic political reasons and had no experience of foreign affairs. His first decisions were dictated by events or plans already laid. In July, two months after the German forces surrendered, he met at Potsdam, Ger., with Soviet leader Joseph Stalin and British Prime Minister Winston Churchill (who was succeeded at the conference by Clement Attlee) to discuss future operations against Japan and a peace settlement for Europe. Little was accomplished, and there would not be another meeting between Soviet and American heads of state for 10 years.

Hopes that good relations between the superpowers would ensure world peace soon faded as a result of the Stalinization of eastern Europe and

Potsdam Conference, with U.S. Pres. Harry S. Truman (centre), flanked by Soviet Premier Joseph Stalin (left), and British Prime Minister Winston Churchill (right), near Berlin, Ger., July 1945. U.S. Army Photo

Soviet support of communist insurgencies in various parts of the globe. Events came to a head in 1947 when Britain, weakened by a failing economy, decided to pull out of the eastern Mediterranean. This would leave both Greece, where a communist-inspired civil war was raging, and Turkey to the mercies of the Soviet Union. Truman now came into his own as a national leader, asking Congress to appropriate aid to Greece and Turkey and asserting, in effect, that henceforth the United States must help free peoples in general to resist communist aggression. This policy, known as the Truman Doctrine, has been criticized for committing the United States to the support of unworthy regimes and for taking on greater burdens than it was safe to assume. At first, however, the Truman

Document: Harry S. Truman: The Truman Doctrine (1947)

Throughout 1946, communist forces, supported by the Soviet satellite states of Bulgaria, Yugoslavia, and Albania, carried on a full-scale guerrilla war against the Greek government. At the same time the U.S.S.R. demanded from Turkey the right to establish bases and the surrender of Turkish territory at the eastern end of the Black Sea. Soviet expansionism threatened not only the Mediterranean but the oil-rich Middle East. The civil war in Greece had reached a critical stage when Great Britain informed the United States on Feb. 24, 1947, that it could no longer give aid to the Greek government. President Truman was advised by military experts that Greece might fall to the communists unless American aid was immediately forthcoming. Despite anticipated opposition from Congress, Truman decided to commit the United States to the defense of Greece and Turkey. On March 12, before a joint session of Congress, he set forth what became known as the Truman Doctrine. The doctrine marked the reversal of American foreign policy, from cooperation with the Soviet Union to "containment" of Soviet power.

The gravity of the situation which confronts the world today necessitates my appearance before a joint session of the Congress. The foreign policy and the national security of this country are involved.

One aspect of the present situation which I wish to present to you at this time for your consideration and decision concerns Greece and Turkey. The United States has received from the Greek government an urgent appeal for financial and economic assistance. Preliminary reports from the American economic mission now in Greece and reports from the American ambassador in Greece corroborate the statement of the Greek government that assistance is imperative if Greece is to survive as a free nation.

I do not believe that the American people and the Congress wish to turn a deaf ear to the appeal of the Greek government.

Greece is not a rich country. Lack of sufficient natural resources has always forced the Greek people to work hard to make both ends meet. Since 1940, this industrious and peace-loving country has suffered invasion, four years of cruel enemy occupation, and bitter internal strife....

Doctrine was narrowly applied. Congress appropriated $400 million for Greece and Turkey, saving both from falling into unfriendly hands, and thereafter the United States relied mainly on economic assistance to support its foreign policy.

The keystone of this policy, and its greatest success, was the European Recovery Program, usually called the Marshall Plan. Europe's economy had failed to recover after the war, its paralysis being worsened by the exceptionally severe winter of 1946–47. Thus, in June 1947 Secretary of State George C. Marshall proposed the greatest foreign-aid program in world history in order to bring Europe back to economic health. In 1948 Congress created the Economic

Document: George C. Marshall: The Marshall Plan (1947)

The Truman Doctrine successfully checked the spread of Soviet expansion in the Mediterranean and the Middle East, but the future of western Europe remained in jeopardy. World War II had devastated its economy and widespread popular discontent was fomented by communist propaganda, both from within and without. Of the four great European powers before the war (Germany, France, Britain, and the U.S.S.R.), only the Soviet Union remained a power in Europe. As the economic and political situation deteriorated, the United States deemed it necessary to bolster the economic recovery of Europe in order to check the further spread of communism. In a commencement speech at Harvard University on June 5, 1947, Secretary of State Marshall outlined the principles of what was to become the European Recovery Program, popularly known as the Marshall Plan.

I need not tell you gentlemen that the world situation is very serious. That must be apparent to all intelligent people. I think one difficulty is that the problem is one of such enormous complexity that the very mass of facts presented to the public by press and radio make it exceedingly difficult for the man in the street to reach a clear appraisement of the situation. Furthermore, the people of this country are distant from the troubled areas of the earth and it is hard for them to comprehend the plight and consequent reactions of the long-suffering peoples, and the effect of those reactions on their governments in connection with our efforts to promote peace in the world.

In considering the requirements for the rehabilitation of Europe, the physical loss of life, the visible destruction of cities, factories, mines, and railroads was correctly estimated; but it has become obvious during recent months that this visible destruction was probably less serious than the dislocation of the entire fabric of European economy. For the past ten years conditions have been highly abnormal. The feverish preparation for war and the more feverish maintenance of the war effort engulfed all aspects of national economies. Machinery has fallen into disrepair or is entirely obsolete. Under the arbitrary and destructive Nazi rule, virtually every possible enterprise was geared into the German war machine. Long-standing commercial ties, private institutions, banks, insurance companies, and shipping companies disappeared through loss of capital, absorption through nationalization, or by simple destruction. In many countries, confidence in the local currency has been severely shaken....

Cooperation Administration and over the next five years poured some $13 billion worth of aid into western Europe. (Assistance was offered to Eastern-bloc countries also, but they were forced by Stalin to decline.) The plan restored economic vitality and confidence to the region, while undermining the local communist parties. In 1949 Truman proposed extending similar aid to underdeveloped countries throughout the world, but the resulting Point Four Program was less successful than the Marshall Plan. Experience showed that it was easier to rebuild a modern industrial economy than to develop one from scratch.

The ideological battle between the United States and the Soviet Union that would mark the Cold War had begun, and U.S. policy for limiting Soviet expansion had developed with remarkable speed. Soon after the collapse of hopes for world peace in 1945 and 1946, the Truman administration had accepted the danger posed by Soviet aggression and resolved to shore up noncommunist defenses at their most critical points. This policy, known as containment, a term suggested by its principal framer, George Kennan, resulted in the Truman Doctrine and the Marshall Plan, as well as in the decision to make the western zones of Germany (later West Germany) a pillar of strength. When the Soviet Union countered this development in June 1948 by blocking all surface routes into the western-occupied zones of Berlin, Britain and the United States supplied the sectors by air for almost a year until the Soviet Union

called off the blockade. A logical culmination of U.S. policy was the creation in 1949 of the North Atlantic Treaty Organization (NATO), a military alliance among 12 countries to resist Soviet aggression. (NATO would outlast the Soviet Union and, by 2009, swell to 28 countries.)

Containment worked less well in Asia. In December 1945 Truman sent General Marshall to China with instructions to work out an agreement between the communist rebels and the Nationalist government of Chiang Kai-shek. This was an impossible task, and in the subsequent fighting Mao Zedong's communist forces prevailed. The Nationalist government fled to Taiwan in 1949, and the United States then decided to concentrate its East Asian policy upon strengthening occupied Japan, with much better results.

POSTWAR DOMESTIC REORGANIZATION

After the end of World War II the vast U.S. military establishment was dismantled, its strength falling from 12 million men and women to about 1.5 million in 1947. The navy and army air forces remained the world's strongest, however, and the U.S. monopoly of atomic weapons seemed to ensure security. In 1946 the United States formed an Atomic Energy Commission for purposes of research and development. The armed forces were reorganized under a secretary of defense by the National Security Act of 1947, which also created the U.S. Air Force as an independent service. In 1949 the services were brought together in a single Department of Defense, though each retained considerable autonomy. In that same year the Soviet Union exploded its own atomic device, opening an era of intense nuclear, and soon thermonuclear, competition.

Peace brought with it new fears. Demobilizing the armed forces might result in massive unemployment and another depression. Or, conversely, the huge savings accumulated during the war could promote runaway inflation. The first anxiety proved groundless, even though government did little to ease the transition to a peacetime economy. War contracts were canceled, war agencies diminished or dissolved, and government-owned war plants sold to private parties. But, after laying off defense workers, manufacturers rapidly tooled up and began producing consumer goods in volume. The housing industry grew too, despite shortages of every kind, thanks to mass construction techniques pioneered by the firm of Levitt and Sons, Inc., and other developers. All this activity created millions of new jobs. The Serviceman's Readjustment Act of 1944, known as the G.I. Bill of Rights, also helped ease military personnel back into civilian life by providing veterans with loans, educational subsidies, and other benefits.

Inflation was more troublesome. Congress lacked enthusiasm for wartime price controls and in June 1946 passed a bill preserving only limited controls. Truman vetoed the bill as inadequate, controls expired, and prices immediately soared. Congress then passed an even weaker price-control bill, which Truman signed. Nevertheless, by the end of the year, most price and wage controls had been lifted. In December the Office of Price Administration began to close down. As a result the consumer price index did not stabilize until 1948, when prices were more than a third above the 1945 level, while wage and salary income had risen by only about 15 percent.

Truman's difficulties with Congress had begun in September 1945 when he submitted a 21-point domestic program, including proposals for an expansion of Social Security and public housing and for the establishment of a permanent Fair Employment Practices Act banning discrimination. These and subsequent liberal initiatives, later known as the Fair Deal, were rejected by Congress, which passed only the Employment Act of 1946. This clearly stated the government's responsibility for maintaining full employment and established a Council of Economic Advisers to advise the president.

Truman's relations with Congress worsened after the 1946 elections. Voters, who were angered by the price-control debacle, a wave of strikes, and Truman's seeming inability to lead or govern, gave control of both houses of Congress to Republicans for the first time since 1928. The president and the extremely conservative 80th Congress battled from beginning to end, not over foreign policy, where bipartisanship prevailed, but over domestic matters. Congress passed two tax reductions over Truman's vetoes and in 1947, again over Truman's veto, passed the Taft–Hartley Act, which restricted unions while extending the rights of management. Congress also rejected various liberal measures submitted by Truman, who did not expect the proposals to pass but wanted Congress on record as having opposed important social legislation.

By 1948, Truman had won support for his foreign policy, but he was expected to lose the presidential election that year because of his poor domestic record. Polls showed him lagging behind Thomas E. Dewey, the governor of New York, who had been the Republican nominee in 1944 and was again the party's standard bearer. To make matters worse the Democratic Party splintered. Former vice president Wallace headed the Progressive Party ticket, which pledged to improve Soviet-American relations whatever the cost. Southerners, known as Dixiecrats, who were alienated by the Democratic Party's strong civil rights plank, formed the States' Rights Democratic Party and nominated Gov. Strom Thurmond of

The Chicago Daily Tribune's *now-famous headline erroneously announced President Truman's loss to challenger Thomas Dewey in the 1948 presidential election, which Truman in fact won.* W. Eugene Smith/Time & Life Pictures/Getty Images

South Carolina for president. These defections appeared to ensure Truman's defeat. Instead Truman won handily (notwithstanding the *Chicago Tribune*'s famously premature headline "Dewey Defeats Truman"), receiving almost as many votes as his opponents combined. His support came largely from labour, which was upset by the Republican passage of the Taft–Hartley Act, from African Americans, who strongly supported the Democrats' civil rights provisions, and from farmers, who preferred the higher agricultural subsidies promised by the Democrats, especially at a time when commodity prices were falling.

The Democrats regained control of Congress in 1948, but Truman's relations with that body continued to be troubled. In January 1949 he asked for a broad range of Fair Deal measures, with uneven results. Congress did approve a higher minimum wage, the extension of Social Security to 10,000,000 additional persons, more public works, larger sums for the Tennessee Valley Authority (TVA) and for rural electrification, and the Housing Act of 1949, which authorized construction of 810,000 units for low-income families. Truman failed, however, to persuade Congress to repeal Taft–Hartley, to reform the agricultural subsidy system, to secure federal aid to education, to adopt his civil rights program, or, most importantly, to accept his proposal for national health insurance. He succeeded nevertheless in protecting the New Deal principle of federal responsibility for social welfare, and he helped form the Democratic agenda for the 1960s.

THE RED SCARE

Truman's last years in office were marred by charges that his administration was lax about, or even condoned, subversion and disloyalty and that communists, called "reds," had infiltrated the government. These accusations were made despite Truman's strongly anticommunist foreign policy and his creation, in 1947, of an elaborate Federal Employee Loyalty Program, which resulted in hundreds of federal workers being fired and in several thousand more being forced to resign.

The excessive fear of communist subversion was fed by numerous sources. China's fall to communism and the announcement of a Soviet atomic explosion in 1949 alarmed many, and fighting between communist and U.S.-supported factions in Korea heightened political emotions as well. Real cases of disloyalty and espionage also contributed, notably the theft of atomic secrets, for which Soviet agent Julius Rosenberg and his wife, Ethel, were convicted in 1951 and executed in 1953. (Later there was significant debate about their guilt, and the two were frequently regarded as victims of cynical and vindictive officials of the FBI; however, Soviet intelligence information released in the 1990s confirmed the Rosenbergs' involvement in espionage.) Republicans had much to gain from exploiting these and related issues.

Sen. Joseph R. McCarthy, a Republican from Wisconsin, stood out among those who held that the Roosevelt and Truman administrations amounted

Document: Joseph R. McCarthy: Communists in the State Department (1950)

The beginning of the meteoric career of Joseph R. McCarthy, who gave his name to an era of American history, may be traced to an address he delivered on the night of Feb. 9, 1950, at Wheeling, W. Va. McCarthy later inserted in the Congressional Record a text of the speech—probably modified—which is reprinted here. McCarthy asserted at that time that American reversals in the postwar period, especially the fall of China to communism, were the result of communist infiltration into the highest levels of the American government, particularly the State Department. The source of the figures cited by McCarthy in the speech was never identified (in fact, no communists were actually ever discovered as a direct result of his charges), but he nevertheless succeeded in keeping both the government and the country in turmoil for several years.

Ladies and gentlemen:

Tonight as we celebrate the one hundred and forty-first birthday of one of the greatest men in American history, I would like to be able to talk about what a glorious day today is in the history of the world. As we celebrate the birth of this man, who with his whole heart and soul hated war, I would like to be able to speak of peace in our time, of war being outlawed, and of worldwide disarmament. These would be truly appropriate things to be able to mention as we celebrate the birthday of Abraham Lincoln.

Five years after a world war has been won, men's hearts should anticipate a long peace, and men's minds should be free from the heavy weight that comes with war. But this is not such a period — for this is not a period of peace. This is a time of the "cold war." This is a time when all the world is split into two vast, increasingly hostile armed camps — a time of a great armaments race. Today we can almost physically hear the mutterings and rumblings of an invigorated god of war. You can see it, feel it, and hear it all the way from the hills of Indochina, from the shores of Formosa, right over into the very heart of Europe itself....

to "20 years of treason." In February 1950 McCarthy claimed that he had a list (whose number varied) of State Department employees who were loyal only to the Soviet Union.

McCarthy offered no evidence to support his charges and revealed only a single name, that of Owen Lattimore, who was not in the State Department and would never be convicted of a single offense. Although he failed to make a plausible case against anyone, McCarthy's colourful and cleverly presented accusations drove some persons out of their jobs and brought popular condemnation to others. The persecution of innocent persons on the charge of being communists and the forced conformity that this practice engendered in American public life came to be known as McCarthyism, and the period of its dominance was labeled the McCarthy era. McCarthy won a large personal following by making charges of disloyalty that, though mostly undocumented, badly hurt the Democrats. Many others—including the House

Un-American Activities Committee (HUAC), which conducted investigations through the 1940s and '50s into alleged communist activities—promoted the scare in various ways, leading to few convictions but loss of employment by many government employees, teachers, scholars, and people in the mass media. Those investigated by HUAC included a number of artists and entertainers, such as Elia Kazan, Pete Seeger, Bertolt Brecht, Arthur Miller, and the Hollywood Ten.

The committee's most celebrated case was perhaps that of Alger Hiss, a former U.S. State Department official. Hiss was convicted in January 1950 of perjury concerning his dealings with Whittaker Chambers, who accused him of membership in a communist espionage ring. (Hiss proclaimed his innocence until his death in 1996, but Soviet documents released in the 1990s confirmed that he had been a spy.)

THE KOREAN WAR

On June 25, 1950, a powerful invading force from the Soviet-supported Democratic People's Republic of Korea (North Korea) swept south of the 38th parallel into the Republic of Korea (South Korea). Within days, President Truman resolved to defend South Korea, even though there were few Americans in Korea and few troops ready for combat. The UN Security Council, acting during

Annie Lee Moss, who worked at the Pentagon for the Army Signal Corps, sitting with her lawyer, George Hayes, at one of Sen. Joseph McCarthy's hearings. Her sympathetic disposition, obvious unfamiliarity with Karl Marx, and the lack of evidence connecting her to the Communist Party undermined McCarthy's attempt to cast her as a communist threat and his cause. Hank Walker/ Time & Life Pictures/Getty Images

a Soviet boycott, quickly passed a resolution calling upon UN members to resist North Korean aggression.

After almost being driven into the sea, UN forces, made up largely of U.S. troops and commanded by U.S. Gen. Douglas MacArthur, counterattacked successfully and in September pushed the North Korean forces back across the border. Not content with this victory, the United States attempted to unify Korea by force, advancing almost to the borders of China and the Soviet Union. China, after its warnings were ignored, then entered the war, driving the UN forces back into South Korea. The battle line was soon stabilized along the 38th parallel, and armistice talks began on July 10, 1951, three months after Truman had relieved MacArthur for openly challenging U.S.

policies. The talks dragged on fruitlessly, interrupted by outbreaks of fighting, until Dwight D. Eisenhower became president. The United States sustained some 142,000 casualties in this limited war, most of them occurring after China's entry.

In addition to militarizing the Cold War, the Korean conflict widened its field. The United States assumed responsibility for protecting Taiwan against invasion from mainland China. Additional military aid was extended to the French in Indochina. In December 1950 Truman called for a crash program of rearmament, not just to support the forces in Korea but especially to expand the U.S. presence in Europe. As a result defense expenditures rose to $53.6 billion in 1953, four times the pre-Korean level, and would decline only modestly after the armistice.

The Hollywood Ten

Ten motion-picture producers, directors, and screenwriters who appeared before the House Un-American Activities Committee in October 1947 refused to answer questions regarding their possible communist affiliations, and, after spending time in prison for contempt of Congress, were mostly blacklisted by the Hollywood studios. The 10 were Alvah Bessie, Herbert Biberman, Lester Cole, Edward Dmytryk, Ring Lardner, Jr., John Howard Lawson, Albert Maltz, Samuel Ornitz, Adrian Scott, and Dalton Trumbo.

The group originally included the German writer Bertolt Brecht, but Brecht fled the country on the day following his inquest, and the remaining 10 were voted in contempt of Congress on Nov. 24, 1947. Convicted in federal court the following year, they were given sentences of six months to one year in prison. (While in prison, Dmytryk broke with the rest and agreed to cooperate, admitting being a communist and giving the names of 26 others.)

With the exception of Dmytryk, the group was severely blacklisted by the film industry. Most were never again employed in Hollywood, but some did write scripts under pseudonyms. As "Robert Rich," Trumbo won an Academy Award Oscar for best screenplay for The Brave One (1956). The red blacklist disappeared by the early 1960s, and Trumbo and Lardner subsequently wrote screenplays under their own names.

CHAPTER 2

LIKING IKE: THE DWIGHT EISENHOWER ADMINISTRATION

The stalemated Korean War, a renewal of inflation, and the continuing Red Scare persuaded Truman not to stand for reelection in 1952 and also gravely handicapped Gov. Adlai E. Stevenson of Illinois, the Democratic nominee. His opponent, Gen. Dwight D. Eisenhower, who had been the supreme commander of the Allied forces in western Europe during World War II, was an immensely popular war hero with great personal charm and no political record, making him extremely hard to attack. Although he disliked their methods, Eisenhower allowed Republican campaigners, including his running mate, Sen. Richard M. Nixon of California, to capitalize on the Red Scare by accusing the Truman administration of disloyalty. Eisenhower himself charged the administration with responsibility for the communist invasion of Korea and won wide acclaim when he dramatically promised that if elected he would visit Korea in person to end the war.

Dwight D. Eisenhower's campaign slogan during his run for presidency in 1952, "I Like Ike," found its way onto various forms of memorabilia, including this dress. Keystone-France/Gamma-Keystone/Getty Images

PEACE, GROWTH, AND PROSPERITY

Eisenhower won over many farmers, ethnic whites, workers, and Roman Catholics who had previously voted Democratic. He defeated Stevenson by a large margin, carrying 39 states, including three in the once solidly Democratic South. Despite Eisenhower's overwhelming victory, Republicans gained control of the House by just eight votes and managed only a tie in the Senate. Because the Republican margin was so slight, and because many right-wing Republicans in Congress disagreed with his policies, Eisenhower would increasingly depend upon Democrats to realize his objectives.

Eisenhower had promised to end the Korean War, hold the line on government spending, balance the budget, abolish inflation, and reform the Republican Party. On July 27, 1953, an armistice was signed in Korea freezing the status quo. By cutting defense spending while taxes remained fairly high, and by keeping a tight rein on credit, Eisenhower was able to avoid serious deficits, abolish inflation, and, despite several small recessions, encourage steady economic growth that made Americans more prosperous than they had ever been before. Eisenhower also supported public works and a modest expansion of government social programs. In 1954 the St. Lawrence Seaway Development Corporation was established by Congress. In 1956 Congress authorized the National System of Interstate and Defense Highways, Eisenhower's pet project and the largest public works program in history. Amendments to the Social Security Act in 1954 and 1956 extended benefits to millions not previously covered. Thus, Eisenhower achieved all but the last of his goals, and even in that he was at least partially successful. At first Eisenhower did little to check the Red Scare, but in 1954 Senator McCarthy unwisely began to investigate the administration and the U.S. Army. (In the midst of the hearings, Joseph Welch, an attorney for the Army, challenged McCarthy with a question that still echoes through American history: "Have you no sense of decency, sir? At long last, have you left no sense of decency?") This led to a full-scale investigation of McCarthy's own activities, and on December 2 the Senate, with Eisenhower playing a behind-the-scenes role, formally censured McCarthy for abusing his colleagues. McCarthy soon lost all influence, and his fall did much to remove the poison that had infected American politics. In short, Eisenhower was so successful in restoring tranquillity that, by the end of his first term, some people were complaining that life had become too dull.

Tensions eased in foreign affairs as well. On March 5, 1953, Stalin died, opening the door to better relations with the Soviet Union. In 1955 the Soviets agreed to end the four-power occupation of Austria, and that July Eisenhower met in Geneva with the new Soviet leader, Nikita S. Khrushchev, for talks that were friendly though inconclusive.

As for military policy, Eisenhower instituted the "New Look," which entailed reducing the army from 1.5 million men in 1953 to 900,000 in 1960. The navy experienced smaller reductions, while air force expenditures rose. Eisenhower was primarily interested in deterring a nuclear attack and to that end promoted expensive developments in nuclear weaponry and long-range missiles.

EISENHOWER'S SECOND TERM

Despite suffering a heart attack in 1955 and a case of ileitis that required surgery the next year, Eisenhower stood

for reelection in 1956. His opponent was once again Stevenson. Two world crises dominated the campaign. On October 23, Hungarians revolted against communist rule, an uprising that was swiftly crushed by Red Army tanks. On October 29, Israel invaded Egypt, supported by British and French forces looking to regain control of the Suez Canal and, perhaps, to destroy Egypt's president, Gamal Abdel Nasser, who had nationalized the canal in July.

Eisenhower handled both crises deftly, forcing the invaders to withdraw from Egypt and preventing events in Hungary from triggering a confrontation between the superpowers. Owing in part to these crises, Eisenhower carried all but seven states

American soldiers, invited by Lebanese Pres. Camille Chamoun to help quell an armed rebellion, patrol the streets of a village in Lebanon, July 1958. U.S. Army Photo

Document: Dwight D. Eisenhower: The Crisis in the Middle East (1957)

On July 26, 1956, the Egyptian government announced that it was nationalizing the Suez Canal and would henceforth use canal revenues to finance its Aswan Dam project, from which the United States earlier had withdrawn financial support. On October 29 Israel, whose existence had been for eight years a thorn in the side of its Arab neighbors, invaded Egypt; the next day Great Britain and France issued a joint ultimatum threatening intervention in the conflict unless an immediate cease-fire occurred and both Israel and Egypt pulled back 10 miles from the canal. Israel complied with the order, but Egypt did not. British and French aircraft began bombing Egyptian targets, and Great Britain vetoed a U.S. resolution in the UN Security Council calling for a cessation of hostilities. The actual fighting was over quickly, and British and French troops withdrew by the end of the year. The short-lived conflict had several results. Occurring as it did at the end of a U.S. presidential campaign, it helped assure the reelection of Eisenhower over Democratic challenger Stevenson; it led American policy-makers to fear the increase of Soviet influence in the Middle East; and it showed people everywhere how unstable was the peace that had followed the armistice in Korea. Eisenhower discussed both the events of the previous six months and their meaning for the world in an address to the American people on Feb. 20, 1957, that is reprinted here in part.

I come to you again to talk about the situation in the Middle East. The future of the United Nations and peace in the Middle East may be at stake.

In the four months since I talked to you about the crisis in that area, the United Nations has made considerable progress in resolving some of the difficult problems. We are now, however, faced with a fateful moment as the result of the failure of Israel to withdraw its forces behind the armistice lines as contemplated by the United Nations resolutions on this subject.

I have already today met with leaders of both parties from the Senate and the House of Representatives and we have had a very useful exchange of views. It was the general feeling of that meeting that I should lay the situation before the American people.

Before talking about the specific issues involved, I want to make clear that these issues are not something remote and abstract, but involve matters vitally touching upon the future of each one of us....

in the election. It was a purely personal victory ("I Like Ike," Eisenhower's campaign slogan in 1952, had become "We Still Like Ike"), however, for the Democrats retained control of both houses of Congress.

DOMESTIC ISSUES

Although the Eisenhower administration can, in general, be characterized as a period of growth and prosperity, some problems did begin to arise during the second term. In 1957–58 an economic recession hit, and unemployment rose to its highest level since 1941. Labour problems increased in intensity, with some 500,000 steelworkers going on strike for 116 days in 1959. There was even evidence of corruption in the Eisenhower staff. The president remained personally popular, but public discontent was demonstrated in the large majorities gained by the Democrats in the congressional elections of 1958.

Problems associated with postwar population trends also began to be recognized. The U.S. population, which had grown markedly throughout the 1950s, passed 179 million in 1960. Growth was concentrated in the West, and the country became increasingly urbanized as the middle class moved from the cities to new suburban developments. The migration left cities without their tax base but with responsibility for an increasing number of poor residents. It also resulted in a huge increase in commuters, which in turn led to continuing problems of traffic and pollution.

During Eisenhower's second term, race became a central national concern for the first time since Reconstruction. Some civil rights advances had been made in previous years. In 1954 the Supreme Court had ruled that racially segregated schools were unconstitutional. The decision provoked intense resistance in the South but was followed by a chain of rulings and orders that continually narrowed the right to discriminate. In 1955 Martin Luther King, Jr., led a boycott of segregated buses in Montgomery, Ala., giving rise to the nonviolent civil rights movement. But neither the president nor Congress became involved in the race issue until 1957, when the segregationist governor of Arkansas blocked the integration of a high school in Little Rock. Eisenhower then sent federal troops to enforce the court's order for integration.

Congress was similarly prompted to pass the first civil rights law in 82 years, the Civil Rights Act of 1957, which set the stage for the more far-reaching legislation that would follow in the 1960s.

WORLD AFFAIRS

On Oct. 4, 1957, the Soviet Union orbited the first artificial satellite, arousing fears that the United States was falling behind the Soviets technologically. This prompted Eisenhower, who generally held the line on spending, to sign the National Defense Education Act of 1958, which provided extensive aid to schools and students in order to bring American education up to what were regarded as Soviet levels of achievement. The event also strengthened demands for the acceleration of the arms and space races, which eventually led to the U.S. Moon landing on July 20, 1969, and to a remarkable expansion of scientific knowledge. In 1958, threatened and actual conflicts between governments friendly to Western powers and unfriendly or communist forces in Lebanon, the islands of Quemoy and Matsu offshore of China, Berlin, and Cuba caused additional concern. Only a minority believed that the United States was still ahead in military and space technology, though in fact this was true.

The illness of Secretary of State John Foster Dulles in March 1959, and his subsequent resignation, led the president to increase his own activity in foreign affairs. He now traveled more and met more often with heads of state. The most

(From left) *William H. Pickering, James Van Allen, and Wernher von Braun raising a model of the first U.S. satellite, Explorer I, at a press conference; Explorer I was launched Jan. 31, 1958.* NASA/JPL

important meeting was to be a summit in 1960 with Khrushchev and Western leaders to discuss such matters as Berlin, German reunification, and arms control. But shortly before the summit's scheduled date Khrushchev announced, on May 5, to the Supreme Soviet of the U.S.S.R. that an American spy plane had been shot down four days earlier over Sverdlovsk (now Yekaterinburg), referring to the flight as an "aggressive act" by the United States.

On May 7 Khrushchev revealed that the pilot of the plane, Francis Gary Powers, had parachuted to safety, was alive and well in Moscow, and had testified that he had taken off from Peshawar, in Pakistan, with the mission of flying across the Soviet Union over the Aral Sea and via Sverdlovsk, Kirov, Arkhangelsk, and Murmansk to Bodö military airfield in Norway, collecting intelligence information en route. Powers admitted to working for the U.S. Central Intelligence Agency (CIA). The United States responded that there had been no authorization for any such flight as Khrushchev had described, although a U-2 probably had flown over Soviet territory. The Soviet Union refused to accept that the U.S. government had had no knowledge of the flights. On May 16 in Paris Khrushchev declared that the Soviet Union could not take part in the summit talks unless the U.S. government immediately stopped flights over Soviet territory, apologized for those already made, and punished the persons responsible.

Eisenhower's response, promising to suspend all such flights during the remainder of his presidency, did not satisfy the Soviet Union, and the summit was adjourned on May 17. Through its disruption of the Paris summit, the strife caused by this incident (which became known as the U-2 Affair) darkened any hopes of improved U.S.-Soviet relations. (Powers was tried in August and sentenced to 10 years' confinement, but he was exchanged for the Soviet spy Rudolf Abel in 1962.)

AN ASSESSMENT OF THE POSTWAR ERA

Despite great differences in style and emphasis, the administrations of Truman and Eisenhower were notable for their continuity. Both were essentially periods of reconstruction. After 15 years of depression and war, people were not interested in social reform but in rebuilding and expanding the educational and transportation systems, achieving stable economic growth, and, in the case of the younger generation whose lives had been most disrupted by World War II, in marrying and having children.

Thus, the postwar era was the age of the housing boom, the television boom, and the baby boom, of high birth and comparatively low divorce rates, of proliferating suburbs and a self-conscious emphasis upon family "togetherness." Though frustrating to social reformers, this was probably a necessary phase of development. Once the country had been physically rebuilt, the practical needs of a rapidly growing population had been met, and standards of living had risen, there would come another age of reform.

Document: Dwight D. Eisenhower: Farewell Address (1961)

A "new" Eisenhower seemed to emerge during 1959 and 1960, when the president, at last in health and acting without the advisers—Secretary of the Treasury George M. Humphrey, Secretary of State John Foster Dulles, and Presidential Assistant Sherman Adams—who had dominated the early years of his administration, began to use the powers of his office to implement his policies and to check the rise of certain influential factions in the government. One group that particularly worried Eisenhower was the alliance that he dubbed the "military-industrial complex." He warned on several occasions, most notably in his farewell address of Jan. 17, 1961, that advances in technology combined with the growing defense needs of the country had created an opportunity for the military establishment and the armaments industry to exert undue and improper influence on the formation and conduct of national policy. The warning was especially striking coming from Eisenhower, a product of the military and good friend, as it had been assumed, of "Big Business." Eisenhower's address is reprinted here.

My Fellow Americans:

Three days from now, after half a century in the service of our country, I shall lay down the responsibilities of office as, in traditional and solemn ceremony, the authority of the presidency is vested in my successor.

This evening I come to you with a message of leavetaking and farewell, and to share a few final thoughts with you, my countrymen.

Like every other citizen, I wish the new President and all who will labor with him Godspeed. I pray that the coming years will be blessed with peace and prosperity for all.

Our people expect their President and the Congress to find essential agreement on issues of great moment, the wise resolution of which will better shape the future of the nation.

My own relations with the Congress, which began on a remote and tenuous basis, when long ago a member of the Senate appointed me to West Point, have since ranged to the intimate during the war and immediate postwar period and, finally, to the mutually interdependent during these past eight years....

CHAPTER 3

FROM CAMELOT ALL THE WAY WITH LBJ: THE JOHN F. KENNEDY AND LYNDON B. JOHNSON ADMINISTRATIONS

The arrival of the age of reform was indicated in 1960 by the comparative youth of the presidential candidates chosen by the two major parties. The Democratic nominee, Sen. John F. Kennedy of Massachusetts, was age 43; the Republican, Vice President Nixon, was 47. They both were ardent cold warriors and political moderates. Kennedy's relative inexperience and his religion (he was the first Roman Catholic presidential nominee since Al Smith) placed him at an initial disadvantage.

Kennedy created a favourable first impression with voters during a series of four televised debates with Nixon, the most important and most watched of which was the first, reaching a then-record audience estimated to be about 70 million. Many argued that television was changing the political process and that how one looked and presented oneself

The televised debates between Richard Nixon (left) *and John F. Kennedy* (right) *during the presidential campaign of 1960 contributed to Kennedy's victory in the election that year.* Pictorial Parade/Archive Photos/Getty Images

on TV was more important than what one said. This seemed to be the case during the first debate. Younger, tanned, and dressed in a dark suit, Kennedy appeared to overshadow the more haggard, gray-suited Nixon, whose hastily applied makeup job scarcely covered his late-in-the-day stubble of facial hair. Informal surveys taken after the debate indicated that audiences who listened on the radio tended to think Nixon had won, while those who watched on TV claimed victory for Kennedy. Many also believed that Kennedy ultimately won the closely contested election because he had won the first debate.

THE NEW FRONTIER

During the campaign Kennedy had stated that America was "on the edge of a New Frontier"; in his inaugural speech he spoke of "a new generation of Americans"; and during his presidency he seemed to be taking government in a new direction, away from the easygoing Eisenhower

Document: John F. Kennedy: Inaugural Address (1961)

Jan. 20, 1961, in Washington, D.C., was a cold, windy day. A brilliant sun shone on snow that had fallen the night before. A rabbi, a Protestant minister, a Catholic cardinal, and a Greek Orthodox archbishop prayed for guidance; all four emphasized freedom of religion. Robert Frost, a friend of the Kennedy family, read a poem. John F. Kennedy, the man who stepped to the rostrum to take the oath as chief executive, was the youngest man ever to be elected president. Many noted his youthfulness, and as they spoke of the hopes for his administration they did so in terms of a new kind of politics that would be appropriate to the needs of a new generation of citizens and of a new world. "The inauguration of JFK as 35th President of the U.S. will stand," asserted Commonweal, "as one of the most dramatic political events of this century." The even more dramatic event that was to occur on Nov. 22, 1963, would cause people to remember the inaugural address of that January day with a special regard. The address is reprinted here.

We observe today not a victory of party but a celebration of freedom — symbolizing an end as well as a beginning — signifying renewal as well as change. For I have sworn before you and Almighty God the same solemn oath our forebears prescribed nearly a century and three-quarters ago.

The world is very different now. For man holds in his mortal hands the power to abolish all forms of human poverty and all forms of human life. And yet the same revolutionary beliefs for which our forebears fought are still at issue around the globe — the belief that the rights of man come not from the generosity of the state but from the hand of God.

We dare not forget today that we are the heirs of that first revolution. Let the word go forth from this time and place, to friend and foe alike, that the torch has been passed to a new generation of Americans — born in this century, tempered by war, disciplined by a hard and bitter peace, proud of our ancient heritage — and unwilling to witness or permit the slow undoing of those human rights to which this nation has always been committed, and to which we are committed today at home and around the world.

Let every nation know, whether it wishes us well or ill, that we shall pay any price, bear any burden, meet any hardship, support any friend, oppose any foe to assure the survival and the success of liberty....

style. His administration was headed by strong, dedicated personalities. The Kennedy staff was also predominantly young. Its energy and commitment revitalized the country, but its competence was soon called into question.

In April 1961 Kennedy authorized a plan that had been initiated under Eisenhower for a covert invasion of Cuba to overthrow the newly installed, Soviet-supported communist regime of Fidel Castro. The invasion was repulsed at the Bay of Pigs, embarrassing the administration and worsening relations between the United States and the Soviet Union. These deteriorated further at a private meeting

Document: John F. Kennedy: Soviet Missiles in Cuba (1962)

On Sunday, Oct. 14, 1962, a U.S. surveillance flight over Cuba took photographs furnishing incontrovertible evidence that Soviet medium-range missiles were already in place on the island and that sites for more advanced missiles were under construction. President Kennedy received the information on October 16 and immediately assembled a group of key government personnel to determine a course of action for the United States. For five days the group discussed various alternatives; surveillance of Cuba was intensified and strict security measures were implemented. In the interim, on October 18, Soviet Foreign Secretary Andrei Gromyko told Kennedy and Secretary of State Dean Rusk in the course of a conversation that Soviet aid to Cuba was for defense purposes only; Kennedy did not reveal that he had evidence to the contrary. On Saturday the 20th, a naval quarantine of Cuba was decided on and letters were drafted to the heads of 43 allied governments, to all Latin American governments, and to Soviet Premier Khrushchev. On Monday the 22nd, Kennedy delivered a televised address to the country, part of which is reprinted here, explaining the situation and outlining the American government's course of action. Within 48 hours, 12 of 25 Soviet ships carrying cargoes to Cuba turned around, and on Sunday, October 28, Moscow Radio broadcast what was obviously an official response to the American position, accepting Kennedy's assurance that no invasion of Cuba was contemplated by the United States and announcing that construction of military sites on the island would be discontinued and that those already in existence would be dismantled. Secretary Rusk summed up the tensions of that unforgettable week in a later remark: "We're eyeball to eyeball, and I think the other fellow just blinked."

This government, as promised, has maintained the closest surveillance of the Soviet military buildup on the island of Cuba. Within the past week unmistakable evidence has established the fact that a series of offensive missile sites is now in preparation on that imprisoned island. The purpose of these bases can be none other than to provide a nuclear strike capability against the Western Hemisphere.

Upon receiving the first preliminary hard information of this nature last Tuesday morning [October 16] at 9 a.m., I directed that our surveillance be stepped up. And having now confirmed and completed our evaluation of the evidence and our decision on a course of action, this government feels obliged to report this new crisis to you in fullest detail.

The characteristics of these new missile sites indicate two distinct types of installations. Several of them include medium-srange ballistic missiles capable of carrying a nuclear warhead for a distance of more than 1,000 nautical miles. Each of these missiles, in short, is capable of striking Washington, D.C., the Panama Canal, Cape Canaveral, Mexico City, or any other city in the south-eastern part of the United States, in Central America, or in the Caribbean area....

between Kennedy and Khrushchev in June 1961 when the Soviet leader was perceived as attempting to bully his young American counterpart. Relations hit bottom in October 1962 when the Soviets secretly began to install long-range offensive missiles in Cuba, which threatened to tip the balance of nuclear power. Kennedy forced the removal of the missiles, gaining back the status he had lost at the Bay of Pigs and in his meeting with Khrushchev. Kennedy then began to work toward improving international relations, and in July 1963 he concluded

a treaty with Britain and the Soviet Union banning atomic tests in the atmosphere and underwater. His program of aid to Latin America, the Alliance for Progress, raised inter-American relations to their highest level since the days of Franklin Roosevelt.

Kennedy's domestic policies were designed to stimulate international trade, reduce unemployment, provide medical care for the aged, reduce federal income taxes, and protect the civil rights of African Americans. The latter issue, which had aroused national

Lady Bird Johnson (left) and Jacqueline Kennedy standing by U.S. Pres. Lyndon B. Johnson as he takes the oath of office aboard Air Force One *after the assassination of John F. Kennedy, November 22, 1963.* Lyndon B. Johnson Library Photo

concern in 1962 when federal troops were employed to assure the admission of an African American (James Meredith) at the University of Mississippi, caused further concern in 1963, when similar action was taken at the University of Alabama and mass demonstrations were held in support of desegregation. Although the Democrats controlled both houses of Congress, the administration's proposals usually encountered strong opposition from a coalition of Republicans and Southern Democrats. With Congress's support, Kennedy was able to increase military spending substantially. This led to greater readiness but also to a significant rise in the number of long-range U.S. missiles, which prompted a similar Soviet response.

On Nov. 22, 1963, President Kennedy was assassinated in Dallas, Texas, most probably by a lone gunman, though conspiracy theories abounded. Vice Pres. Lyndon B. Johnson took the oath of office immediately.

THE GREAT SOCIETY

Johnson's first job in office was to secure enactment of New Frontier bills that had been languishing in Congress. By far the most important of these was the Civil Rights Act of 1964, which Johnson pushed through despite a filibuster by Southern senators that lasted 57 days. The act provided machinery to secure equal access to accommodations, to prevent discrimination in employment by federal contractors, and to cut off funds to

segregated school districts. It also authorized the Justice Department to take a more active role in civil rights cases. Johnson went beyond the New Frontier in 1964 by declaring war on poverty. His Economic Opportunity Act provided funds for vocational training, created a Job Corps to train youths in conservation camps and urban centres, encouraged community action programs, extended loans to small businessmen and farmers, and established Volunteers in Service to America (VISTA), a domestic counterpart of a popular foreign Peace Corps program created by President Kennedy.

Johnson provided dynamic and successful leadership at a time of national trauma, and in the election of 1964 he won a landslide victory over his Republican opponent, the conservative senator Barry Goldwater of Arizona. More importantly, the Democrats gained 38 seats in the House of Representatives that year, enough to override the conservative bloc and enact a body of liberal social legislation.

With this clear mandate, Johnson submitted the most sweeping legislative program to Congress since the New Deal. He outlined his plan for achieving a "Great Society" in his 1965 State of the Union address, and over the next two years he persuaded Congress to approve most of his proposals.

The Appalachian Regional Development Act provided aid for that economically depressed area. The Housing and Urban Development Act of 1965 established a Cabinet-level

Document: Lyndon B. Johnson: The Great Society (1964)

The programs of most 20th-century American presidents were given slogan-nicknames, either by the presidents themselves or by the press, which prefers short phrases that fit headlines. Thus Theodore Roosevelt had his Square Deal, Woodrow Wilson his New Freedom, FDR his New Deal, Harry Truman his Fair Deal, JFK his New Frontier; Lyndon Johnson outlined his own program in a speech at the University of Michigan on May 22, 1964, naming it the Great Society.

I have come today from the turmoil of your Capitol to the tranquility of your campus to speak about the future of our country. The purpose of protecting the life of our nation and preserving the liberty of our citizens is to pursue the happiness of our people. Our success in that pursuit is the test of our success as a nation. For a century we labored to settle and to subdue a continent. For half a century we called upon unbounded invention and untiring industry to create an order of plenty for all of our people. The challenge of the next half century is whether we have the wisdom to use that wealth to enrich and elevate our national life and to advance the quality of our American civilization.

Your imagination, your initiative, and your indignation will determine whether we build a society where progress is the servant of our needs or a society where old values and new visions are buried under unbridled growth. For, in your time, we have the opportunity to move not only toward the rich society and the powerful society but upward to the Great Society....

department to coordinate federal housing programs. Johnson's Medicare bill fulfilled President Truman's dream of providing health care for the aged. The Elementary and Secondary Education Act of 1965 provided federal funding for public and private education below the college level. The Higher Education Act of 1965 provided scholarships for more than 140,000 needy students and authorized a National Teachers Corps. The Immigration Act of 1965 abolished the discriminatory national-origins quota system. The minimum wage was raised and its coverage extended in 1966. In 1967, Social Security pensions were raised and coverage expanded. The Demonstration Cities and Metropolitan

Area Redevelopment Act of 1966 provided aid to cities rebuilding blighted areas. Other measures dealt with mass transit, truth in packaging and lending, beautification, conservation, water and air quality, safety, and support for the arts.

THE CIVIL RIGHTS MOVEMENT

The civil rights revolution came to a head under the Johnson administration. Many had seen the March on Washington in August 1963 as the apotheosis of the nonviolent struggle for civil rights. Some 200,000 people had come from all over the country to gather at the Lincoln Memorial, where Martin Luther

Martin Luther King, Jr., at the Lincoln Memorial waving to a crowd of March on Washington demonstrators in 1963. A seminal moment in the civil rights movement came when Dr. King delivered his "I Have a Dream" speech, calling for full equality for all Americans. Francis Miller/Time & Life Pictures/Getty Images

King, Jr., delivered his "I Have a Dream" speech. Earlier in the decade, black and white Freedom Riders had been violently attacked when they rode through the South together on buses, hoping to provoke the federal government into enforcing its bans on segregation in interstate bus travel and in bus terminals, restrooms, and other facilities associated with interstate travel. With passage of the Civil Rights Act of 1964, the civil rights movement saw many of its goals embodied in federal law.

Despite the Civil Rights Act, however, most African Americans in the South found it difficult to exercise their voting rights. In the summer of 1964, the Congress of Racial Equality (CORE) and the Student Nonviolent Coordinating Committee (SNCC)—which both had been instrumental in the Freedom Rides—along with the National Association for the Advancement of Colored People (NAACP)—whose history reached back to W.E.B. Du Bois and the Niagara Movement—organized a massive effort

Civil Rights Act

The Civil Rights Act of 1964 is often called the most important U.S. law on civil rights since Reconstruction (1865–77). Title I of the act guarantees equal voting rights by removing registration requirements and procedures biased against minorities and the underprivileged. Title II prohibits segregation or discrimination in places of public accommodation involved in interstate commerce. Title VII bans discrimination by trade unions, schools, or employers involved in interstate commerce or doing business with the federal government. The latter section also applies to discrimination on the basis of sex and established a government agency, the Equal Employment Opportunity Commission (EEOC), to enforce these provisions. The act also calls for the desegregation of public schools (Title IV), broadens the duties of the Civil Rights Commission (Title V), and assures nondiscrimination in the distribution of funds under federally assisted programs (Title VI).

The Civil Rights Act was a highly controversial issue in the United States as soon as it was proposed by President Kennedy in 1963. Although Kennedy had been unable to secure passage of the bill in Congress, a stronger version was eventually passed with the urging of President Johnson, who signed the bill into law on July 2, 1964, following one of the longest debates in Senate history. White groups opposed to integration responded to the act with a significant backlash that took the form of protests, increased support for pro-segregation candidates for public office, and racial violence. The constitutionality of the act was immediately challenged and was upheld by the Supreme Court in the test case Heart of Atlanta Motel v. U.S. *(1964). The act gave federal law enforcement agencies the power to prevent racial discrimination in employment, voting, and the use of public facilities.*

to register voters in Mississippi. They also conducted "Freedom Schools" in which the philosophy of the civil rights movement, African American history, and leadership development were taught. A large number of white student activists from the North had joined the "Freedom Summer" effort, and when one black and two white volunteers were killed, it made headlines nationally and greatly heightened awareness of the movement. These murders echoed, on a small scale, the violence visited upon countless African Americans—those who had participated in demonstrations and many who had not—during the

previous decade, in forms that ranged from beatings by police to bombings of residences and black institutions. In 1965 mass demonstrations were held to protest the violence and other means used to prevent black voter registration. After a peaceful protest march was halted by police violence on the Edmund Pettus Bridge in Selma, Ala., Johnson responded with the Voting Rights Act of 1965, which abolished literacy tests and other voter restrictions and authorized federal intervention against voter discrimination. The subsequent rise in black voter registration ultimately transformed politics in the South.

These gains were considerable, but many African Americans remained dissatisfied by the slow progress. The nonviolent civil rights movement was challenged by "black power" advocates, such as Stokely Carmichael, who called for a freedom struggle that sought political, economic, and cultural objectives beyond narrowly defined civil rights reform. By the late 1960s not just King's Southern Christian Leadership Conference and the NAACP but also SNCC and CORE were challenged by militant organizations, such as the Black Panther Party, whose leaders dismissed nonviolent principles, often quoting black nationalist Malcolm X's imperative: "by any means necessary." Race riots broke out in most of the country's large cities, notably in 1965 in the Watts district of Los Angeles, leaving 34 dead, and two years later in Newark and Detroit. Four summers of violence resulted in many deaths and property losses that left whole neighborhoods ruined and their residents more distressed than ever. After a final round provoked by the assassination of King in April 1968, the rioting abated. Yet the activist pursuit of political and economic empowerment for African Americans continued, reflected culturally in the Black Arts movement—which pursued populist art that promoted the ideas of black separatism—and in the politicized soul music that replaced gospel and folk music as the sound track of the freedom struggle.

LATINO AND NATIVE AMERICAN ACTIVISM

In September 1965 Cesar Chavez, who had founded the National Farm Workers Association (later the United Farm Workers of America) in 1962, began leading what became a five-year strike by California grape pickers and a nationwide boycott of California grapes that attracted liberal support from throughout the country. Many of those farm workers were, like Chavez, Latino, and the 1960s—particularly during the strike and boycott—arguably marked the first time the Latino population in the United States drew sustained attention. People of Hispanic origin had lived in the United States since the country's origin, and their presence increased after huge portions of Mexico became part of the United States in the wake of the Mexican-American War (1846–48) and following the acquisition of Puerto Rico in the Spanish-American War (1898). Large-scale Hispanic immigration to the United States began in the 20th century as Mexicans sought to escape the Mexican Revolution (1910–20) or to seek economic opportunity.

In 1954, in *Hernandez* v. *Texas*, the U.S. Supreme Court ruled unanimously that the conviction of an agricultural labourer, Pete Hernandez, for murder should be overturned because Mexican Americans had been barred from participating in both the jury that indicted and the jury that convicted him. In this landmark ruling, the court recognized that the Fourteenth Amendment's guarantee of equal protection under the law extended to Mexican Americans. The Chicano (Mexican American) civil rights movement of the 1960s encompassed not only the Chavez-led efforts of agricultural workers in California but also the land grant movement in New Mexico spearheaded by Reies Lopez Tijerina as well as the struggle for equal education in Los Angeles. Yet it would not be until the 1980s that Latinos—such as Henry Cisneros, who was elected mayor of San Antonio, Texas, in 1981—began to hold prominent political office in the United States. By that point Hispanic servicemen had already racked up scores of medals in World War I, World War II, Korea, and Vietnam. And by 2010 the 50 million Latinos living in all 50 states constituted 16 percent of the U.S. population.

Activism on behalf of Native Americans also grew substantially during the 1960s. In 1968 the American Indian Movement (AIM) was founded by Russell Means and others to help Native Americans in urban ghettos who had been displaced by government programs that had the effect of forcing them from their reservations. Its goals eventually encompassed the entire spectrum of Indian demands—economic independence, revitalization of traditional culture, protection of legal rights, and, most especially, autonomy over tribal areas and the restoration of lands that they believed had been illegally seized. AIM was involved in many highly publicized protests; it was one of the American Indian groups involved in the occupation (1969–71) of Alcatraz Island, the march (1972) on Washington, D.C., to protest violation of treaties (in which AIM members occupied the office of the Bureau of Indian Affairs), and the takeover (1973) of a site at Wounded Knee to protest the government's Indian policy.

SOCIAL CHANGES

The 1960s were marked by the greatest changes in morals and manners since the 1920s. Young people, college students in particular, rebelled against what they viewed as the repressed, conformist society of their parents. They advocated a sexual revolution, which was aided by the increasing prominence of the birth control pill and later by *Roe* v. *Wade* (1973), a Supreme Court ruling that legalized abortion.

In the 1960s "recreational" drugs such as marijuana and LSD were increasingly used. Opposition to U.S. involvement in Vietnam promoted the rise of a New Left, which was anticapitalist as well as antiwar. The political activists of the New Left drew on the theories of political philosopher Herbert Marcuse, sociologist C. Wright Mills, and psychoanalyst and social psychologist Erich Fromm, among others. A "counterculture" sprang up that legitimized radical standards of taste and behaviour in the arts as well as in life. Feminism was reborn and joined the ranks of radical causes.

Roe v. Wade

In 1973 in a 7-2 vote the Supreme Court held that a set of Texas statutes criminalizing abortion in most instances violated a woman's constitutional right of privacy, which the court found implicit in the liberty guarantee of the due process clause of the Fourteenth Amendment.

Harry A. Blackmun, 1976. Library of Congress, Washington, D.C. (neg. no. LC-USZC6-24)

The case began in 1970 when Jane Roe (a fictional name used to protect the identity of Norma McCorvey) instituted federal action against Henry Wade, the district attorney of Dallas county, Texas, where Roe resided. The court disagreed with Roe's assertion of an absolute right to terminate pregnancy in any way and at any time and attempted to balance a woman's right of privacy with a state's interest in regulating abortion. Writing for the majority, Justice Harry A. Blackmun noted that only a "compelling state interest" justifies regulations limiting "fundamental rights" such as privacy and that legislators must therefore draw statutes narrowly "to express only the legitimate state interests at stake." The court then attempted to balance the state's distinct compelling interests in the health of pregnant women and in the potential life of fetuses. It placed the point after which a state's compelling interest in the pregnant woman's health would allow it to regulate abortion "at approximately the end of the first trimester" of pregnancy. With regard to fetuses, the court located that point at "capability of meaningful life outside the mother's womb," or viability.

Repeated challenges since 1973, such as Planned Parenthood of Southeastern Pennsylvania v. Casey (1992) narrowed the scope of Roe v. Wade but failed to overturn it. In Gonzales v. Carhart (2007) the Supreme Court upheld the federal Partial-Birth Abortion Ban Act (2003), which prohibited a rarely used abortion procedure known as intact dilation and evacuation.

Except for feminism, most organized expressions of the counterculture and the New Left, including the influential Students for a Democratic Society (SDS), did not long survive the sixties. Nevertheless they changed American life. Drug taking, previously confined largely to the impoverished inner cities, became part of middle-class life. The sexual revolution reduced government censorship, changed attitudes toward traditional sexual roles, and enabled homosexuals to organize and acknowledge their identities as never before. Although there had been earlier protests by gay groups, the Stonewall riots—a series of violent confrontations between police and gay rights activists outside the Stonewall Inn, a bar in New York City, in the summer of 1969—was perhaps the first time lesbians, gays, and transvestites saw the value in uniting behind a common cause.

Hippies

During the 1960s and 1970s, a countercultural movement that rejected the mores of mainstream American life originated on and around college campuses in the United States. Its members, called hippies, soon were found elsewhere, especially in Canada, Britain, and other western European countries. Their name was derived from "hip," a term often invoked by and used to describe the Beat Generation, the bohemian literary and social movement of the 1950s whose formative figures included Allen Ginsberg and Jack Kerouac. The youth-oriented counterculture of the 1960s and '70s evolved from two main strains, the social iconoclasm of the Beats and the political radicalism of the New Left, which developed with the Free Speech and civil rights movements. The hippie movement arose in part in opposition to U.S. involvement in the Vietnam War (1955–75); however, many hippies were not directly engaged in politics, and not all of those involved in the radical politics of the period considered themselves hippies. One group where the two strains met most directly and flamboyantly was the Youth International Party ("Yippies"), cofounded by Abbie Hoffman and Jerry Rubin.

Hippies felt alienated from middle-class society, which they saw as dominated by materialism and repression, and they developed their own distinctive lifestyle. They favoured long hair and casual, often unconventional, dress, sometimes in "psychedelic" colours or emblazoned with wild tie-dyed patterns. Many males grew facial hair, and both men and women often wore sandals and beads. Long, flowing dresses were popular with women, and rimless "granny" glasses with both men and women. Hippies commonly took up communal or cooperative living arrangements, and they often adopted vegetarian diets based on unprocessed foods and practiced holistic medicine. For many The Whole Earth Catalog, which first appeared in 1968, became an essential guide to living. Many hippies "dropped out" from society, forgoing regular jobs and careers, although some developed small businesses that catered to the alternative lifestyles of hippies.

Hippies advocated nonviolence and love. "Make love, not war" became the guiding aphorism for these "flower children," who transformed Winston Churchill's "V for victory" hand gesture into the ubiquitous "peace sign" by reversing it (i.e., palm and fingers out). Equally totemic was the "peace symbol" (four prongs in a circle), borrowed from the British Campaign for Nuclear Disarmament of the 1950s and '60s. The hippies promoted openness and tolerance as alternatives to the restrictions and regimentation they saw in middle-class society. Hippies often practiced open sexual relationships and lived in various types of family groups. They commonly sought spiritual guidance from sources outside the Judeo-Christian tradition, particularly Buddhism and other Eastern religions, and sometimes in various combinations, guided by "gurus" such as Alan Watts and Baba Ram Das (Richard Alpert). Astrology was popular, and the period was often referred to as the Age of Aquarius. Hippies (most prominently psychologist Timothy Leary) promoted the recreational use of hallucinogenic drugs, particularly marijuana and LSD (lysergic acid diethylamide), in so-called head trips, justifying the practice as a way of expanding consciousness.

Opposition to the Vietnam War sparked numerous anti-war demonstrations around the country, such as this one held in New York City's Bryant Park. Such rallies often drew large crowds of young people, many of whom embraced the counterculture movement. Bernard Gotfryd/Premium Archive/Getty Images

Both folk and rock music were an integral part of hippie culture. Singers such as Bob Dylan and Joan Baez and groups such as the Beatles, Grateful Dead, Jefferson Airplane, and Rolling Stones were among those most closely identified with the movement. The musical Hair, a celebration of the hippie lifestyle, opened on Broadway in 1968, and the film Easy Rider, which reflected hippie values and aesthetics, appeared in 1969. Novelist Ken Kesey, one of the best-known literary spokesmen for the movement, was equally famous for the Acid (LSD) Test celebrations hosted by him and a group called the Merry Pranksters.

Public gatherings—part music festivals, sometimes protests, often simply excuses for celebrating life—were an important part of the hippie movement. The first "be-in," called the Gathering of the Tribes, was held in San Francisco in 1967. A three-day music festival known as Woodstock, held in rural New York state in 1969, drew an estimated 400,000–500,000 people and became virtually synonymous with the movement. Hippies participated in a number of teach-ins at colleges and universities in which opposition to the Vietnam War was explained, and they took part in antiwar protests and marches. They joined other protesters in the "moratorium"—a nationwide demonstration—against the war in 1969. They were involved in the development of the environmental movement. The first Earth Day was held in 1970.

By the mid-1970s the movement had waned, and by the 1980s hippies had given way to or followed the path of a new generation of young people who were intent on making careers for themselves in business and who came to be known as yuppies (young urban professionals). Nonetheless, hippies continued to have an influence on the wider culture, seen, for example, in more relaxed attitudes toward sex, in the new concern for the environment, and in a widespread lessening of formality.

Unrestrained individualism altered traditional family values. People began marrying later and having fewer children. The divorce rate accelerated to the point that the number of divorces per year was roughly half the number of marriages. The number of abortions rose, as did the illegitimacy rate. By the 1980s one in six families was headed by a single woman, and over half of all people living in poverty, including some 12 million children, belonged to such families. Because inflation and recession made it hard to support even traditional families on a single income, a majority of mothers entered the work force. Thus the stable, family-oriented society of the 1950s became a thing of the past.

THE VIETNAM WAR

U.S. involvement in Vietnam dated to the Truman administration, when economic and military aid was provided to deter a communist takeover of French Indochina. When France withdrew and Vietnam was divided in two in 1954, the United States continued to support anticommunist forces in South Vietnam. By 1964, communist insurgents were winning their struggle against the government of South Vietnam, which a decade of American aid had failed to strengthen or reform. In August, following an allegedly unprovoked attack on U.S. warships patrolling the Gulf of Tonkin, a resolution pledging complete support for American action in Vietnam was passed unanimously in the House of Representatives and with only two dissenting votes in the Senate.

After the fall elections, Johnson began deploying a huge force in Vietnam (more than half a million troops in 1968, together with strong air and naval units). This power was directed not only against the Viet Cong insurgents but also against North Vietnam, which increased its efforts as American participation escalated. Despite massive U.S.

Document: Lyndon B. Johnson: Withdrawal Speech (1968)

As 1967 drew to a close it was evident that the Vietnam War was causing serious divisions in the United States. Public disenchantment with the conduct of the war and with the war itself was becoming more widespread. Even President Johnson's own party was sharply divided on the issue—so much so, in fact, that Sen. Eugene McCarthy of Minnesota began campaigning for the Democratic presidential nomination on an antiwar platform. By his impressive showing in the New Hampshire primary election in March 1968, Senator McCarthy demonstrated the reality of the divided opinions about the war. Hawkish candidates for office started to sound more dovelike, and other antiwar candidates entered the field. Then on March 31 President Johnson made an address to the nation on Vietnam policy, in which he announced a cutback in the bombing of North Vietnam and made another offer to start peace negotiations with the Hanoi regime. But the most startling—and totally unanticipated—portion of the speech was his closing announcement that he would not be a candidate for reelection. This statement, coupled with the fact that North Vietnam did accept the offer to begin talks toward a negotiated settlement, radically changed the political picture in the United States in an election year. Portions of President Johnson's address are reprinted below.

Tonight I want to speak to you on peace in Vietnam and Southeast Asia.

No other question so preoccupies our people. No other dream so absorbs the 250 million human beings who live in that part of the world. No other goal motivates American policy in Southeast Asia.

For years, representatives of our government and others have traveled the world — seeking to find a basis for peace talks. Since last September, they have carried the offer I made public at San Antonio.

It was this: that the United States would stop its bombardment of North Vietnam when that would lead promptly to productive discussions — and that we would assume that North Vietnam would not take military advantage of our restraint.

Hanoi denounced this offer, both privately and publicly. Even while the search for peace was going on, North Vietnam rushed their preparations for a savage assault on the people, the government, and the allies of South Vietnam.

Their attack — during the Tet holidays — failed to achieve its principal objectives. It did not collapse the elected government of South Vietnam or shatter its Army — as the Communists had hoped. It did not produce a "general uprising" among the people of the cities. The Communists were unable to maintain control of any city. And they took very heavy casualties....

bombing of North Vietnam, the communists refused to yield. On Jan. 30, 1968, disregarding a truce called for the Tet (lunar new year) holiday, the communists launched an offensive against every major urban area in South Vietnam. Although the Tet Offensive was a military failure, it proved to be a political victory for the communists because it persuaded many Americans that the war could not be ended at a bearable price. Opposition to U.S. involvement became the major issue of the 1968 election. After Sen. Eugene McCarthy, a leading critic of the war, ran strongly against him in the New Hampshire primary, Johnson announced that he would not seek or accept renomination. He also curtailed bombing operations, opened peace talks with the North Vietnamese, and on November 1 ended the bombing of North Vietnam.

While war efforts were being reduced, violence within the United States seemed to be growing. Just two months after King's assassination, Sen. Robert F. Kennedy, a leading contender for the Democratic presidential nomination, was assassinated. President Johnson then secured the nomination of Vice President Hubert H. Humphrey at the Democratic National Convention at Chicago, where violence again erupted as antiwar demonstrators were manhandled by local police.

CHAPTER 4

"NIXON'S THE ONE": THE RICHARD M. NIXON ADMINISTRATION

Hubert Humphrey lost the 1968 presidential election to the Republican nominee, former vice president Richard Nixon. The narrowness of Nixon's margin resulted from a third-party campaign by the former governor of Alabama, George Wallace, who attracted conservative votes that would otherwise have gone to Nixon. Democrats retained large majorities in both houses of Congress.

FOREIGN AFFAIRS

Nixon and his national security adviser, Henry Kissinger, believed that American power relative to that of other countries had declined to the point where a fundamental reorientation was necessary. They sought improved relations with the Soviet Union to make possible reductions in military strength while at the same time enhancing American security. In 1969 the Nixon Doctrine called for allied countries, especially in Asia, to take more responsibility for their own defense. Nixon's policy of détente led to Strategic Arms

Henry Kissinger (right) *meeting with Chinese Premier Zhou Enlai during the American envoy's secret visit to Peking (now Beijing) in 1971.* AFP/Getty Images

Limitation Talks (SALT), which resulted in a treaty with the Soviet Union all but terminating antiballistic missile systems. In 1972 Nixon and Kissinger negotiated an Interim Agreement that limited the number of strategic offensive missiles each side could deploy in the future. Nixon also dramatically reversed Sino-American relations with a secret visit by Kissinger to Peking in July 1971. This led to a presidential visit the following year and to the establishment of strong ties between the two countries. Nixon then visited Moscow as well, showing that détente with the rival communist powers did not mean that he would play them off against one another.

The limits of détente were tested by the Arab-Israeli Yom Kippur War of October 1973, in which the United States supported Israel and the Soviet Union the Arabs. Nixon managed the crisis well, preventing the confrontation with the Soviets from getting out of hand and negotiating a cease-fire that made possible later improvements in Israeli-Egyptian relations. Nixon and Kissinger dramatically altered U.S. foreign relations, modifying containment, reducing the importance of alliances, and making

Document: Richard M. Nixon: The Moscow Summit (1972)

Coming three months after his trip to China, President Nixon's visit to the Soviet Union from May 22 to 29, 1972, inaugurated a new era of détente with both the major communist powers and raised hopes internationally that the Cold War was drawing to a close. While in the Soviet Union, the president met with Premier Aleksei N. Kosygin and Communist Party leader Leonid I. Brezhnev to discuss such matters as preventing nuclear war, arms limitation, China-Soviet relations, and increased trade between the United States and the U.S.S.R. The most important immediate outcome of the summit meeting was the signing, on May 26, of a strategic arms limitation treaty. On June 1, just after his return from Russia, President Nixon addressed a joint session of Congress in a televised broadcast to the nation detailing the results of his trip. Portions of his speech are reprinted here.

Mr. Speaker, Mr. President, Members of the Congress, our distinguished guests, my fellow Americans: Your welcome in this great Chamber tonight has a very special meaning to Mrs. Nixon and to me. We feel very fortunate to have traveled abroad so often representing the United States of America. But we both agree after each journey that the best part of any trip abroad is coming home to America again.

During the past 13 days we have flown more than 16,000 miles and we visited four countries. Everywhere we went—to Austria, the Soviet Union, Iran, Poland—we could feel the quickening pace of change in old international relationships and the people's genuine desire for friendship for the American people. Everywhere new hopes are rising for a world no longer shadowed by fear and want and war, and as Americans we can be proud that we now have an historic opportunity to play a great role in helping to achieve man's oldest dream: a world in which all nations can enjoy the blessings of peace....

I have not come here this evening to make new announcements in a dramatic setting. This summit has already made its news. It has barely begun, however, to make its mark on our world, and I ask you to join me tonight—while events are fresh, while the iron is hot—in starting to consider how we can help to make that mark what we want it to be....

the balance of power and the dual relationship with the Soviet Union and China keystones of national policy.

Meanwhile, inconclusive fighting continued in Vietnam, and unproductive peace talks continued in Paris. Although in 1969 Nixon announced his policy of "Vietnamization," according to which more and more of the fighting was to be assumed by South Vietnam itself, he began by expanding the fighting in Southeast Asia with a 1970 "incursion" into Cambodia. This incident aroused strong protest; student demonstrations at Kent State University in Ohio led on May 4 to a confrontation with troops of the Ohio National Guard, who fired on the students without orders, killing four and wounding several others. National revulsion at this act led to serious disorders at many universities and forced some of them to close for the remainder of the term. Further antiwar demonstrations followed the 1971 U.S. invasion of Laos and Nixon's decision to resume intensive bombing of North Vietnam in 1972.

Peace negotiations with North Vietnam slowly progressed, and a cease-fire agreement was finally signed on Jan. 27, 1973. The agreement, which provided for exchange of prisoners of war and for U.S. withdrawal from South Vietnam without any similar commitment from the North Vietnamese, ended 12 years of U.S. military effort that had taken some 58,000 American lives.

DOMESTIC AFFAIRS

When Chief Justice Earl Warren, who had presided over the most liberal Supreme Court in history, retired in 1969, Nixon replaced him with the conservative Warren Burger. Three other retirements enabled Nixon to appoint a total of four moderate or conservative justices. The Burger court, though it was expected to, did not reverse the policies laid down by its predecessor.

Equal Rights Amendment (ERA)

The text of the proposed Equal Rights Amendment stated that "Equality of rights under the law shall not be denied or abridged by the United States or by any State on account of sex" and further that "the Congress shall have the power to enforce, by appropriate legislation, the provisions of this article." The amendment was first introduced to Congress in 1923, shortly after women in the United States were granted the right to vote, and it was finally approved by the U.S. Senate 49 years later, in March 1972. It was then submitted to the state legislatures for ratification within seven years but, despite a deadline extension to June 1982, was not ratified by the requisite majority of 38 states. It would have become the 27th Amendment to the Constitution.

Although the ERA gained ratification of 30 states within one year of its Senate approval, mounting intense opposition from conservative religious and political organizations effectively brought ratification to a standstill. The main objections to the ERA were based on fears that women would lose privileges and protections such as exemption from compulsory military service and combat duty and economic support from husbands for themselves and their children.

Advocates of the ERA, led primarily by the National Organization for Women (NOW), maintained, however, that the issue was mainly economic. NOW's position was that many sex-discriminatory state and federal laws perpetuated a state of economic dependence among a large number of women and that laws determining child support and job opportunities should be designed for the individual rather than for one sex. Many advocates of the ERA believed that the failure to adopt the measure as an amendment would cause women to lose many gains and would give a negative mandate to courts and legislators regarding feminist issues.

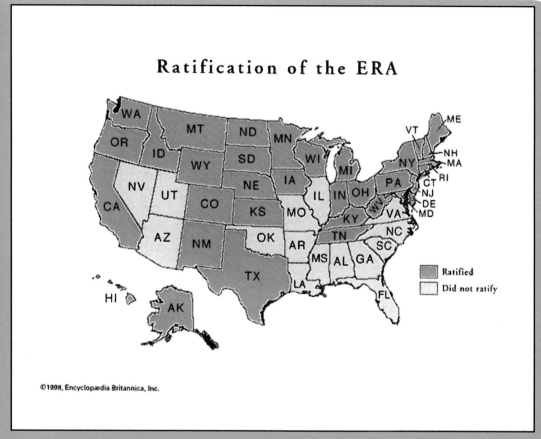

Ratification of the ERA

©1998, Encyclopædia Britannica, Inc.

Even after the seven-year deadline for its ratification was extended by three years, the Equal Rights Amendment failed to be ratified by the required 38 states. This map shows the 35 states that ratified the ERA and the 15 that did not.

Congress enacted Nixon's revenue-sharing program, which provided direct grants to state and local governments. Congress also expanded Social Security and federally subsidized housing. In 1972 the Congress, with the support of the president, adopted a proposed constitutional amendment guaranteeing equal rights for women. Despite widespread support, the Equal Rights Amendment, or ERA, as it was called, failed to secure ratification in a sufficient number of states. (Subsequent legislation and court decisions, however, gave women in substance what the ERA had been designed to secure.)

The cost of living continued to rise, until by June 1970 it was 30 percent above the 1960 level; industrial production declined, as did the stock market. By mid-1971 unemployment reached a 10-year peak of 6 percent, and inflation continued. Wage and price controls were instituted, the dollar was devalued, and the limitation on the national debt was raised three times in 1972 alone. The U.S. trade deficit improved, but inflation remained unchecked.

THE WATERGATE SCANDAL

A scandal surfaced in June 1972, when five men were arrested for breaking into the Democratic national headquarters at the Watergate office-apartment-hotel complex in Washington, D.C. When it was learned that the burglars had been hired by the Committee to Re-Elect the President (CREEP or CRP), John Mitchell, a former U.S. attorney general, resigned as director of CREEP. These events, however, had no effect on the election that fall. Even though the Democrats retained majorities in both the Senate and the House, Nixon won a landslide victory over Democratic nominee Sen. George McGovern of South Dakota, who won only Massachusetts and the District of Columbia.

In 1973, however, it was revealed that an attempt to suppress knowledge of the connection between the Watergate affair and CREEP involved highly placed

White House reporters watching the telecast of U.S. Pres. Richard M. Nixon's first Watergate-related address, April 30, 1973. © Archive Photos

members of the White House staff. In addition to the trial of the burglars conducted in federal court by Judge John J. Sirica, a Senate select committee—the Select Committee on Presidential Campaign Activities—was formed. That committee, under the leadership of Sen. Samuel J. Ervin, Jr., opened hearings in May, and Nixon appointed Archibald Cox as a special prosecutor to investigate the scandal. Amid conflicting testimony, almost daily disclosures of further scandals, and continuing resignations of administrative personnel, a battle developed between the legislative and executive branches of government. Nixon attempted to stop the investigation by firing Cox, leading Attorney General Elliot Richardson and Deputy Attorney General William D. Ruckelshaus to resign. This "Saturday night massacre" of Justice Department officials did not, however, stem the flow

Document: Richard M. Nixon: Resignation from the Presidency (1974)

Following the release of the tape transcripts on Aug. 5, 1974, many members of Congress urged President Nixon to resign to save the country the ordeal of a protracted debate on impeachment in the House and a trial in the Senate. On August 7, three leading congressional Republicans—Sen. Barry Goldwater, Sen. Hugh Scott, and Rep. John Rhodes—went to the White House to tell the president he had virtually no support left in Congress, even among members of his own party. Therefore, on Thursday evening, August 8, President Nixon addressed the nation via television to announce that he would be resigning his office the next day. On the morning of the 9th, he bid farewell to the White House staff. Both of President Nixon's final speeches are offered in this volume beginning with his television address to the country.

This is the 37th time I have spoken to you from this office, where so many decisions have been made that shaped the history of this Nation. Each time I have done so to discuss with you some matter that I believe affected the national interest.

In all the decisions I have made in my public life, I have always tried to do what was best for the Nation. Throughout the long and difficult period of Watergate, I have felt it was my duty to persevere, to make every possible effort to complete the term of office to which you elected me.

In the past few days, however, it has become evident to me that I no longer have a strong enough political base in the Congress to justify continuing that effort. As long as there was such a base, I felt strongly that it was necessary to see the constitutional process through to its conclusion, that to do otherwise would be unfaithful to the spirit of that deliberately difficult process and a dangerously destabilizing precedent for the future.

But with the disappearance of that base, I now believe that the constitutional purpose has been served, and there is no longer a need for the process to be prolonged.

I would have preferred to carry through to the finish whatever the personal agony it would have involved, and my family unanimously urged me to do so. But the interest of the Nation must always come before any personal considerations....

of damaging revelations, confessions, and indictments.

The Watergate affair itself was further complicated by the revelation of other irregularities. It became known that a security unit in the White House (the "Plumbers") had engaged in illegal activities under the cloak of national security. Nixon's personal finances were questioned, and Vice Pres. Spiro T. Agnew resigned amid accusations of financial improprieties and pled no contest to a single, negotiated criminal charge. On Dec. 6, 1973, Nixon's nominee, Congressman Gerald R. Ford of Michigan, was approved by Congress as the new vice president.

On May 9, 1974, the Judiciary Committee of the House of Representatives began hearing evidence relating to a possible impeachment proceeding. On July 27–30 it voted to recommend that Nixon be impeached on three charges. On August 5 the president obeyed a Supreme Court order to release transcripts of three tape-recorded conversations (from among Nixon's secret recordings of his phone calls and conversations in the Oval Office), and he admitted that, as evidenced in the recordings, he had taken steps to direct the Federal Bureau of Investigation away from the White House when its inquiries into the Watergate burglary were leading it toward his staff.

Nixon's support in Congress vanished, and it seemed probable that he would be impeached. On the evening of August 8, in a television address, Nixon announced his resignation, effective the next day.

After his final good-byes, Nixon and his family flew to their home in California. His resignation became effective while he was airborne.

CHAPTER 5

THE NATIONAL NIGHTMARE ENDS, THE NATIONAL MALAISE BEGINS: THE GERALD FORD AND JIMMY CARTER ADMINISTRATIONS

At noon on Aug. 9, 1974, Vice Pres. Gerald R. Ford was sworn in as Richard Nixon's successor as president of the United States, stating, "Our long national nightmare is over." The shadow of Watergate, however, would loom long over the American political and cultural landscape. For the rest of the decade paranoia and disillusionment were never far from the consciousness of Americans.

THE GERALD R. FORD ADMINISTRATION

Ford, the first president not elected either to the office or to the vice presidency, had served in Congress for 25 years.

Pres. Gerald Ford with his wife, Betty, during his inauguration. Bill Pierce/Time & Life Pictures/ Getty Images

He had been a football star during his undergraduate days at the University of Michigan. Well-liked and ideologically flexible, he had won the role of House minority leader in 1965 and held this position until 1973. Ford's was essentially a caretaker government. He had no mandate and no broad political base, and his party was tainted by Watergate.

PARDONING NIXON

One of Ford's early acts as president was the announcement of a conditional amnesty program for those who had evaded the draft or deserted during the Vietnam War. The most attention-getting act of his years in office, and the move that for many destroyed his credibility, followed in the next month. On Sept. 8, 1974, declaring that in the end "it is not the ultimate fate of Richard Nixon that most concerns me" but rather "the immediate future of this great country," Ford pardoned Nixon "for all offenses against the United States" that he had committed "or may have committed' while in office. The pardon, later alleged to have been the result of blackmail (that if Ford did not pardon him, Nixon would blacken the new president's reputation by publicly claiming that Ford had promised a pardon in exchange for the presidency), effectively squelched any criminal prosecutions to which Nixon might have been liable. Ford annoyed members of his own party by naming Nelson A. Rockefeller, both a party liberal and a representative of the so-called "Eastern establishment," as his vice president.

Troubled Economy

Kissinger remained secretary of state and conducted foreign policy along the lines previously laid down by Nixon and himself. Ford's principal concern was the economy, which had begun to show signs of weakness. A brief Arab oil embargo during the Yom Kippur War had led to a quadrupling of oil prices, and the oil shock produced both galloping inflation and a recession. Prices rose more than 10 percent in 1974 and unemployment reached 9.2 percent in May 1974. Ford was no more able than Nixon to deal with the combination of inflation and recession, called "stagflation," and Congress had no remedies either. For the most part Congress and the president were at odds. Ford vetoed no fewer than 50 bills during his short term in office.

During the final days of the Vietnam War, in March 1975, Ford ordered an airlift of some 237,000 anticommunist Vietnamese refugees from Da Nang, most of whom were taken to the United States. Two months later, Cambodia seized the American cargo ship *Mayaguez*. Ford declared the event an "act of piracy" and sent the Marines to seize the ship. They succeeded, but the rescue operation to save the 39-member crew resulted in the loss of 41 American lives and the wounding of 50 others. Twice in September 1975, Ford was the target of assassination attempts. In the first instance, Secret Service agents intervened before shots were fired; in the second, the would-be assassin fired one shot at Ford but missed by several feet.

The 1976 Election

In the election of 1976 Ford won the nomination of his party, fighting off a strong challenge by Ronald Reagan, the former governor of California. In a crowded field of contenders, the little-known ex-governor of Georgia, Jimmy Carter, won the Democratic nomination by starting early and making a virtue of his inexperience in Washington politics. Ford, despite Watergate and stagflation, nearly won the general election. He was defeated by a popular vote of 40.8 million to 39.1 million and an electoral vote of 297 to 240. Carter's electoral margin was the smallest since 1916.

THE JIMMY CARTER ADMINISTRATION

Although lacking a national political base or major backing, Carter had managed through tireless and systematic campaigning to assemble a broad constituency. In the aftermath of the Watergate scandal, which had raised widespread concern about the power of the presidency and the integrity of the executive branch, Carter styled himself as an outsider to Washington, D.C., a man of strong principles who could restore the faith of the American people in their leaders. Beginning with his inaugural walk with his wife, Rosalynn, down Pennsylvania Avenue, Carter tried to reinforce his image as a man of the people. He adopted an informal style of dress and speech in public appearances, held frequent press conferences, and reduced the pomp of the presidency.

FOREIGN AFFAIRS

More than any other president, Carter used diplomacy to promote human rights, especially with regard to the governments of South Korea, Iran, Argentina, South Africa, and Rhodesia (Zimbabwe). Efforts to continue the détente with the U.S.S.R. foundered as the Soviets supported revolutions in Africa, deployed medium-range nuclear weapons in

Israeli Prime Minister Menachem Begin (left), *Egyptian Pres. Anwar el-Sadat* (right), *and U.S. Pres. Jimmy Carter meeting at the Camp David presidential retreat in Maryland.* Karl Schumacher/AFP/Getty Images

Europe, and occupied Afghanistan. Relations with the People's Republic of China, on the other hand, improved, and full diplomatic recognition of the communist government took effect on Jan. 1, 1979. In September 1977 the United States and Panama signed two treaties giving control of the Panama Canal to Panama in the year 2000 and providing for the neutrality of the waterway.

In 1978 Carter brought together Egyptian Pres. Anwar el-Sadat and Israeli Prime Minister Menachem Begin at the presidential retreat in Camp David, Md., and secured their agreement to the Camp David Accords, which ended the state of war that had existed between the two countries since Israel's founding in 1948. The difficult negotiations—which lasted 13 days and were salvaged only by Carter's tenacious intervention—provided for the establishment of full diplomatic and economic relations on condition that Israel return the occupied Sinai Peninsula to Egypt. On September 17 Carter announced that two accords had been signed establishing the terms for a peace treaty between Egypt and Israel. Further torturous negotiations followed before the peace treaty was signed in Washington, D.C., on March 26, 1979.

On Jan. 1, 1979, Carter established full diplomatic relations between the United States and China and simultaneously broke official ties with Taiwan. Also in 1979, in Vienna, Carter and Soviet leader Leonid Brezhnev signed a new bilateral strategic arms limitation treaty (SALT II) intended to establish parity in strategic nuclear weapons delivery systems between the two superpowers on terms that could be adequately verified. Carter removed the treaty from consideration by the Senate in January 1980, however, after the Soviet Union invaded Afghanistan. He also placed an embargo on the shipment of American grain to the Soviet Union and pressed for a U.S. boycott of the 1980 Summer Olympics due to be held in Moscow.

Carter's substantial foreign policy successes were overshadowed, however, by a groundswell of popular discontent over his economic policies and by the emergence of a serious crisis in foreign affairs. On Nov. 4, 1979, a mob of Iranian students stormed the U.S. embassy in Tehran and took the diplomatic staff there hostage. Their actions, in response to the arrival of the deposed shah (Mohammad Reza Shah Pahlavi) in the United States for medical treatment, were sanctioned by Iran's revolutionary government, led by Shi'ite cleric Ayatollah Ruhollah Khomeini. A standoff developed between the United States and Iran over the issue of the captive diplomats. Carter responded by trying to negotiate the hostages' release while avoiding a direct confrontation with the Iranian government, but, as the crisis wore on (documented nightly on American television by a special news program that would become the influential *Nightline*), his inability to obtain the release of the hostages became a major political liability. The failure of a secret U.S. military mission to rescue the hostages (which ended almost before it began with a crash in the desert of a plane and helicopter) in April 1980 seemed to typify the inefficacy and misfortune of the Carter administration. The hostages were not released until Carter left office in January 1981. Carter's inability to either resolve the hostage crisis or to manage American perceptions of it disabled him as a leader.

Domestic Policy

Early on in his administration, Carter had introduced a dizzying array of ambitious programs for social, administrative, and economic reform. Most of those programs, however, met with opposition in Congress despite the Democratic majorities in both the House of Representatives and the Senate. On one hand, Congress, in the post-Watergate environment, was more willing to challenge the executive branch; on the other, Carter the populist

Paul Volcker (left) *shakes hands with Pres. Jimmy Carter at his swearing-in ceremony as chairman of the Federal Reserve Board, the post formerly held by G. William Miller, who stands to the right of the president.* © AP Images

was quick to criticize Congress and to take his agenda to the American people. In either case, Carter's difficulties with Congress undermined the success of his administration, and by 1978 his initial popularity had dissipated in the face of his inability to convert his ideas into legislative realities.

Carter's management of the economy aroused widespread concern. The inflation rate climbed higher each year he was in office, rising from 6 percent in 1976 to more than 12 percent by 1980;

unemployment remained high at 7.5 percent; and volatile interest rates reached a high of 20 percent or more twice during 1980. The faltering economy was due in part to the energy crisis that had originated in the early 1970s as a result of the country's overdependence on foreign oil. In 1977 the president, whose mistrust of special interest groups such as the oil companies was well known, proposed an energy program that included an oil tax, conservation, and the use of alternative sources of energy. The House supported

Document: Jimmy Carter: A National Malaise (1979)

The second half of Jimmy Carter's presidency was a time of troubles for him, for his administration, and for the country. Inflation and the energy crisis persisted despite all efforts to deal with them, and the situation in Iran looked as if it would get worse and worse—which indeed it did. On July 15, 1979, Carter addressed the country on the subject of energy for the fifth time. He spoke at length of his plans to solve the problem. But before discussing the energy problem he discoursed to the American people on another problem, a deeper one, he felt, and one that required a greater national effort to solve. He referred to a "crisis of confidence"; several days later he talked of "a national malaise." Reprinted here is a portion of the July 15th speech, in which he stated some ideas that have been remembered longer than many of his other presidential acts and words.

I know, of course, being President, that government actions and legislation can be very important. That's why I've worked hard to put my campaign promises into law—and I have to admit, with just mixed success. But after listening to the American people I have been reminded again that all the legislation in the world can't fix what's wrong with America. So, I want to speak to you first tonight about a subject even more serious than energy or inflation. I want to talk to you right now about a fundamental threat to American democracy.

I do not mean our political and civil liberties. They will endure. And I do not refer to the outward strength of America, a nation that is at peace tonight everywhere in the world, with unmatched economic power and military might.

The threat is nearly invisible in ordinary ways. It is a crisis of confidence. It is a crisis that strikes at the very heart and soul and spirit of our national will. We can see this crisis in the growing doubt about the meaning of our own lives and in the loss of a unity of purpose for our Nation....

the program, but the Senate quashed it. In the summer of 1979 Carter appointed Paul Volcker as chairman of the Federal Reserve Board. Volcker raised interest rates to unprecedented levels, which resulted in a severe recession but brought inflation under control. Both business leaders and the public at large blamed Carter for the nation's economic woes, charging that the president lacked a coherent strategy for taming inflation without causing a painful increase in unemployment.

In the election of 1980 Ronald Reagan was the Republican nominee, while Republican John B. Anderson of Illinois headed a third ticket and received 5,600,000 votes. Carter was overwhelmingly defeated by Reagan, who pointed to what he called Carter's "misery index"—the inflation rate plus the unemployment rate, whose sum was over 20—and asked two poignant questions that the public took to heart: "Are you better off than you were four years ago?" and "Is America as respected throughout the world?" The Republicans gained control of the Senate for the first time since 1954.

CHAPTER 6

MORNING IN AMERICA: THE RONALD REAGAN AND GEORGE H.W. BUSH ADMINISTRATIONS

Jimmy Carter had come into office asking, "Why not the best?" But the interlude of hope at the beginning of his administration was short-lived. Whether his vision of an energy-efficient America of diminished expectations was prescient or presumptuous, he failed to restore Americans' faith in the executive office and perhaps in themselves. Ultimately, Ronald Reagan's ascent to the presidency in 1980 had very much to do with his rhetorical ability to break the cloud of gloom that Watergate, along with the U.S. failure in the Vietnam War, had cast upon the country.

THE RONALD REAGAN ADMINISTRATION

Reagan's presidency began on a dramatic note when, after the inaugural ceremony, he announced that Iran had agreed

Pres. Ronald Reagan with his wife, Nancy, at his inaugural ball in 1981. Bill Pierce/Time & Life Pictures/Getty Images

to release the remaining American hostages. Then, on March 30, 1981, a deranged drifter named John W. Hinckley, Jr., shot the president as he left a Washington, D.C., hotel. Reagan underwent emergency surgery, spent 12 days in the hospital, and was weakened for months. In August 1981, 13,000 members of the national union of air traffic controllers walked off their jobs, demanding higher pay and better working conditions. As federal employees, they were forbidden by law to strike, and Reagan refused to negotiate. Most of the striking controllers ignored the ultimatum Reagan gave them to return to work in 48 hours and were promptly fired. Although the firings disrupted air traffic until replacements were hired and trained, many Americans saw Reagan's action as a sign of decisiveness and conviction.

REAGONOMICS

Following the so-called supply-side economic program he propounded in

Document: Ronald Reagan:
A Tax System that Is Unwise, Unwanted, and Unfair (1985)

In May 1985, President Reagan delivered an impassioned TV speech in which he strongly criticized the U.S. tax system, which he declared was "unwise, unwanted, and unfair," and proposed that Congress adopt a new system, which he described in detail. This speech, from Reagan's second term, was reflective of the economic policy he had championed since the beginning of his tenure in office. Presidents before him had made similar proposals, but despite widespread agreement that the tax code was a veritable grab bag of special interest legislations, with more loopholes than anyone but an expert could count, nothing really significant had ever been done. The cynics predicted that even now nothing would be done. But, astonishingly, something was done, although not immediately. A new tax system was agreed on by both houses of Congress and signed into law by the President before the 1986 congressional elections. Reprinted here is most of Reagan's May 28, 1985, speech.

My fellow citizens, I'd like to speak to you tonight about our future, about a great historic effort to give the words freedom, fairness and hope new meaning and power for every man and woman in America.

Specifically, I want to talk about taxes; about what we must do as a nation this year to transform a system that's become an endless source of confusion and resentment into one that is clear, simple and fair for all; a tax code that no longer runs roughshod over Main Street America, but insures your families and firms incentives and rewards for hard work and risk-taking in an American future of strong economic growth.

No other issue goes so directly to the heart of our economic life; no other issue will have more lasting impact on the well-being of your families and your future.

In 1981 our critics charged that letting you keep more of your earnings would trigger an inflationary explosion, send interest rates soaring and destroy our economy. Well, we cut your tax rates anyway by nearly 25 percent. And what that helped trigger was falling inflation, falling interest rates and the strongest economic expansion in 30 years....

his campaign, along with a pledge to reverse the trend toward big government, Reagan proposed 30 percent reductions in both individual and corporate income taxes over a three-year period, which he believed would stimulate the economy and eventually increase revenues from taxes as income levels grew. At the same time, he proposed large increases in military expenditures and significant cuts in spending on social welfare. In 1981 Congress passed most of the president's budget proposals, though the tax cut was scaled back slightly, to 25 percent.

The results were mixed. A severe recession in 1982 pushed the country's unemployment rate to nearly 11 percent, the highest it had been since the Great

Depression. The country's trade deficit increased from $25 billion in 1980 to $111 billion in 1984. In addition, the huge increases in military spending, combined with insufficient cuts in other programs, produced massive budget deficits, the largest in the country's history to date. In order to address the deficit, Reagan backed away from strict supply-side theories to support a $98.3 billion tax increase in 1982. By early 1983 the economy had begun to recover, and by the end of that year unemployment and inflation were significantly reduced; they remained relatively low in the later years of Reagan's administration.

THE REAGAN DOCTRINE

Believing that the United States had grown weak militarily and had lost the respect it once commanded in world affairs, Reagan aimed to restore the country to a position of moral and military preeminence. In addition to massive increases in the defense budget, he urged a more aggressive approach to combating communism and related forms of leftist totalitarianism. His administration expanded military and economic assistance to friendly governments in the less-developed world battling leftist insurgencies, and he actively supported guerrilla movements in countries with leftist governments. This policy, which became known as the Reagan Doctrine, was applied with particular zeal in Latin America.

During the 1980s the United States supported military-dominated governments in El Salvador in a bloody civil war, providing military and economic aid and helping to train elite units of the Salvadoran army. After the Sandinista government—which had overthrown the dictatorship of Anastasio Somoza in Nicaragua in 1979—strengthened its ties to Cuba and other communist-bloc countries, Reagan authorized $20 million to recruit and train a band of anti-Sandinista guerrillas. The "Contras," as they came to be called, were never a serious military threat to the Sandinistas, but the destruction caused by their attacks, along with the Reagan administration's trade embargo and efforts to influence international lending agencies to refuse Nicaraguan loan requests, augmented by the Sandinistas' own mismanagement, effectively undermined the Nicaraguan economy by the end of the 1980s.

Reagan's decision to send a battalion of U.S. marines to Lebanon in support of a cease-fire in that country's civil war resulted in a terrorist attack in 1983, in which some 260 marines were killed. On Oct. 21, 1983, Reagan launched an invasion of the Caribbean nation of Grenada, where Cuban influence was growing. U.S. forces prevailed, despite much bungling. Popular at home, the invasion was criticized almost everywhere else. Relations with China worsened at first but improved in 1984 with an exchange of state visits.

At the time of the presidential election of 1984, Reagan was at the height of his popularity. Using slogans such as "It's morning in America" and "America is back," his reelection campaign emphasized the country's reduction in inflation, the beginnings of its economic recovery, and its renewed leadership role in world affairs. This combination proved too much for the Democratic nominee, former vice president Walter Mondale of Minnesota, and his running mate, Congresswoman Geraldine Ferraro of New York, the first female vice presidential candidate ever to be named by a major party. Reagan won 59 percent of the popular vote to Mondale's 41 percent; in the electoral college, Reagan received 525 votes to Mondale's 13, the largest number of electoral votes of any candidate in history.

Second Term and the Iran-Contra Affair

Reagan's second term was more successful than his first in regard to foreign affairs. It had begun as an especially chilly period in Soviet-American relations, owing in no small part to the president's penchant for harsh anti-Soviet rhetoric. Reagan's massive military spending program, the largest in American peacetime history (which included plans for a space-based missile defense system popularly referred to as "Star Wars"), undoubtedly contributed to this climate. On the other hand, some observers argued that the buildup—through the strain it imposed on the Soviet economy—was responsible

for a more accommodating Soviet position in arms negotiations. Some argued further that it had led to a weakening of the influence of hard-liners in the Soviet leadership, making possible the glasnost ("openness") and perestroika ("restructuring") policies of the moderate new Soviet leader Mikhail Gorbachev after 1985 and even for the dissolution of the Soviet Union itself in 1990–91.

Reagan and Gorbachev met for the first time in November 1985, in Geneva, to discuss reductions in nuclear weapons. At a dramatic summit meeting in Reykjavík, Ice., in October 1986, Gorbachev proposed a 50 percent reduction in the nuclear arsenals of each side, and for a time it seemed as though a historic agreement would be reached. Although the summit ended in failure owing to differences over "Star Wars," it was followed up in December 1987 (just months after Reagan had challenged Gorbachev to tear down the Berlin Wall) by a treaty eliminating intermediate-range nuclear forces (INF) on European soil. The INF Treaty was the first arms-control pact to require an actual reduction in nuclear arsenals rather than merely restricting their proliferation. Relations between the superpowers had improved radically by 1988, primarily as a result of the reforms Gorbachev initiated at home and that were matched by equally great changes in foreign policy, but also in response to a softening of Reagan's anticommunist rhetoric. An exchange of unusually warm state visits in 1988 was followed by Soviet

Document: Ronald Reagan:
Remarks at the Brandenburg Gate in West Berlin (1987)

In the early 1980s relations between the United States and the Soviet Union had deteriorated to a level of hostility not seen since the Cuban Missile Crisis of 1962. By the summer of 1987, however, the Cold War rivalry between the United States and Soviet Union had begun to thaw again. The détente between the two superpowers had come with startling speed, largely as a result of the emergence of Mikhail Gorbachev as Soviet premier in 1985. A liberal-minded reformer, Gorbachev launched an unprecedented public relations campaign with the explicit goal of defusing Cold War tensions. Nevertheless, the Soviet Union still maintained uncompromising control over eastern Europe. In June 1987 President Reagan traveled to West Germany to visit the city of Berlin, which, divided by the Berlin Wall, symbolically represented the division of Europe between East and West. Reagan called on Gorbachev to pull down the Berlin Wall and to end Soviet domination of eastern Europe. Two years later, in November 1989, the Berlin Wall did fall. Excerpts of Reagan's speech are reprinted here.

Thank you very much. Chancellor Kohl, Governing Mayor Diepgen, ladies and gentlemen: Twenty four years ago, President John F. Kennedy visited Berlin, speaking to the people of this

Pres. Ronald Reagan at the Brandenburg Gate in Berlin in 1987, delivering a speech in which he famously called on Soviet premier Mikhail Gorbachev to "tear down" the Berlin Wall and to end Soviet control of eastern Europe. AFP/Getty Images

city and the world at the city hall. Well, since then two other presidents have come, each in his turn, to Berlin. And today, I, myself, make my second visit to your city.

We come to Berlin, we American Presidents, because it's our duty to speak, in this place, of freedom. But I must confess, we're drawn here by other things as well: by the feeling of history in this city, more than 500 years older than our own nation; by the beauty of the Grunewald and the Tiergarten; most of all, by your courage and determination. Perhaps the composer, Paul Lincke, understood something about American Presidents. You see, like so many Presidents before me, I come here today because wherever I go, whatever I do: "Ich hab noch einen koffer in Berlin." [I still have a suitcase in Berlin.]...

promises of substantial force reductions, especially in Europe.

Reagan's domestic policies were unchanged. His popularity remained consistently high until 1987, when it was learned that his administration had secretly sold arms to Iran in exchange for American hostages and then had illegally used the profits to subsidize the Contras. In the process he was embroiled in the worst scandal of his political career, one that would cost him much popular and party support and significantly impair his ability to lead the country. Reagan

Iran-Contra Affair

In early 1985 the head of the National Security Council (NSC), Robert C. McFarlane, undertook the sale of antitank and antiaircraft missiles to Iran in the mistaken belief that such a sale would secure the release of a number of American citizens who were being held captive in Lebanon by Shīʿite terrorist groups loyal to Iran. This and several subsequent weapon sales to Iran in 1986 directly contradicted the U.S. government's publicly stated policy of refusing either to bargain with terrorists or to aid Iran in its war with Iraq, a policy based on the belief that Iran was a sponsor of international terrorism. A portion of the $48 million that Iran paid for the arms was diverted by the NSC and given to the Contras, the U.S.-backed rebels fighting to overthrow the Marxist-oriented Sandinista government of Nicaragua. The monetary transfers were undertaken by NSC staff member Lieut. Col. Oliver North with the approval of McFarlane's successor as head of the NSC, Rear Adm. John M. Poindexter. North and his associates also raised private funds for the Contras. These activities violated the Boland Amendment, a law passed by Congress in 1984 that banned direct or indirect U.S. military aid to the Contras.

The NSC's illegal activities came to light in November 1986 and aroused an immediate public uproar. The investigation of the affair was the focus of televised hearings held by the Joint House-Senate Iran-Contra Committee. Poindexter and North lost their jobs and were prosecuted, President Reagan's public image was tarnished, and the United States suffered a serious though temporary loss of credibility as an opponent of terrorism.

accepted responsibility for the arms-for-hostages deal but denied any knowledge of the diversion.

Although no evidence was revealed that indicated that Reagan was more deeply involved, many in Congress and the public remained skeptical. Nevertheless, most of the public eventually appeared willing to forgive him for whatever they thought he had done, and his popularity, which had dropped dramatically during the first months of the crisis, rebounded.

ECONOMIC LEGACY

In the short run Reagan's economic measures succeeded. Inflation remained low, as did unemployment, while economic growth continued. Nonetheless, while spending for domestic programs fell, military spending continued to rise, and revenues did not increase as had been predicted. The result was a staggering growth in the budget deficit. The United States, which had been a creditor nation in 1980, was by the late 1980s the world's largest debtor nation.

Furthermore, although economic recovery had been strong, individual income in constant dollars was still lower than in the early 1970s, and family income remained constant only because many more married women were in the labour force. Savings were at an all-time low, and productivity gains were averaging only about 1 percent a year. Economic growth had continued through the remainder of

Reagan's presidency, a period that his supporters hailed as "the longest peacetime expansion in American history." Critics charged that the tax cuts and the fruits of economic growth benefited mainly the wealthy and that the gap between rich and poor had grown wider. Reagan had solved the short-term problems of inflation and recession, but he did so with borrowed money and without touching the deeper sources of America's economic decline.

THE GEORGE BUSH ADMINISTRATION

In 1988 Vice Pres. George Bush of Texas faced Democratic nominee Michael Dukakis, the governor of Massachusetts, in the presidential election. Trailing Dukakis in the polls late in the summer Bush made a risky decision; instead of stressing his qualifications for the job and his plans for the country, he campaigned against his opponent's alleged weaknesses. Accordingly, Bush's speeches and campaign advertising focused on such issues as a Massachusetts prison furlough plan and Dukakis's veto of a state law requiring public school students to recite the Pledge of Allegiance. Dukakis, whose three terms as governor had seemingly marked him as a moderate, was slow to respond to Bush's depiction of him as a dangerous liberal. In the election Bush won 54 percent of the vote to Dukakis's 46 percent. The vice president carried all but 10 states and the District of Columbia to secure a 426–112 margin in the electoral college.

FOREIGN POLICY

From the outset of his presidency, Bush demonstrated far more interest in foreign than domestic policy. Generally, he continued the key policies of the Reagan administration, especially by retaining cordial relations with the Soviet Union and its successor states. In December 1989, Bush ordered a military invasion of Panama in order to topple that country's leader, Gen. Manuel Antonio Noriega, who—though at one time of service to the U.S. government—had become notorious for his brutality and his involvement in the drug trade. The invasion, which lasted four days, resulted in hundreds of deaths, mostly of Panamanians, and the operation was denounced by both the Organization of American States and the UN General Assembly.

Bush's presidency coincided with world events of large proportion, including the collapse of communism in eastern Europe and the Soviet Union and the reunification of Germany. In November 1990 Bush met with Gorbachev in Paris and signed a mutual nonaggression pact, a symbolic conclusion to the Cold War. They also signed treaties sharply reducing the number of weapons that the two superpowers had stockpiled over the decades of Cold War hostility.

IRAQ WAR

Bush's leadership and diplomatic skills were severely tested by the Iraqi invasion of Kuwait, which began on Aug. 2, 1990. At risk was not only the sovereignty of this small sheikhdom but also U.S. interests in the Persian Gulf, including access to the region's vast oil supplies. Fearing that Iraqi aggression would spill over into Saudi Arabia, Bush swiftly organized a multinational coalition composed mostly of NATO and Arab countries. Under the auspices of the United Nations, some 500,000 U.S. troops (the largest mobilization of U.S. military personnel since the Vietnam War) were brought together with other coalition forces in Saudi Arabia. Lasting from January 16 to February 28, the war was easily won by the coalition at only slight material and human cost, but its sophisticated weapons caused heavy damage to Iraq's military and civilian infrastructure and left many Iraqi soldiers dead.

With the declining power (and subsequent collapse in 1991) of the Soviet Union, the war also emphasized the role of the United States as the world's single military superpower.

"READ MY LIPS"

This short and relatively inexpensive war, paid for largely by U.S. allies, was popular while it lasted. On the strength of the victory over Iraq and his competent leadership in foreign affairs, Bush's approval rating soared to about 90 percent. This popularity soon waned, however, as an economic recession that began in late 1990 persisted into 1992. Throughout this period, Bush

Pres. George Bush (left) *meeting with Soviet Pres. Mikhail Gorbachev at the American Embassy in Paris in 1990. The mutual nonaggression pact they signed there effectively represented the end of the Cold War.* © AP Images

showed much less initiative in domestic affairs, though he initially worked with Congress, which was controlled by the Democrats, in efforts to reduce the federal government's continuing large budget deficits. A moderate conservative, he made no drastic departures from Reagan's policies—except in taxes.

In 1990, in a move that earned him the enmity of his conservative supporters and the distrust of many voters who had backed him in 1988, he reneged on his "read my lips" pledge, in which he promised "no new taxes," and raised taxes in an attempt to cope with the soaring budget deficit.

Document: George Bush: Operation Desert Storm (1991)

In August 1990 Iraqi forces invaded neighbouring Kuwait in an attempt to gain control of its oil reserves, prompting President Bush to direct a massive American military buildup in Saudi Arabia to protect against any further Iraqi aggression. The Bush administration officially dubbed the defense of Saudi Arabia "Operation Desert Shield," but the size and scope of the American presence made clear that a powerful offensive capability existed for U.S. forces. Throughout the military buildup, American officials negotiated with Iraqi dictator Saddam Hussein in an effort to persuade him to withdraw from Kuwait. These efforts failed, as did the UN's effort to mediate an Iraqi withdrawal. When the UN Security Council deadline of Jan. 15, 1991, passed without an Iraqi withdrawal, American and Allied forces launched a massive six-week aerial bombardment that decimated Iraqi supplies, troops, and fortifications in Kuwait and southern Iraq. Excerpts of Bush's speech announcing the opening of the air campaign, known as "Operation Desert Storm," are reprinted here.

Just 2 hours ago, allied air forces began an attack on military targets in Iraq and Kuwait. These attacks continue as I speak. Ground forces are not engaged.

This conflict started August 2d when the dictator of Iraq invaded a small and helpless neighbor. Kuwait—a member of the Arab League and a member of the United Nations—was crushed; its people, brutalized. Five months ago, Saddam Hussein started this cruel war against Kuwait. Tonight, the battle has been joined....

As I report to you, air attacks are underway against military targets in Iraq. We are determined to knock out Saddam Hussein's nuclear bomb potential. We will also destroy his chemical weapons facilities. Much of Saddam's artillery and tanks will be destroyed. Our operations are designed to best protect the lives of all the coalition forces by targeting Saddam's vast military arsenal. Initial reports from General Schwarzkopf are that our operations are proceeding according to plan....

THE 1992 ELECTION

Bush's policy reversal on taxation and his inability to turn around the economy—his failure to put across what he called "the vision thing" to the American public—ultimately proved his downfall. Bush ran a lackluster campaign for reelection in 1992. He faced a fierce early challenge from Patrick Buchanan in the Republican primary and then lost votes in the general election to third-party candidate Ross Perot. Meanwhile, Bush's Democratic opponent, Bill Clinton of Arkansas, hammered away at the issue of the deteriorating economy. Bush, the first vice president since Martin Van Buren in 1836 to succeed directly to the presidency via an election rather than the death of the incumbent, lost to Clinton by a popular vote of 37 percent to Clinton's 43 percent; Perot garnered an impressive 19 percent of the vote.

Upon assuming office, Bush had made a number of notable senior staff appointments, among them that of Gen. Colin Powell to chairman of the U.S. Joint Chiefs of Staff. His other important policy makers included James Baker as secretary of state and William Bennett as director of the Office of National Drug Control Policy. In the course of his presidency, he also nominated two Supreme Court justices, David H. Souter (to replace the retiring William J. Brennan) and the more controversial Clarence Thomas (to replace Thurgood Marshall).

In his last weeks in office, Bush ordered a U.S. military-led mission to feed the starving citizens of war-torn Somalia, thereby placing U.S. marines in the crossfire of warring factions and inadvertently causing the deaths of 18 soldiers. Equally as controversial was his pardoning of six Reagan administration officials charged with illegal actions associated with the Iran-Contra Affair.

CHAPTER 7

"IT'S THE ECONOMY, STUPID": THE BILL CLINTON ADMINISTRATION

The beginning of the 1990s was a difficult time for the United States. The country was plagued not only by a sluggish economy but by violent crime (much of it drug-related), poverty, welfare dependency, problematic race relations, and spiraling health costs. Although Bill Clinton promised to boost both the economy (campaign strategist James Carville had constantly reminded candidate Clinton that the key issue of the day was "the economy, stupid!") and the quality of life, his administration got off to a shaky start, the victim of what some critics have called ineptitude and bad judgment.

EARLY POLICY INITIATIVES

One of Clinton's first acts was to attempt to fulfill a campaign promise to end discrimination against gay men and lesbians in the military. After encountering strong criticism

First lady Hillary Clinton (centre) *and "second lady" Tipper Gore* (left) *meeting with the patients and staff of a medical centre as part of the health care reform initiative that was launched early in Bill Clinton's presidency.* Cynthia Johnson/Time & Life Pictures/Getty Images

from conservatives and some military leaders—including Colin Powell, the chairman of the Joint Chiefs of Staff—Clinton was eventually forced to support a compromise policy—summed up by the phrase "don't ask, don't tell"—that was viewed as being at once ambiguous, unsatisfactory to either side of the issue, and possibly unconstitutional. His first two nominees for attorney general withdrew over ethics questions, and two major pieces of legislation—an economic stimulus package and a campaign finance reform bill—were blocked by a Republican filibuster in the Senate.

In the hope that he could avoid a major confrontation with Congress, he set aside any further attempts at campaign finance reform. During the presidential campaign, Clinton promised to institute a system of universal health insurance. His appointment of his wife, Hillary Rodham Clinton, to chair a task force on health care reform drew stark criticism from Republicans, who objected both to the propriety of the arrangement and to what they considered her outspoken feminism. They campaigned fiercely against the task force's eventual proposal, and none of the numerous

Document: Hillary Clinton: Attempts at Health Care Reform (1993)

During the 1992 presidential campaign, Bill Clinton had promised voters that if they elected him, they would get "two for the price of one." He was speaking of his wife, Hillary, who would become the most politically influential first lady in history. She would also become one of the most controversial, especially after being named by her husband to serve as the chairperson of the national task force on health care reform. First, critics argued that it was inappropriate for a first lady to head a major government task force because unlike any other appointee, she could not be fired. Second, many complained that because her task force conducted secret deliberations which no member of the press was allowed to observe, the task force itself was inherently undemocratic. Third, critics argued that her views on health care were far to the left of the national mainstream and that her policy proposals would "socialize" a significant percentage of the American economy. In the speech excerpted below, Hillary Clinton (who would be elected to the U.S. Senate from New York in 2000, run for the Democratic presidential nomination in 2008, and then serve as the secretary of state) responded to her critics. In the end, however, criticism of the first lady and the goals of her task force proved overwhelming. In early 1994 the Democrat-controlled Congress chose not to put Clinton's health care plan to a vote because it lacked the support necessary for passage, and they did not want an embarrassing defeat for the president. Furthermore, Republican victories in the 1994 midterm elections guaranteed that Clinton's health care plan would never win congressional passage. The following address, excerpted below, was delivered to the American Medical Association in Chicago, Ill., in June 1993.

All of us respond to children. We want to nurture them so they can dream the dreams that free and healthy children should have. This is our primary responsibility as adults. And it is our primary responsibility as a government. We should stand behind families, teachers and others who work with the young, so that we can enable them to meet their own needs by becoming self-sufficient and responsible so that they, in turn, will be able to meet their families and their own children's needs.

When I was growing up, not far from where we are today, this seemed an easier task. There seemed to be more strong families. There seemed to be safer neighborhoods. There seemed to be an outlook for caring and cooperation among adults that stood for and behind children. I remember so well my father saying to me that if you get in trouble at school, you get in trouble at home—no questions asked—because there was this sense among the adult community that all of them, from my child's perspective, were involved in helping their own and others' children....

recommendations were formally submitted to Congress.

Despite these early missteps, the Clinton administration had numerous policy and personnel successes. Although 1992 third-party presidential candidate Ross Perot had spoken vividly of the effects of the North American Free Trade

Agreement, which he said would produce a "giant sucking sound" as American jobs were lost to Mexico, Congress passed the measure and Clinton signed it into law, thereby creating a generally successful free-trade zone between the United States, Canada, and Mexico. During Clinton's first term, Congress enacted with Clinton's support a deficit reduction package to reverse the spiraling debt that had been accrued during the 1980s and '90s, and he signed some 30 major bills related to women and family issues, including the Family and Medical Leave Act and the Brady Handgun Violence Prevention Act. Clinton also changed the face of the federal government, appointing women and minorities to significant posts throughout his administration, including Janet Reno as the first woman attorney general, Donna Shalala as secretary of Health and Human Services, Joycelyn Elders as surgeon general, Madeleine Albright as the first woman secretary of state, and Ruth Bader Ginsburg as a justice on the Supreme Court.

U.S. Pres. Bill Clinton looks on as Israeli Prime Minister Yitzhak Rabin (left) *shakes hands with PLO chairman Yāsir 'Arafāt* (right), *at the White House in 1993 after the signing of the Israel-PLO accords.* Cynthia Johnson/Time & Life Pictures/Getty Images

Document: Contract with America (1994)

In November 1994 the Republican Party won control of both the House of Representatives and the Senate. It was a victory of historic proportions; Republicans had not held a majority in both houses of Congress since 1954. Moreover, since 1932 Republicans had controlled the House of Representatives only twice. Much of the credit for the Republicans' victory was given to Representative Newt Gingrich of Georgia. A former history professor, Gingrich had spent the better part of two decades laying the groundwork for a Republican congressional majority. When President Clinton's popularity plummeted in the summer and fall of 1994, Gingrich skillfully positioned House Republicans as a viable alternative to what he described as Clinton's "failed" liberal policies. Their program for change was encapsulated in the Contract with America, reprinted below. In the aftermath of the 1994 midterm elections, Gingrich was elected Speaker of the House by his fellow House Republicans.

As Republican Members of the House of Representatives and as citizens seeking to join that body we propose not just to change its policies, but even more important, to restore the bonds of trust between the people and their elected representatives. That is why, in this era of official evasion and posturing, we offer instead a detailed agenda for national renewal, a written commitment with no fine print.

This year's election offers the chance, after four decades of one-party control, to bring to the House a new majority that will transform the way Congress works. That historic change would be the end of government that is too big, too intrusive, and too easy with the public's money. It can be the beginning of a Congress that respects the values and shares the faith of the American family. Like Lincoln, our first Republican president, we intend to act "with firmness in the right, as God gives us to see the right." To restore accountability to Congress. To end its cycle of scandal and disgrace. To make us all proud again of the way free people govern themselves....

MID-TERM CHALLENGE

With Clinton's popularity sagging after the health care debacle, the 1994 elections resulted in the opposition Republican Party winning a majority in both houses of Congress for the first time in 40 years. This historic victory was viewed by many—especially the House Republicans led by Speaker Newt Gingrich—as the voters' repudiation of the Clinton presidency.

A chastened Clinton subsequently accommodated some of the Republican proposals—offering a more aggressive deficit reduction plan and a massive overhaul of the nation's welfare system—while opposing Republican efforts to slow the growth of government spending on popular programs such as Medicare. Ultimately the uncompromising and confrontational behaviour of the congressional Republicans produced the opposite of what they intended, and after a budget impasse between the Republicans and Clinton in 1995 and 1996—which forced two partial government shutdowns, including one for 22 days (the longest closure of government operations to date)—Clinton won considerable public support for his more moderate approach.

Clinton's foreign policy ventures included a successful effort in 1994 to reinstate Haitian President Jean-Bertrand Aristide, who had been ousted by a military coup in 1991; a commitment of U.S. forces to a peacekeeping initiative in Bosnia and Herzegovina; and a leading role in the ongoing initiatives to bring a permanent resolution to the dispute between Palestinians and Israelis. In 1993 he invited Israeli Prime Minister Yitzhak Rabin (who was later assassinated by a Jewish extremist opposed to territorial concessions to the Palestinians) and Palestine Liberation Organization (PLO) chairman Yāsir ʿArafāt to Washington to sign a historic agreement that granted limited Palestinian self-rule in the Gaza Strip and Jericho.

During the Clinton administration the United States remained a target for international terrorists with bomb attacks on the World Trade Center in New York City (1993), on U.S. embassies in Kenya and Tanzania (1998), and on the U.S. Navy in Yemen (2000). The domestic front, though, was the site of unexpected antigovernment violence when on April 19, 1995, an American, Timothy McVeigh, detonated a bomb in a terrorist attack on the Alfred P. Murrah Federal Building in Oklahoma City, Okla., killing 168 and injuring more than 500.

THE 1996 ELECTION

Although scandal was never far from the White House—a fellow Arkansan who had been part of the administration committed suicide; there were rumours of financial irregularities that had occurred while Clinton was governor of Arkansas; opponents charged that the first lady engineered the firing of staff in the White House travel office ("Travelgate"); former associates were indicted and convicted of crimes; and rumours of sexual impropriety persisted—the economy made a slow but steady recovery after 1991, marked by dramatic gains in the stock market in the mid-1990s. Buoyed by the economic growth, Clinton was easily reelected in 1996, capturing 49 percent of the popular vote to 41 percent for Republican challenger Bob Dole and 8 percent for Perot. In the electoral college Clinton won 379 votes to Dole's 159.

Economic growth continued during Clinton's second term, eventually setting a record for the nation's longest peacetime economic expansion. After enormous budget deficits throughout the 1980s and early 1990s—including a $290 billion deficit in 1992—by 1998 the Clinton administration oversaw the first balanced budget and budget surpluses since 1969. The vibrant economy produced a tripling

President Clinton, with wife, Hillary, by his side, vehemently denying having an affair with White House intern Monica Lewinsky after allegations of their relationship surfaced. Diana Walker/ Time & Life Pictures/Getty Images

in the value of the stock market, historically high levels of home ownership, and the lowest unemployment rate in nearly 30 years.

THE LEWINSKY AFFAIR

During Clinton's first term Attorney General Reno approved an investigation into Clinton's business dealings in Arkansas. The resulting inquiry, known as Whitewater—the name of the housing development corporation at the centre of the controversy—was led from 1994 by independent counsel Kenneth Starr. Although the investigation lasted several years and cost more than $50 million, Starr was unable to find conclusive evidence of wrongdoing by the Clintons. When a three-judge panel allowed him to expand the scope of his investigation, however, he uncovered evidence of an affair between Clinton and Monica Lewinsky, a White House intern. Clinton

Document: Kenneth Starr: Starr Report (1998)

When Bill Clinton ran for president in 1992, he was besieged with allegations of marital infidelity. On Super Bowl Sunday 1992, Clinton and wife Hillary appeared on the CBS television program 60 Minutes to respond to the allegations. Clinton claimed that while he had "caused pain" in his marriage in the past, he and his wife had a solid marriage. Two years later, an Arkansas woman, Paula Jones, accused Clinton of sexually harassing her while he was governor of Arkansas. As before, the allegations had little impact on Clinton's popularity. In January 1998 a new and far more damaging allegation of sexual impropriety emerged against Clinton. While serving as independent counsel for the "Whitewater" investigation, Kenneth Starr learned that Clinton was involved in a sexual relationship with a former White House intern, Monica Lewinsky. Word of Starr's revelation soon leaked to the press and set off a year-long media firestorm. Clinton initially denied the allegations, but, when DNA evidence surfaced that proved the affair, Clinton reversed course. In a nationally televised address in August 1998, he admitted to the relationship with Lewinsky but denied lying under oath. Reprinted below are portions of Starr's official report on the Clinton-Lewinsky affair.

As required by Section 595(c) of Title 28 of the United States Code, the Office of the Independent Counsel ("OIC" or "Office") hereby submits substantial and credible information that President William Jefferson Clinton committed acts that may constitute grounds for an impeachment.

The information reveals that President Clinton:

- lied under oath at a civil deposition while he was a defendant in a sexual harassment lawsuit;
- lied under oath to a grand jury;
- attempted to influence the testimony of a potential witness who had direct knowledge of facts that would reveal the falsity of his deposition testimony;
- attempted to obstruct justice by facilitating a witness's plan to refuse to comply with a subpoena;
- attempted to obstruct justice by encouraging a witness to file an affidavit that the President knew would be false, and then by making use of that false affidavit at his own deposition;
- lied to potential grand jury witnesses, knowing that they would repeat those lies before the grand jury; and
- engaged in a pattern of conduct that was inconsistent with his constitutional duty to faithfully execute the laws....

repeatedly and publicly denied that the affair had taken place. After conclusive evidence of the affair surfaced, Clinton admitted to the affair and apologized to his family and to the American public.

On the basis of Starr's 445-page report and supporting evidence, hearings conducted before the 1998 midterm elections resulted in Clinton's impeachment for perjury and obstruction of justice by a lame-duck session of the House of Representatives after the election.

Clinton was acquitted of the charges by the Senate in 1999. During the impeachment proceedings, foreign policy also dominated the headlines. In December 1998 Clinton, citing Iraqi noncompliance with UN resolutions and weapons inspectors, ordered a four-day bombing campaign against Iraq; the military action prompted Iraq to halt further weapons inspections.

When the dust had settled, the Clinton administration was damaged but not broken. Bill Clinton's job approval rating remained high during the final years of his presidency, and in 1999 Hillary Clinton launched a successful campaign for the U.S. Senate seat being vacated by Democrat Daniel Patrick Moynihan in New York, thereby becoming the first first lady to win elective office. During the final year of his presidency, Clinton invited Yasir 'Arafat and Israeli Prime Minister Ehud Barak to the United States in an attempt to broker a final settlement between the Israelis and the Palestinians. The eventual breakdown of the talks, along with subsequent events in Jerusalem and elsewhere, resulted in some of the deadliest conflicts between Israelis and Palestinians in more than a decade. Clinton also became the first American president to visit Vietnam since the end of the Vietnam War.

CHAPTER 8

AMERICA AFTER 9-11: THE GEORGE W. BUSH ADMINISTRATION

Despite continued economic growth, the 2000 presidential election between the Democratic candidate, Vice Pres. Al Gore, and the Republican candidate, Texas Gov. George W. Bush, the former president's eldest son, was one of the closest and most controversial in the republic's history. Although Gore won the nationwide popular vote by more than 500,000 votes, the presidency hinged on the outcome in Florida, whose 25 electoral votes would give the winner of that state a narrow majority in the electoral college. With Bush leading in Florida by fewer than 1,000 votes after a mandatory statewide recount, the presidency remained undecided for five weeks as Florida state courts and federal courts heard numerous legal challenges. After a divided Florida Supreme Court ordered a statewide manual recount of the approximately 45,000 "undervotes" (i.e., ballots that machines recorded as not clearly expressing a presidential vote) and the inclusion of hand-counted ballots in two counties that had not been previously certified by Florida's

U.S. ELECTION 2000

Gore (Democratic)
266 electoral votes*

Bush (Republican)
271 electoral votes

© 2001 Encyclopædia Britannica, Inc.

* Protesting D.C.'s lack of congressional representation,
one D.C. elector cast a blank ballot.

In the 2000 presidential election, one of the most controversial elections in American history, Al Gore won the nationwide popular vote over George W. Bush by more than 500,000 votes but narrowly lost in the electoral college, 271–266. This map shows the distribution of electoral votes by state.

secretary of state—which reduced Bush's margin to under 200 votes before the manual recounting began—the Bush campaign quickly filed an appeal to halt the manual recount, which the U.S. Supreme Court granted by a 5–4 vote pending oral arguments. Concluding (7–2) that a quick statewide recount could not be performed fairly unless elaborate ground rules were established, the court issued a controversial 5-to-4 decision to reverse the Florida Supreme Court's

recount order, effectively awarding the presidency to Bush. With his 271-to-266 victory in the electoral college, Bush became the first president since 1888 to win the election despite losing the nationwide popular vote.

CONGRESSIONAL RESISTANCE

Bush became the first Republican president since the 1950s to enjoy a majority in both houses of Congress. Among the initial domestic challenges that faced the Bush administration were a weakening national economy and an energy crisis in California. Bush, who had campaigned as a "compassionate conservative," promoted traditionally conservative policies in domestic affairs, the centrepiece of which was a $1.35 trillion tax-cut bill he signed into law in June 2001. That month, however, Republican Sen. Jim Jeffords became an independent, giving the Democrats control of the Senate. Subsequently Bush encountered strong congressional resistance to some of his initiatives, such as an educational voucher program that would provide subsidies to parents who send their children to private schools, the creation of a nuclear missile defense system, and federal funding for selected social programs of religious groups. In foreign affairs, the administration attempted to liberalize U.S. immigration

Pres. George W. Bush (centre), *along with New York City Mayor Rudolph Giuliani* (left) *and an official of the New York City Fire Department, surveying the site of the World Trade Center after the devastating attacks of September 11, 2001.* Paul J. Richards/AFP/Getty Images

policy with regard to Mexico, with which it struck closer ties. But it faced sharp criticism from China for its outspoken support of Taiwan and from Europe and elsewhere for its abandonment of the Kyoto Protocol, a 1997 treaty aimed at reducing the emission of greenhouse gases, and for its declared intention to withdraw from the 1972 Treaty on the Limitation of Anti-Ballistic Missile Systems (it formally withdrew from the treaty in 2002).

THE SEPTEMBER 11 ATTACKS

The greatest challenge of Bush's first year in office came on the heels of a massive terrorist attack on September 11, 2001, in which hijacked commercial airliners were employed as suicide bombs. Two of the four hijacked planes leveled the twin towers of the World Trade Center and collapsed or damaged many of the surrounding buildings in New York City,

Document: George W. Bush: Declaration of War on Terrorism (2001)

On the morning of Sept. 11, 2001, 19 Middle Eastern terrorists hijacked four American passenger jets and used the planes as guided missiles to attack symbolic targets on the eastern seaboard of the United States. Two planes slammed into the World Trade Center Towers in New York City, causing both towers to collapse. A third plane crashed into the Pentagon, near Washington, D.C., and a fourth went down in the Pennsylvania countryside when passengers resisted the hijackers. More people perished in the devastating attacks than had died in the Japanese attack at Pearl Harbor, Hawaii, 60 years previously. On September 20, President Bush spoke before a Joint Session of Congress and outlined America's response to the events of September 11. That address is printed here.

Mr. Speaker, Mr. President Pro Tempore, members of Congress, and fellow Americans: In the normal course of events, Presidents come to this chamber to report on the state of the Union. Tonight, no such report is needed. It has already been delivered by the American people.

We have seen it in the courage of passengers, who rushed terrorists to save others on the ground—passengers like an exceptional man named Todd Beamer. And would you please help me to welcome his wife, Lisa Beamer, here tonight. We have seen the state of our Union in the endurance of rescuers, working past exhaustion. We have seen the unfurling of flags, the lighting of candles, the giving of blood, the saying of prayers—in English, Hebrew, and Arabic. We have seen the decency of a loving and giving people who have made the grief of strangers their own. My fellow citizens, for the last nine days, the entire world has seen for itself the state of our Union—and it is strong. Tonight we are a country awakened to danger and called to defend freedom. Our grief has turned to anger, and anger to resolution. Whether we bring our enemies to justice, or bring justice to our enemies, justice will be done....

another destroyed a large section of the Pentagon outside Washington, D.C., and still another crashed in the southern Pennsylvania countryside. Some 3,000 people were killed in this, the worst act of terrorism in U.S. history. Bush responded with a call for a global war on terrorism.

Identifying exiled Saudi millionaire and terrorist mastermind Osama bin Laden as the primary suspect in the acts, Bush built an international coalition against bin Laden (who later claimed responsibility for the attacks) and his network, al-Qaeda ("the Base"), and the Taliban government of Afghanistan, which had harboured bin Laden and his followers. On October 7 the United States launched aerial attacks against Afghanistan; by the end of the year the Taliban and bin Laden's forces were routed or forced into hiding, and the Bush administration was negotiating with Afghanistan's many factions in an attempt to establish a stable regime there.

In 2002 the U.S. economy worsened, as consumer confidence and the stock market continued to fall and corporate scandals dominated the headlines. Nevertheless, Bush remained popular, and he led the Republican Party to majorities in both the House and Senate in the midterm elections of 2002.

THE IRAQ WAR

Despite the economic difficulties, foreign affairs continued to dominate the Bush administration's agenda. In 2002 Bush focused world attention on Iraq, accusing Saddam Hussein's government of having ties to al-Qaeda and of continuing to possess and develop weapons of mass destruction, contrary to UN mandates. In November Bush's secretary of state, Colin Powell, engineered a UN Security Council resolution authorizing the return of weapons inspectors to Iraq. Soon thereafter Bush declared that Iraq was in breach of the new resolution for its failure to cooperate fully with the inspectors. In mid-March, declaring that diplomacy was at an end, he issued an ultimatum giving Saddam 48 hours to leave Iraq or face removal by force (though he indicated that, even if Saddam chose to leave, U.S.-led military forces would enter the country to search for weapons of mass destruction and to stabilize the new government). On March 20 (local time), following Saddam's public refusal to leave, the United States and allied forces launched an attack on Iraq, called Operation Iraqi Freedom.

With some international assistance, notably from the United Kingdom, the United States launched a brief air bombing campaign in Iraq followed by a massive ground invasion, arising from Kuwait in the south. The resistance encountered was heavier than expected, especially in the major cities, which nevertheless capitulated and fell under U.S. or British control by the end of April; on May 1 President Bush declared an end to major combat. Armed resistance, however, continued and even increased, primarily as guerrilla attacks on

Document: John P. Murtha: War in Iraq (2005)

By November 2005 many of the 81 Democratic Representatives and 29 Democratic Senators who had voted in 2002 to authorize the invasion of Iraq had begun to criticize the administration's handling of the war; however, few position reversals by American politicians have shaken the Washington establishment and shaped debate as forcefully as that of Rep. John P. "Jack" Murtha, a conservative Democrat from Pennsylvania who called for the withdrawal of U.S. troops. The hawkish ranking Democrat on the House Appropriations Committee, a strong supporter of the Persian Gulf War, and a marine veteran who reenlisted to serve in Vietnam (where he earned a bronze star, two purple hearts, and the Vietnamese Cross of Gallantry), Murtha was a most unlikely opponent of the war. His speech to the House of Representatives (reprinted below) evoked passionate responses on both sides of the aisle. White House spokesman Scott McClellan denounced Murtha's call as a "surrender to the terrorists," and many Republicans decried it as a "cut and run" policy, none more sensationally than Rep. Jean Schmidt of Ohio, who told the House that a constituent had asked her to tell Murtha that "cowards cut and run, Marines never do." Even many Democrats were reluctant to endorse Murtha's plan.

The war in Iraq is not going as advertised. It is a flawed policy wrapped in illusion. The American public is way ahead of us. The United States and coalition troops have done all they can in Iraq, but it is time for a change in direction. Our military is suffering. The future of our country is at risk. We can not continue on the present course. It is evident that continued military action in Iraq is not in the best interest of the United States of America, the Iraqi people or the Persian Gulf Region.

General Casey said in a September 2005 Hearing, "the perception of occupation in Iraq is a major driving force behind the insurgency." General Abizaid said on the same date, "Reducing the size and visibility of the coalition forces in Iraq is a part of our counterinsurgency strategy."

For 2 years I have been concerned about the U.S. policy and the plan in Iraq. I have addressed my concerns with the Administration and the Pentagon and have spoken out in public about my concerns. The main reason for going to war has been discredited. A few days before the start of the war I was in Kuwait—the military drew a red line around Baghdad and said when U.S. forces cross that line they will be attacked by the Iraqis with Weapons of Mass Destruction—but the US forces said they were prepared. They had well trained forces with the appropriate protective gear....

U.S. soldiers and on Iraqis assuming positions of leadership. The American goal of a rebuilt, democratic state in Iraq proved elusive, as U.S. administrators struggled to reinstitute basic infrastructure to the country following the victory. Just as elusive were Iraq's former leader, Saddam Hussein, who was eventually captured in December, and hard evidence of weapons of mass destruction. The lack of such evidence and continuing American casualties emboldened critics of the administration, who questioned the prewar intelligence gathered to support the invasion.

THE 2004 ELECTION

The Iraq War became a major issue in the campaign for the 2004 presidential election between Bush and his Democratic challenger, Sen. John Kerry of Massachusetts. Other campaign issues included joblessness, homeland security, free trade, health care, and the role of the country in the international community, as well as debates over religion, abortion, marriage, and civil rights. Candidate spending, voter turnout, and partisan dissension were high, and Bush defeated Kerry in a contentious and close election, which seemed, like the 2000 election, to hinge on the electoral votes of a single state, this time Ohio.

Bush began his second term emboldened by a larger Republican majority in both the House of Representatives and the Senate, with promises to prop up the sagging economy, allay domestic security fears, reduce the national debt, lower unemployment, and help usher in an era of democracy in Iraq. In particular, he sought to privatize Social Security and overhaul the tax system.

By mid-decade the economy showed strong signs of revival, based partly on the continuing upsurge of the housing market. Bush's plan for Social Security reform, however, proved unpopular and never even came to a vote. The president's personal popularity and that of his

party began to wane as it was beset with a series of ethics-related scandals. In 2005 Republican House majority leader Tom Delay was forced to step down after a Texas grand jury indicted him on election-law violations; later, he was further linked to influence-peddling indiscretions that led to the conviction and imprisonment of lobbyist Jack Abramoff. In 2006, reports of national security-related government wiretapping and allegations of torture of some suspected terrorists alarmed civil libertarians. The next year Attorney General Alberto Gonzales was forced to resign after a probe into the "political" firing of eight U.S. attorneys; and Lewis ("Scooter") Libby, special assistant to Vice President Dick Cheney, was convicted of lying to a special counsel regarding his involvement in the politically motivated leak of a CIA agent's covert identity.

HURRICANE KATRINA AND GROWING DISENCHANTMENT WITH THE IRAQ WAR

Even more damaging to Bush's standing with many Americans was what was widely seen as the federal government's failure to deal promptly and effectively with the fallout from Hurricane Katrina, which devastated parts of Alabama, Mississippi, Florida, and Louisiana, especially New Orleans, in late August and early September 2005. Moreover, with casualties mounting in Iraq, more people had come to believe that the Bush

A flooded street in New Orleans. The devastation of Hurricane Katrina was apparent long after the storm subsided, as many residents of the Gulf Coast lost their homes and faced flooding, power outages, and food and water shortages, among a host of other problems. New York Daily News Archive/Getty Images

administration had misled the country into war. As a result of all these factors, the Democrats were able to win narrow majorities in both houses of Congress following the 2006 midterm election. Determined to stay the course in Iraq and in spite of strong Democratic opposition, Bush authorized a "surge" of an additional 30,000 troops that brought the total of U.S. combatants in the country to some 160,000 by autumn 2007. But even as the surge reduced violence in

Iraq, the war and the president remained unpopular.

THE FINANCIAL CRISIS

The election to succeed Bush was between Sen. John McCain of Arizona, the Republican candidate, and Sen. Barack Obama of Illinois, who had triumphed over the favourite, Sen. Hillary Clinton of New York, in a long primary battle to win the Democratic nomination.

At the height of the contest, the U.S. economy was thrown into turmoil by a financial crisis. From September 19 to October 10, the Dow Jones Average dropped 26 percent. At the same time, there was a severe contraction of liquidity in credit markets worldwide, caused in part by a debacle related to subprime mortgages. While the housing market boomed, individuals lacking the credit ratings necessary for conventional mortgages had been able to obtain subprime mortgages, most of which were adjustable-rate mortgages (ARM) at low, so-called teaser, interest rates that ballooned after a few years. The rates for many of those ARMs jumped at the same time that overbuilding undercut the housing market; foreclosures mounted, and investment banks that under recent deregulation had been allowed to overleverage their assets foundered, resulting in the bankruptcy or sale of several major financial institutions. The U.S. economic and political establishment reacted by passing (after an unsuccessful first attempt) the Emergency Economic Stabilization Act, which sought to prevent further collapse and to bail out the economy. In the process, the U.S. government provided loans to, and in some cases took an ownership stake in, financial institutions through the Troubled Assets Relief Program (TARP), which allocated $700 billion to the recovery effort.

CHAPTER 9

"YES WE CAN": THE BARACK OBAMA ADMINISTRATION

The financial crisis worked against the presidential candidacy of Republican John McCain, whom many voters associated with the unpopular policies of the administration, and worked for the highly charismatic Democratic candidate Barack Obama, whose campaign from its outset had been based on the theme of sweeping political change. Obama defeated McCain, becoming the first African American elected to the presidency. He captured nearly 53 percent of the popular vote and 365 electoral votes

THE GREAT RECESSION

In the interim between the election and Obama's inauguration, the Bush administration's handling of the distribution of the first half of the TARP funds was criticized. There were accusations that it had infused too much money into large banks without placing adequate conditions on them, rather than purchasing "toxic" assets as it had promised. Obama and his transition team, working with Bush, persuaded the Senate to release the last half of the TARP funds, promising that they

Document: Barack Obama: Inaugural Address (2009)

On Jan. 20, 2009, a frigid morning in Washington, D.C., and across much of the country, Barack Obama became the 44th president of the United States. He was only the second man to swear his oath of office on the Bible used by Abraham Lincoln for that purpose. The Washington Post estimated that 1.8 million people filled the National Mall to witness (the vast majority by means of strategically placed large-screen televisions) the emotion-filled inauguration of America's first African American president, and countless others filled living rooms and other meeting places throughout the country and, indeed, the world. The event's general air of celebration was tempered with sober evaluation of the nation's enormous hurdles and hard work ahead.

My fellow citizens:

I stand here today humbled by the task before us, grateful for the trust you have bestowed, mindful of the sacrifices borne by our ancestors. I thank President Bush for his service to our nation, as well as [for] the generosity and cooperation he has shown throughout this transition.

Forty-four Americans have now taken the presidential oath. The words have been spoken during rising tides of prosperity and the still waters of peace. Yet, every so often

U.S. Pres. Barack Obama delivering his inaugural address, Washington, D.C., Jan. 20, 2009. SMSgt Thomas Meneguin, U.S. Air Force/U.S. Department of Defense

the oath is taken amidst gathering clouds and raging storms. At these moments, America has carried on not simply because of the skill or vision of those in high office, but because we the people have remained faithful to the ideals of our forebears, and true to our founding documents.

So it has been. So it must be with this generation of Americans.

That we are in the midst of crisis is now well understood. Our nation is at war, against a far-reaching network of violence and hatred. Our economy is badly weakened, a consequence of greed and irresponsibility on the part of some, but also our collective failure to make hard choices and prepare the nation for a new age. Homes have been lost; jobs shed; businesses shuttered. Our health care is too costly; our schools fail too many; and each day brings further evidence that the ways we use energy strengthen our adversaries and threaten our planet....

would be targeted at relief for home owners and at stimulating the credit markets.

The economic downturn, widely referred to as the "Great Recession" (which officially dated from December 2007 in the United States), included the two most dismal quarters for the U.S. economy in more than 60 years: GDP contracted by 6.3 percent in late 2008 and by 5.7 percent in early 2009. Efforts to stabilize the economy included extending $80 billion to automakers Chrysler and General Motors, with the government assuming ownership of 8 percent and 61 percent of each, respectively; the Federal Reserve pumping well over $1 trillion into the economy by purchasing Treasury bonds; and the passage of a $787 billion stimulus spending measure. In the third quarter of 2009, GDP finally turned positive, gaining 2.2 percent on an annualized basis. However, unemployment, which had stood at 7.2 percent at the beginning of the year, hovered around 10 percent in early 2010. Moreover, the stimulative policies had helped balloon the U.S. federal deficit to $1.42 trillion, earning widespread criticism from Republicans.

HEALTH CARE REFORM AND THE TEA PARTY

Obama had entered office vowing to reduce partisanship in Washington, but he made little progress in that direction in his first year. With Democrats holding substantial majorities in both houses, Republicans, claiming that they were being largely excluded from substantive negotiations on key bills, took what most Democrats saw as an obstructionist approach, earning the nickname the "Party of No" from liberal commentators. In the meantime, a populist reaction emerged among libertarian-minded conservatives that was generally opposed to what they considered excessive taxation, to illegal immigration, and to government intervention in the private sector. This Tea Party movement gained steam during the summer of 2009, when town hall meetings were held across the country to debate proposed health care insurance reform, the signature issue of the Obama presidential campaign.

Republicans uniformly opposed Democratic proposals for health care reform, branding them a "government takeover" of health care and protesting that the price tag would be devastatingly high. Some Republicans also claimed—falsely—that the Democratic plan would establish "death panels" that would deny coverage to seniors. Although there was also strong opposition to aspects of the plan within the Democratic Party, the House of Representatives passed a sweeping reform bill in November 2009. The Senate version of the bill, which barely survived a filibuster attempt by the Republicans, called for considerably less change than the House bill (most notably excluding the "public option" through which a government-run program would have provided lower-cost competition for private insurance companies).

Before the two houses could attempt to bridge the differences in their bills, the Democrats lost their filibuster-proof majority in the Senate as a result of the victory of a Republican in a special election in Massachusetts. Nevertheless, the president and the Democratic leadership, especially Speaker of the House Nancy Pelosi, pushed on. In March 2010, having secured the support of a sufficient number of House Democrats who had been opposed to aspects of the Senate plan, Pelosi engineered passage of the Senate bill in a 219–212 vote (with all Republicans and 34 Democrats in opposition). Ultimately, the Democrats obtained passage of the bill through the use of a relatively seldom-used procedure known as reconciliation, which requires a simple majority for passage. No Republicans in either house voted for the final bill.

On March 23 Obama signed into law the Patient Protection and Affordable Care Act, which—once all its elements had taken effect over the next nine years—would extend health care to some 32 million previously uninsured Americans and prohibit insurers from denying coverage to those with preexisting conditions. The bill required that all citizens obtain health care insurance.

In the spring of 2010, one of the Obama administration's big economic initiatives, the financial rescue of General Motors, bore fruit as the automaker recorded its first profits in three years. In general, the U.S. economy seemed to be rebounding—if slowly. However, as the summer approached, unemployment stagnated at near 10 percent. Although the Republicans and some economists criticized the economic stimulus as ineffective and predicted the onset of another recession, others argued that it may have added more than three million new jobs.

THE DEEPWATER HORIZON OIL SPILL AND THE WARS IN IRAQ AND AFGHANISTAN

Responding to the banking and finance meltdown that had precipitated the economic downturn, Congress in July enacted comprehensive financial regulations. However, the headlines in spring and summer were dominated by another event, a massive oil spill off the coast of Louisiana in the Gulf of Mexico caused by the explosion and collapse of the Deepwater Horizon drilling platform in April. Efforts to contain the spill—which endangered marine life, fouled beaches, and brought a halt to fishing in a huge area—proved largely futile until July.

A hallmark of Obama's campaign had been his contention that the Bush administration's preoccupation with Iraq had been to the detriment of the situation in Afghanistan; Obama argued that Afghanistan should have been the focus of U.S. military efforts. As security conditions in Iraq continued to improve, the new administration began slowly removing U.S. military personnel, with an announced goal of ending U.S. combat operations by mid-2010 and exiting the country entirely by late 2011.

Meanwhile, in response to the resurgence of the Taliban in Afghanistan, in February 2009 Obama raised the total troop commitment there to 68,000, and then, after three months of deliberation, he acceded to the military's request for another 30,000 troops, over the objections of many Democrats.

MID-TERM ELECTIONS

As the economy continued to struggle and as high levels of unemployment and underemployment persisted, much of the American electorate was commonly characterized as angry. The groundswell of opposition to the policies of the Obama administration and to "big government" that had given birth to the Tea Party movement took on an anti-Washington, anti-incumbent cast. In the 2010 general election Tea Party candidates had mixed success, but the Republican Party as a whole experienced a dramatic resurgence, recapturing leadership of the House with a gain of some 60 seats (the biggest swing since 1948) and reducing but not overturning the Democrats' Senate majority.

In 2010 the administration was stung by three major releases of classified documents by the Web site WikiLeaks that were published in several periodicals. In

Pres. Barack Obama (his back to the camera) *holding a meeting in the Oval Office concerning the repeal of "Don't Ask, Don't Tell," Nov. 29, 2010.* Pete Souza—Official White House Photo

Don't Ask, Don't Tell (DADT)

In the period between winning election as president in November 1992 and his inauguration in January 1993, Bill Clinton announced his intention to quickly seek an end to the U.S. military's long-standing ban on homosexuals in the ranks. Although the move was popular among many Americans, notably gay activists who had supported Clinton's campaign, and Clinton had promised action during the election campaign, few political analysts thought he would move on such a potentially explosive issue so quickly. Indeed, the move met with strong opposition and put the president at odds with top military leaders and with a number of key civilians who had oversight responsibilities for the armed forces. After heated debate, Clinton managed to gain support for a compromise measure under which homosexual servicemen and servicewomen could remain in the military if they did not openly declare their sexual orientation, a policy that quickly became known as "Don't Ask, Don't Tell." Yet military officers were overwhelmingly opposed to that approach, fearing that the mere presence of homosexuals in the armed forces would undermine morale. The policy was further subverted by discrimination suits that upheld the right of gays to serve in the military without fear of discrimination.

Under the terms of the law, homosexuals serving in the military were not allowed to talk about their sexual orientation or engage in sexual activity, and commanding officers were not allowed to question service members about their sexual orientation. Although Clinton introduced "Don't Ask, Don't Tell" as a liberalization of existing policy, saying it was a way for gays to serve in the military when they had previously been excluded from doing so, many gay rights activists criticized the policy for forcing military personnel into secrecy and because it had fallen far short of a policy of complete acceptance. For a variety of reasons, the policy did little to change the behaviour of commanders; gay and lesbian soldiers continued to be discharged from service.

U.S. military leaders testifying at the Senate Armed Services Committee hearing about the Pentagon's DADT report, Dec. 3, 2010. Scott M. Ash—USAF/U.S. Department of Defense

By the 15-year anniversary of the law in 2008, more than 12,000 officers had been discharged from the military for refusing to hide their homosexuality. When Barack Obama campaigned for the presidency in 2008, he pledged to overturn "Don't Ask, Don't Tell" and to allow gay men and lesbians to serve openly in the military (a stance that was, according to public opinion polls, backed by a large majority of the public). In October 2010 "Don't Ask, Don't Tell" was halted after a federal judge in California issued an injunction banning the military from enforcing the policy. Later that month, however, "Don't Ask, Don't Tell" was reinstated after a stay was granted as the U.S. Justice Department appealed the injunction.

On Nov. 30, 2010, the Pentagon released a report of its study on "Don't Ask, Don't Tell," which found that repealing the policy would pose little risk to military effectiveness. Some 70 percent of service members surveyed believed that ending the policy would have mixed, positive, or no impact. In December a bill that would repeal "Don't Ask, Don't Tell" passed in the House of Representatives (250-174) and overcame a Republican filibuster attempt to pass in the Senate (65-31). President Obama praised the vote, releasing a statement that said, "It is time to recognize that sacrifice, valor and integrity are no more defined by sexual orientation than they are by race or gender, religion or creed." Obama signed the bill on December 22. Before the law could be officially enacted, however, the Pentagon had to devise a plan for implementing the repeal, which included updating various policies and regulations as well as developing education and training programs for troops. On July 22, 2011, Obama certified that the military was ready to end "Don't Ask, Don't Tell." After a mandatory 60-day time period passed, the repeal took effect on Sep. 20, 2011.

general, the information released in July and October—raw intelligence related to the wars in Iraq and Afghanistan—added detail but few new revelations to what was already known and did not radically change the public understanding of either war. Nevertheless, the Obama administration condemned the release of the documents as a security breach. It was also quick to criticize WikiLeaks' November release of some 250,000 diplomatic cables between the U.S. State Department and its embassies and consulates throughout the world, dating mostly from 2007 to 2010.

Legislative gridlock eased temporarily in Congress at the end of its lame-duck session as the Obama administration and the Republicans forged compromises on several significant pieces of legislation, including extensions of the Bush tax cuts for another two years and of unemployment benefits, as well as the repeal of the "Don't Ask, Don't Tell" policy that had prohibited gays and lesbians from serving openly in the military.

The Senate also ratified a new Strategic Arms Reduction Talks (START) treaty with Russia. When a gunman killed six people and critically wounded Gabrielle Giffords, a member of the U.S. House of Representatives, as she met with constituents in Tucson, Ariz., on Jan. 8, 2011, however, there was a renewed national discussion about the vehemence of political polarization in the United States.

BUDGET BATTLE

That polarization remained at the fore as the new Republican majority in the House locked heads with the Democratic-controlled Senate and the Obama administration over the federal budget for fiscal year 2011. Unable to agree on that budget, the previous Congress, in October 2010, had passed the first in a series of stopgap measures to keep the federal government operating until agreement could be reached on a long-term budget. Both Republicans and Democrats believed that reductions to the budget were necessary in response to the federal government's soaring deficit; however, they disagreed vehemently on the extent, targets, and timing of budget cuts. House Republicans announced that they would not vote for another temporary budget and demanded deep reductions. The threat of a shutdown of all but essential services of the federal government came within a few hours of being realized, but on April 8, 2011, an agreement on a compromise budget for the remainder of the fiscal year was reached that was passed by both houses. Neither side was completely satisfied. Democrats and Republicans were also engaged in dramatic ideological battle on the state level, perhaps most notably in Wisconsin and Indiana, where collective

bargaining for state employees and the role of unions were at issue.

FOREIGN POLICY

American foreign policy was tested by the huge changes that were taking place early in 2011 in the Middle East as a result of the so-called Arab Spring, in which popular uprisings led to regime change in Tunisia and Egypt and to widespread demonstrations aimed at achieving government reform throughout the region. When Libyan strongman Muammar al-Qaddafi brutally turned the considerable forces of his military on those rebelling against his rule, a coalition of U.S. and European forces sought to prevent a humanitarian catastrophe by intervening militarily with warplanes and cruise missiles. On March 27, as the conflict continued, the United States handed over the primary leadership of the effort to the North Atlantic Treaty Organization. By September rebel forces were in control of most of the country, and in October Qaddafi was captured and killed by them.

The threat of and responses to terrorism also shaped Obama's foreign policy. On May 1 Obama made a dramatic late-night television appearance to announce that U.S. special forces had killed Osama bin Laden, the mastermind of the September 11 attacks of 2001, in a firefight at a fortified compound in Abbottabad, Pak. U.S. forces took custody of the body, confirmed bin Laden's identity through

DNA testing, and buried his body at sea. Earlier in the Obama administration, a bombing attempt by a Nigerian trained by extremists in Yemen was thwarted on an airliner bound for Detroit (December 2009), and another terrorist bombing attempt, this time involving explosive devices that were intercepted en route via air from Yemen to two Chicago-area synagogues, was also foiled (October 2010).

DEFICIT DEADLOCK

In the spring and summer of 2011, the national government faced the possibility of default on the public debt and a downgrading of its credit rating unless Democrats and Republicans could agree on whether and how to increase the congressionally mandated national debt ceiling. That ceiling of $14.29 trillion was reached in mid-May, but, by shifting funds, the Treasury Department was able to push out the anticipated deadline for default until August 2. Although the debt ceiling had been raised more than three dozen times since 1980, House Republicans, responding in large measure to Tea Party initiatives, insisted that the ceiling not be raised unless there were commensurate cuts in government spending. Republican proposals called for from $4 trillion to $6.2 trillion in spending cuts, especially to entitlement programs, including radical overhauls of Medicare and Medicaid. While Democrats also advocated spending cuts, they insisted that Medicare and Medicaid be protected,

and they proposed tax increases for the wealthiest Americans as well as an end to tax breaks for some corporations, especially oil companies.

Efforts at compromise by the leadership of both parties repeatedly collapsed in partisan rancor. In July Obama and Republican Speaker of the House John A. Boehner, meeting privately, nearly reached agreement on a "grand bargain" that would have included trillions in spending cuts, changes to Medicare and Social Security, and tax reform. The deal fell through near the end of the month, however, when the two could not agree on the level of additional tax revenue to be generated. In any case, many believed that the speaker would have been unable to win sufficient support for the agreement from House Republicans, who remained adamantly opposed to tax hikes and had passed a bill requiring a cap on spending and a balanced budget.

Nevertheless, as the threat of default grew more imminent, there was increasing consensus in both parties that the debt ceiling should be raised. With a broad agreement seemingly out of reach, compromise appeared to hang on whether the ceiling would be increased in one step (which would extend the limit past the 2012 election) or two (which would raise the issue again sooner). On July 31, just two days before the deadline, an agreement was reached by the White House and congressional leaders that called for an increase of about $2.4 trillion to the debt ceiling through November

2012, to be imposed in stages. The initial increase of $900 billion would be offset by budget cuts of some $917 billion that would result from an immediate cap on domestic and defense spending. The deal, which did not provide for tax increases, also stipulated that both houses of Congress had to vote on an amendment to the Constitution requiring a balanced budget. The final bill was approved by the House of Representatives by a vote of 269–161 (with centrists from both parties largely voting for it, while many of those farther on the right or the left voted against it) and by the Senate by a bipartisan vote of 74–26.

The bill also created a congressional "super committee" tasked with recommending by the end of November 2011 the measures by which an additional $1.2 to $1.5 trillion would be cut from the deficit over a 10-year period. If the committee had agreed on a set of proposals and had those proposals been approved by Congress, the debt ceiling would have been raised by a commensurate amount. In the event, however, the super committee failed to arrive at a consensus plan, which, according to the stipulations of the bill, triggered some $1.2 trillion in across-the-board cuts (evenly divided between defense

An "Occupy Wall Street" demonstrator protesting in New York City's Zuccotti Park in October 2011. Emmanuel Dunand/AFP/Getty Images

and nondefense spending) to be implemented in 2013.

As these events unfolded in the autumn of 2011, another populist movement, this time on the left of the political spectrum, gained steam. Inspired by the mass protests of the Arab Spring and those that had occurred in Spain and Greece in response to government austerity measures, a disparate group of protesters, calling themselves Occupy Wall Street, had taken up residence in a park near New York City's financial district to call attention to a list of what they saw as injustices. Among the protesters' demands were that the wealthy pay what they considered a fairer share of income taxes, that more efforts be directed at reducing unemployment, and that major corporations—particularly banks and other financial institutions—be held more accountable for risky practices. They identified themselves as the "99 percent," the have-nots who would no longer put up with the corruption and greed that they perceived among the "1 percent," the wealthiest Americans. In the succeeding weeks the movement spread to other cities across the country. As the winter approached and the last U.S. troops left Baghdad in December, bringing to a close the Iraq War, Americans prepared for the 2012 presidential campaign and another referendum on the future of the United States.

CONCLUSION

"There are two ideas of government," William Jennings Bryan said in his famous "Cross of Gold" speech at the Democratic National Convention in 1896. "There are those who believe that if you just legislate to make the well-to-do prosperous that their prosperity will leak through on those below. The Democratic idea has been that if you legislate to make the masses prosperous their prosperity will find its way up and through every class that rests upon it."

More than 100 years later, the debate over these two approaches to government and the economy were still at the centre of American political life. For the most part, Republicans maintained an unbending faith in the free market and inventive entrepreneurial spirit, believing, as Ronald Reagan had said, that government was the problem. On the other hand, most Democrats remained convinced that government intervention was necessary to mitigate the abuses of corporate power, to ensure a level playing field, and to see that the neediest in society were not left behind. "Get rid of big government and handouts," cried one side; "Increase taxes on the wealthiest and maintain the safety net," shouted the other. By the final decades of the 20th century, the country seemed polarized as never before. With the so-called Culture Wars at full tilt, Republican George W. Bush ascended to the presidency in 2000

promising to be a "uniter not a divider." Yet even in the wake of the shared tragedy of the September 11 attacks, Americans seemed unwilling to bridge their ideological divide and Republicans and Democrats unable to get beyond legislative gridlock.

By the time of the 2004 election, it had become common to divide the United States into blue and red states, colours that indicated not only the dominant political party in a state but also the social and cultural values widely believed to hold sway there. Located primarily in the Northeast, the Upper Midwest, and on the coasts, the Democratic blue states were, it was said, urban, liberal, secular, pro-choice, politically correct, and full of wine, cheese, and latte lovers. Generally situated in the West, the lower Midwest, and the South, the Republican red states, on the other hand, were characterized as small-town and suburban, conservative, God-fearing, pro-life, opposed to big government and same-sex marriage, and devoted to NASCAR. These stereotypes were firmly in place when the incumbent President Bush faced Democratic Sen. John F. Kerry of Massachusetts in what is often described as one of the most partisan and polarizing presidential elections in American history.

A closer look at that history reveals that again and again Americans have survived deeply divisive differences—even civil war—to come together to forge a common future. It is fitting that this history of the United States told through its documents should end in the hopeful words of a prominent American, Barack Obama, four years before he became president, as he debunked the country's artificial red-blue division and offered "the audacity of hope":

> *Yet even as we speak, there are those who are preparing to divide us, the spin masters, the negative ad peddlers who embrace the politics of anything goes. Well, I say to them tonight, there is not a liberal America and a conservative America—there is the United States of America. There is not a black America and a white America and Latino America and Asian America; there's the United States of America. The pundits like to slice-and-dice our country into Red States and Blue States; Red States for Republicans, Blue States for Democrats. But I've got news for them, too. We worship an awesome God in the Blue States, and we don't like federal agents poking around in our libraries in the Red States. We coach Little League in the Blue States and have gay friends in the Red States. There are patriots who opposed the war in Iraq and there are patriots who supported it. We are one people, all of us pledging allegiance to the stars and stripes, all of us defending the United States of America.*

APPENDICES (DOCUMENTS)

HARRY S. TRUMAN: THE TRUMAN DOCTRINE (1947)

Source: *Congressional Record*, Washington, 80 Cong., 1 Sess., pp. 1980–1981.

The gravity of the situation which confronts the world today necessitates my appearance before a joint session of the Congress. The foreign policy and the national security of this country are involved.

One aspect of the present situation which I wish to present to you at this time for your consideration and decision concerns Greece and Turkey. The United States has received from the Greek government an urgent appeal for financial and economic assistance. Preliminary reports from the American economic mission now in Greece and reports from the American ambassador in Greece corroborate the statement of the Greek government that assistance is imperative if Greece is to survive as a free nation.

I do not believe that the American people and the Congress wish to turn a deaf ear to the appeal of the Greek government.

Greece is not a rich country. Lack of sufficient natural resources has always forced the Greek people to work hard to make both ends meet. Since 1940, this industrious and peace-loving country has suffered invasion, four years of cruel enemy occupation, and bitter internal strife.

When forces of liberation entered Greece they found that the retreating Germans had destroyed virtually all the railways, roads, port facilities, communications, and merchant marine. More than a thousand villages had been burned. Eighty-five percent of the children were tubercular. Livestock, poultry, and draft animals had almost disappeared. Inflation had wiped out practically all savings. As a result of these tragic conditions, a militant minority, exploiting human want and misery, was able to create political chaos which, until now, has made economic recovery impossible.

Greece is today without funds to finance the importation of those goods which are essential to bare subsistence. Under these circumstances the people of Greece cannot make progress in solving their problems of reconstruction. Greece is in desperate need of financial and economic assistance to enable it to resume purchases of food, clothing, fuel, and seeds. These are indispensable for the subsistence of its people and are obtainable only from abroad. Greece must have help to import the goods necessary to restore internal order and security so essential for economic and political recovery.

The Greek government has also asked for the assistance of experienced American administrators, economists, and technicians to insure that the financial and other aid given to Greece shall be used effectively in creating a stable and self-sustaining economy and in improving its public administration.

The very existence of the Greek state is today threatened by the terrorist activities of several thousand armed men, led by Communists, who defy the government's authority at a number of points, particularly along the northern boundaries. A commission appointed by the United Nations Security Council is at present investigating disturbed conditions in northern Greece and alleged border violations along the frontier between Greece, on the one hand, and Albania, Bulgaria, and Yugoslavia, on the other. Meanwhile, the Greek government is unable to cope with the situation. The Greek Army is small and poorly equipped. It needs supplies and equipment if it is to restore the authority of the government throughout Greek territory.

Greece must have assistance if it is to become a self-supporting and self-respecting democracy. The United States must supply this assistance. We have already extended to Greece certain types of relief and economic aid but these are inadequate. There is no other country to which democratic Greece can turn. No other nation is willing and able to provide the necessary support for a democratic Greek government.

The British government, which has been helping Greece, can give no further financial or economic aid after March 31. Great Britain finds itself under the necessity of reducing or liquidating its commitments in several parts of the world, including Greece.

We have considered how the United Nations might assist in this crisis. But the situation is an urgent one requiring immediate action, and the United Nations and its related organizations are not in a position to extend help of the kind that is required.

It is important to note that the Greek government has asked for our aid in utilizing effectively the financial and other assistance we may give to Greece and in improving its public administration. It is of the utmost importance that we supervise the use of any funds made available to Greece in such a manner that each dollar spent will count toward making Greece self-supporting and will help to build an economy in which a healthy democracy can flourish.

No government is perfect. One of the chief virtues of a democracy, however, is that its defects are always visible and under democratic processes can be pointed out and corrected. The government of Greece is not perfect. Nevertheless, it represents 35 percent of the members of the Greek Parliament who were chosen in an election last year. Foreign observers, including 692 Americans, considered this election to be a fair expression of the views of the Greek people.

The Greek government has been operating in an atmosphere of chaos and extremism. It has made mistakes. The extension of aid by this country does not mean that the United States condones everything that the Greek government has done or will do. We have condemned in the past, and we condemn now, extremist measures of the right or the left. We have in the past advised tolerance, and we advise tolerance now.

Greece's neighbor, Turkey, also deserves our attention. The future of Turkey as an independent and economically sound state is clearly no less important to the freedom-loving peoples of the world than the future of Greece. The circumstances in which Turkey finds itself today are considerably different from those of Greece. Turkey has been spared the disasters that have beset Greece. And during the war, the United States and Great Britain furnished Turkey with material aid. Nevertheless, Turkey now needs our support.

Since the war, Turkey has sought financial assistance from Great Britain and the United States for the purpose of effecting that modernization necessary for the maintenance of its national integrity. That integrity is essential to the preservation of order in the Middle East.

The British government has informed us that, owing to its own difficulties, it can no longer extend financial or economic aid to Turkey. As in the case of Greece, if Turkey is to have the assistance it needs, the United States must supply it. We are the only country able to provide that help.

I am fully aware of the broad implications involved if the United States extends assistance to Greece and Turkey, and I shall discuss these implications with you at this time.

One of the primary objectives of the foreign policy of the United States is the creation of conditions in which we and other nations will be able to work out a way of life free from coercion. This was a fundamental issue in the war with Germany and Japan. Our victory was won over countries which sought to impose their will and their way of life upon other nations.

To insure the peaceful development of nations, free from coercion, the United States has taken a leading part in establishing the United Nations. The United Nations is designed to make possible lasting freedom and independence for all its members. We shall not realize our objectives, however, unless we are willing to help free peoples to maintain their free institutions and their national integrity against aggressive movements that seek to impose upon them totalitarian regimes. This is no more than a frank recognition that totalitarian regimes imposed on free peoples, by direct or indirect aggression, undermine the foundations of international peace and hence the security of the United States.

The peoples of a number of countries of the world have recently had totalitarian regimes forced upon them against their will. The government of the United States has made frequent protests against coercion and intimidation, in violation of the Yalta Agreement, in Poland, Rumania, and Bulgaria. I must also state that in a number of other countries there have been similar developments.

At the present moment in world history nearly every nation must choose between alternative ways of life. The choice is too often not a free one.

One way of life is based upon the will of the majority, and is distinguished by free institutions, representative government, free elections, guarantees of individual liberty, freedom of speech and religion, and freedom from political oppression. The second way of life is based upon the will of a minority forcibly imposed upon the majority. It relies upon terror and oppression, a controlled press and radio, fixed elections, and the suppression of personal freedoms.

I believe that it must be the policy of the United States to support free peoples who are resisting attempted subjugation by armed minorities or by outside pressures. I believe that we must assist free peoples to work out their own destinies in their own way. I believe that our help should be primarily through economic and financial aid, which is essential to economic stability and orderly political processes.

The world is not static and the status quo is not sacred. But we cannot allow changes in the status quo in violation of the Charter of the United Nations by such methods as coercion or by such subterfuges as political infiltration. In helping free and independent nations to maintain their freedom, the United States will be giving effect to the principles of the Charter of the United Nations.

It is necessary only to glance at a map to realize that the survival and integrity of the Greek nation are of grave importance in a much wider situation. If Greece should fall under the control of an armed minority, the effect upon its neighbor, Turkey, would be immediate and serious. Confusion and disorder might well spread throughout the entire Middle East. Moreover, the disappearance of Greece as an independent state would have a profound effect upon those countries in Europe whose peoples are struggling against great difficulties to maintain their freedoms and their independence while they repair the damages of war.

It would be an unspeakable tragedy if these countries, which have struggled so long against overwhelming odds, should lose that victory for which they sacrificed so much. Collapse of free institutions and loss of independence would be disastrous not only for them but for the world. Discouragement and possibly failure would quickly be the lot of neighboring peoples striving to maintain their freedom and independence.

Should we fail to aid Greece and Turkey in this fateful hour, the effect will be far-reaching to the West as well as to the East. We must take immediate and resolute action.

I therefore ask the Congress to provide authority for assistance to Greece and Turkey in the amount of $400 million for the period ending June 30, 1948. In requesting these funds, I have taken into consideration the maximum amount of relief assistance which would be furnished to Greece out of the $350 million which I recently requested that the Congress authorize for the prevention of starvation and suffering in countries devastated by the war.

In addition to funds, I ask the Congress to authorize the detail of American civilian and military personnel to Greece and Turkey, at the request of those countries, to assist in the tasks of reconstruction, and for the purpose of supervising the use of such financial and material assistance as may be furnished. I recommend that authority also be provided for the instruction and training of selected Greek and Turkish personnel.

Finally, I ask that the Congress provide authority which will permit the speediest and most effective use, in terms of needed commodities, supplies, and equipment, of such funds as may be authorized.

If further funds, or further authority, should be needed for purposes indicated in this message, I shall not hesitate to bring the situation before the Congress. On this subject the executive and legislative branches of the government must work together.

This is a serious course upon which we embark. I would not recommend it except that the alternative is much more serious.

The United States contributed $341 billion toward winning World War II. This is an investment in world freedom and world peace. The assistance that I am recommending for Greece and Turkey amounts to little more than one-tenth of 1 percent of this investment. It is only

common sense that we should safeguard this investment and make sure that it was not in vain.

The seeds of totalitarian regimes are nurtured by misery and want. They spread and grow in the evil soil of poverty and strife. They reach their full growth when the hope of a people for a better life has died. We must keep that hope alive.

The free peoples of the world look to us for support in maintaining their freedoms. If we falter in our leadership, we may endanger the peace of the world — and we shall surely endanger the welfare of our own nation.

Great responsibilities have been placed upon us by the swift movement of events. I am confident that the Congress will face these responsibilities squarely.

GEORGE C. MARSHALL: THE MARSHALL PLAN (1947)

Source: *Congressional Record Appendix*, Washington, 80 Cong., 1 Sess., p. A3248.

I need not tell you gentlemen that the world situation is very serious. That must be apparent to all intelligent people. I think one difficulty is that the problem is one of such enormous complexity that the very mass of facts presented to the public by press and radio make it exceedingly difficult for the man in the street to reach a clear appraisement of the situation. Furthermore, the people of this country are distant from the troubled areas of the earth and it is hard for them to comprehend the plight and consequent reactions of the long-suffering peoples, and the effect of those reactions on their governments in connection with our efforts to promote peace in the world.

In considering the requirements for the rehabilitation of Europe, the physical loss of life, the visible destruction of cities, factories, mines, and railroads was correctly estimated; but it has become obvious during recent months that this visible destruction was probably less serious than the dislocation of the entire fabric of European economy. For the past ten years conditions have been highly abnormal. The feverish preparation for war and the more feverish maintenance of the war effort engulfed all aspects of national economies. Machinery has fallen into disrepair or is entirely obsolete. Under the arbitrary and destructive Nazi rule, virtually every possible enterprise was geared into the German war machine. Long-standing commercial ties, private institutions, banks, insurance companies, and shipping companies disappeared through loss of capital, absorption through nationalization, or by simple destruction. In many countries, confidence in the local currency has been severely shaken.

The breakdown of the business structure of Europe during the war was complete. Recovery has been seriously retarded by the fact that two years after the close of hostilities a peace settlement with Germany and Austria has not been agreed upon. But even given a more prompt solution of these difficult problems, the rehabilitation of the economic structure of Europe quite evidently will require a much longer time and greater effort than had been foreseen.

There is a phase of this matter which is both interesting and serious. The farmer has always produced the foodstuffs to exchange with the city dweller for the other necessities of life. This division of labor is the basis of modern civilization. At the present time it is threatened with breakdown. The town and city industries are not producing adequate goods to exchange with the food-producing farmer. Raw materials and fuel are in short supply. Machinery is lacking or worn out. The farmer or the peasant cannot find the goods for sale which he desires to purchase. So the sale of his farm produce for money which he cannot use seems to him an unprofitable transaction. He, therefore, has withdrawn many fields from crop cultivation and is using them for grazing. He feeds more grain to stock and finds for himself and his family an ample supply of food, however short he may be on clothing and the other ordinary gadgets of civilization.

Meanwhile people in the cities are short of food and fuel. So the governments are forced to use their foreign money and credits to procure these necessities abroad. This process exhausts funds which are urgently needed for reconstruction. Thus a very serious situation is rapidly developing which bodes no good for the world. The modern system of the division of labor upon which the exchange of products is based is in danger of breaking down.

The truth of the matter is that Europe's requirements for the next three or four years of foreign food and other essential products — principally from America — are so much greater than her present ability to pay that she must have substantial additional help or face economic, social, and political deterioration of a very grave character.

The remedy lies in breaking the vicious circle and restoring the confidence of the European people in the economic future of their own countries and of Europe as a whole. The manufacturer and the farmer throughout wide areas must be able and willing to exchange their products for currencies the continuing value of which is not open to question.

Aside from the demoralizing effect on the world at large and the possibilities of disturbances arising as a result of the desperation of the people concerned, the consequences to the economy of the United States should be apparent to all. It is logical that the United States should do whatever it is able to do to assist in the return of normal economic health in the world, without which there can be no political stability and no assured peace. Our policy is directed not against any country or doctrine but against hunger, poverty, desperation, and chaos. Its purpose should be the revival of a working economy in the world so as to permit the emergence of political and social conditions in which free institutions can exist.

Such assistance, I am convinced, must not be on a piecemeal basis as various crises develop. Any assistance that this government may render in the future should provide a cure rather than a mere palliative. Any government that is willing to assist in the task of recovery will find full cooperation, I am sure, on the part of the United States government. Any government which maneuvers to block the recovery of other countries cannot expect help from us. Furthermore, governments, political parties, or groups which seek to perpetuate human misery in order to profit therefrom politically or otherwise will encounter the opposition of the United States.

It is already evident that, before the United States government can proceed much further in its efforts to alleviate the situation and help start the European world on its way to recovery, there must be some agreement among the countries of Europe as to the requirements of the situation and the part those countries themselves will take in order to give proper effect to whatever action might be undertaken by this government. It would be neither fitting nor efficacious for this government to undertake to draw up unilaterally a program designed to place Europe on its feet economically. This is the business of the Europeans. The initiative, I think, must come from Europe. The role of this country should consist of friendly aid in the drafting of a European program and of later support of such a program so far as it may be practical for us to do so. The program should be a joint one, agreed to by a number [of], if not all, European nations.

An essential part of any successful action on the part of the United States is an understanding on the part of the people of America of the character of the problem and the remedies to be applied. Political passion and prejudice should have no part. With foresight, and a willingness on the part of our people to face up to the vast responsibility which history has clearly placed upon our country, the difficulties I have outlined can and will be overcome.

JOSEPH R. MCCARTHY: COMMUNISTS IN THE STATE DEPARTMENT (1950)

Source: *Congressional Record*, 81 Cong., 2 Sess., pp. 1952–1957.

Ladies and gentlemen:

Tonight as we celebrate the one hundred and forty-first birthday of one of the greatest men in American history, I would like to be able to talk about what a glorious day today is in the history of the world. As we celebrate the birth of this man, who with his whole heart and soul hated war, I would like to be able to speak of peace in our time, of war being outlawed, and of worldwide disarmament. These would be truly appropriate things to be able to mention as we celebrate the birthday of Abraham Lincoln.

Five years after a world war has been won, men's hearts should anticipate a long peace, and men's minds should be free from the heavy weight that comes with war. But this is not such a period — for this is not a period of peace. This is a time of the "cold war." This is a time when all the world is split into two vast, increasingly hostile armed camps — a time of a great armaments race. Today we can almost physically hear the mutterings and rumblings of an invigorated god of war. You can see it, feel it, and hear it all the way from the hills of Indochina, from the shores of Formosa, right over into the very heart of Europe itself.

The one encouraging thing is that the "mad moment" has not yet arrived for the firing of the gun or the exploding of the bomb which will set civilization about the final task of destroying itself. There is still a hope for peace if we finally decide that no longer can we safely blind our eyes and close our ears to those facts which are shaping up more and more clearly. And that is that we are now engaged in a showdown fight — not the usual war between nations for land areas or other material gains but a war between two diametrically opposed ideologies.

The great difference between our Western Christian world and the atheistic Communist world is not political, ladies and gentlemen, it is moral. There are other differences, of course, but those could be reconciled. For instance, the Marxian idea of confiscating the land and factories and running the entire economy as a single enterprise is momentous. Likewise, Lenin's invention of the one-party police state as a way to make Marx's idea work is hardly less momentous. Stalin's resolute putting across of these two ideas, of course, did much to divide the world. With only those differences, however, the East and the West could most certainly still live in peace.

The real, basic difference, however, lies in the religion of immoralism — invented by Marx, preached feverishly by Lenin, and carried to unimaginable extremes by Stalin. This religion of immoralism, if the Red half of the world wins — and well it may — this religion of immoralism will more deeply wound and damage mankind than any conceivable economic or political system.

Karl Marx dismissed God as a hoax, and Lenin and Stalin have added in clear-cut, unmistakable language their resolve that no nation, no people who believe in a God can exist side by side with their communistic state.

Karl Marx, for example, expelled people from his Communist Party for mentioning such things as justice, humanity, or morality. He called this soulful ravings and sloppy sentimentality.

While Lincoln was a relatively young man in his late thirties, Karl Marx boasted that the Communist specter was haunting Europe. Since that time, hundreds of millions of people and vast areas of the world have fallen under Communist domination. Today, less than 100 years after Lincoln's death, Stalin brags that this Communist specter is not only haunting the world but is about to completely subjugate it.

Today we are engaged in a final, all-out battle between communistic atheism and Christianity. The modern champions of communism have selected this as the time. And, ladies and gentlemen, the chips are down — they are truly down.

Lest there be any doubt that the time has been chosen, let us go directly to the leader of communism today — Joseph Stalin. Here is what he said — not back in 1928, not before the war, not during the war — but two years after the last war was ended: "To think that the Communist revolution can be carried out peacefully, within the framework of a Christian democracy means one has either gone out of one's mind and lost all normal understanding, or has grossly and openly repudiated the Communist revolution."

And this is what was said by Lenin in 1919, which was also quoted with approval by Stalin in 1947: "We are living," said Lenin, "not merely in a state but in a system of states, and the existence of the Soviet Republic side by side with Christian states for a long time is unthinkable. One or the other must triumph in the end. And before that end supervenes, a series of frightful collisions between the Soviet Republic and the bourgeois states will be inevitable."

Ladies and gentlemen, can there be anyone here tonight who is so blind as to say that the war is not on? Can there be anyone who fails to realize that the Communist world has said, "The time is now" — that this is the time for the showdown between the democratic Christian world and the Communist atheistic world? Unless we face this fact, we shall pay the price that must be paid by those who wait too long.

Six years ago, at the time of the first conference to map out the peace — Dumbarton Oaks — there was within the Soviet orbit 180 million people. Lined up on the antitotalitarian side there were in the world at that time roughly 1,625,000,000 people. Today, only six years later, there are 800 million people under the absolute domination of Soviet Russia — an increase of over 400 percent. On our side, the figure has shrunk to around 500 million. In other words, in less than six years the odds have changed from 9 to 1 in our favor to 8 to 5 against us. This indicates the swiftness of the tempo of Communist victories and American defeats in the cold war. As one of our outstanding historical figures once said, "When a great democracy is destroyed, it will not be because of enemies from without but rather because of enemies from within." The truth of this statement is becoming terrifyingly clear as we see this country each day losing on every front.

At war's end we were physically the strongest nation on earth and, at least potentially, the most powerful intellectually and morally. Ours could have been the honor of being a beacon in the desert of destruction, a shining, living proof that civilization was not yet ready to destroy itself. Unfortunately, we have failed miserably and tragically to arise to the opportunity.

The reason why we find ourselves in a position of impotency is not because our only powerful, potential enemy has sent men to invade our shores, but rather because of the traitorous actions of those who have been treated so well by this nation. It has not been the less fortunate or members of minority groups who have been selling this nation out, but rather those who have had all the benefits that the wealthiest nation on earth has had to offer — the finest homes, the finest college education, and the finest jobs in government we can give.

This is glaringly true in the State Department. There the bright young men who are born with silver spoons in their mouths are the ones who have been worst.

Now I know it is very easy for anyone to condemn a particular bureau or department in general terms. Therefore, I would like to cite one rather unusual case — the case of a man who has done much to shape our foreign policy.

When Chiang Kai-shek was fighting our war, the State Department had in China a young man named John S. Service. His task, obviously, was not to work for the communization of China. Strangely, however, he sent official reports back to the State Department urging that we torpedo our ally Chiang Kai-shek and stating, in effect, that communism was the best hope of China.

Later, this man — John Service — was picked up by the Federal Bureau of Investigation for turning over to the Communists secret State Department information. Strangely, however, he was never prosecuted. However, Joseph Grew, the undersecretary of state, who insisted on his prosecution, was forced to resign. Two days after Grew's successor, Dean Acheson, took over as undersecretary of state, this man — John Service — who had been picked up by the FBI and who had previously urged that communism was the best hope of China, was not only reinstated in the State Department but promoted; and, finally, under Acheson, placed in charge of all placements and promotions. Today, ladies and gentlemen, this man Service is on his way to represent the State Department and Acheson in Calcutta — by far and away the most important listening post in the Far East.

Now, let's see what happens when individuals with Communist connections are forced out of the State Department. Gustave Duran, who was labeled as (I quote) "a notorious international Communist," was made assistant to the assistant secretary of state in charge of Latin-American affairs. He was taken into the State Department from his job as a lieutenant colonel in the Communist International Brigade. Finally, after intense congressional pressure and criticism, he resigned in 1946 from the State Department — and, ladies and gentlemen, where do you think he is now? He took over a high-salaried job as chief of Cultural Activities Section in the office of the assistant secretary-general of the United Nations.

Then there was a Mrs. Mary Jane Kenny, from the Board of Economic Warfare in the State Department, who was named in an FBI report and in a House committee report as a courier for the Communist Party while working for the government. And where do you think Mrs. Kenny is — she is now an editor in the United Nations Document Bureau.

Another interesting case was that of Julian H. Wadleigh, economist in the Trade Agreements Section of the State Department for eleven years and was sent to Turkey and Italy and other countries as United States representative. After the statute of limitations had run so he could not be prosecuted for treason, he openly and brazenly not only admitted but proclaimed that he had been a member of the Communist Party ... that while working for the State Department he stole a vast number of secret documents ... and furnished these documents to the Russian spy ring of which he was a part.

You will recall last spring there was held in New York what was known as the World Peace Conference — a conference which was labeled by the State Department and Mr. Truman as the sounding board for Communist propaganda and a front for Russia. Dr. Harlow Shapley was the chairman of that conference. Interestingly enough, according to the new release put out by the Department in July, the secretary of state appointed Shapley on a commission which acts as liaison between UNESCO and the State Department.

This, ladies and gentlemen, gives you somewhat of a picture of the type of individuals who have been helping to shape our foreign policy. In my opinion the State Department, which is one of the most important government departments, is thoroughly infested with Communists.

I have in my hand fifty-seven cases of individuals who would appear to be either card-carrying members or certainly loyal to the Communist Party, but who nevertheless are still helping to shape our foreign policy.

One thing to remember in discussing the Communists in our government is that we are not dealing with spies who get thirty pieces of silver to steal the blueprints of a new weapon. We are dealing with a far more sinister type of activity because it permits the enemy to guide and shape our policy. ...

This brings us down to the case of one Alger Hiss, who is important not as an individual anymore but rather because he is so representative of a group in the State Department. It is unnecessary to go over the sordid events showing how he sold out the nation which had given him so much. Those are rather fresh in all of our minds. However, it should be remembered that the facts in regard to his connection with this international Communist spy ring were made known to the then Undersecretary of State Berle three days after Hitler and Stalin signed the Russo-German Alliance Pact. At that time one Whittaker Chambers — who was also part of the spy ring — apparently decided that with Russia on Hitler's side, he could no longer betray our nation to Russia. He gave Undersecretary of State Berle — and this is all a matter of record — practically all, if not more, of the facts upon which Hiss's conviction was based.

Undersecretary Berle promptly contacted Dean Acheson and received word in return that Acheson (and I quote) "could vouch for Hiss absolutely" — at which time the matter was dropped. And this, you understand, was at a time when Russia was an ally of Germany. This condition existed while Russia and Germany were invading and dismembering Poland, and while the Communist groups here were screaming "warmonger" at the United States for their support of the allied nations.

Again in 1943, the FBI had occasion to investigate the facts surrounding Hiss's contacts with the Russian spy ring. But even after that FBI report was submitted, nothing was done.

Then, late in 1948 — on August 5 — when the Un-American Activities Committee called Alger Hiss to give an accounting, President Truman at once issued a presidential directive ordering all government agencies to refuse to turn over any information whatsoever in regard to the Communist activities of any government employee to a congressional committee.

Incidentally, even after Hiss was convicted, it is interesting to note that the President still labeled the exposé of Hiss as a "red herring."

If time permitted, it might be well to go into detail about the fact that Hiss was Roosevelt's chief adviser at Yalta when Roosevelt was admittedly in ill health and tired physically and mentally ... and when, according to the secretary of state, Hiss and Gromyko drafted the report on the conference.

According to the then Secretary of State Stettinius, here are some of the things that Hiss helped to decide at Yalta: (1) the establishment of a European High Commission; (2) the treatment of Germany — this you will recall was the conference at which it was decided that we would occupy Berlin with Russia occupying an area completely circling the city, which, as you know, resulted in the Berlin airlift which cost thirty-one American lives; (3) the Polish question; (4) the relationship between UNRRA and the Soviet; (5) the rights of Americans on control commissions of Rumania, Bulgaria, and Hungary; (6) Iran; (7) China — here's where we gave away Manchuria; (8) Turkish Straits question; (9) international trusteeships; (10) Korea.

Of the results of this conference, Arthur Bliss Lane of the State Department had this to say: "As I glanced over the document, I could not believe my eyes. To me, almost every line spoke of a surrender to Stalin."

As you hear this story of high treason, I know that you are saying to yourself, "Well, why doesn't the Congress do something about it?" Actually, ladies and gentlemen, one of the important reasons for the graft, the corruption, the dishonesty, the disloyalty, the treason in high government positions — one of the most important reasons why this continues — is a lack of moral uprising on the part of the 140 million American people. In the light of history, however, this is not hard to explain.

It is the result of an emotional hangover and a temporary moral lapse which follows every war. It is the apathy to evil which people who have been subjected to the tremendous evils of war feel. As the people of the world see mass murder, the destruction of defenseless and innocent people, and all of the crime and lack of morals which go with war, they become numb and apathetic. It has always been thus after war. However, the morals of our people have not been destroyed. They still exist. This cloak of numbness and apathy has only needed a spark to rekindle them. Happily, this spark has finally been supplied.

As you know, very recently the secretary of state proclaimed his loyalty to a man guilty of what has always been considered as the most abominable of all crimes — of being a traitor to the people who gave him a position of great trust. The secretary of state, in attempting to justify his continued devotion to the man who sold out the Christian world to the atheistic world, referred to Christ's Sermon on the Mount as a justification and reason therefor, and the reaction of the American people to this would have made the heart of Abraham Lincoln happy. When this pompous diplomat in striped pants, with a phony British accent, proclaimed to the American people that Christ on the Mount endorsed communism, high treason, and betrayal of a sacred trust, the blasphemy was so great that it awakened the dormant indignation of the American people.

He has lighted the spark which is resulting in a moral uprising and will end only when the whole sorry mess of twisted, warped thinkers are swept from the national scene so that we may have a new birth of national honesty and decency in government.

DWIGHT D. EISENHOWER: THE CRISIS IN THE MIDDLE EAST (1957)

Source: *Congressional Record*, 85 Cong., 1 Sess., pp. 2376–2377.

I come to you again to talk about the situation in the Middle East. The future of the United Nations and peace in the Middle East may be at stake.

In the four months since I talked to you about the crisis in that area, the United Nations has made considerable progress in resolving some of the difficult problems. We are now, however, faced with a fateful moment as the result of the failure of Israel to withdraw its forces behind the armistice lines as contemplated by the United Nations resolutions on this subject.

I have already today met with leaders of both parties from the Senate and the House of Representatives and we have had a very useful exchange of views. It was the general feeling of that meeting that I should lay the situation before the American people.

Before talking about the specific issues involved, I want to make clear that these issues are not something remote and abstract, but involve matters vitally touching upon the future of each one of us.

The Middle East is a land bridge between the Eurasian and African continents. Millions of tons of commerce are transmitted through it annually. Its own products, especially petroleum, are essential to Europe and the Western world.

The United States has no ambitions or desires in this region other than that each country there may maintain its independence and live peacefully within itself and with its neighbors, and, by peaceful cooperation with others, develop its own spiritual and material resources. But that much is vital to the peace and well-being of us all. This is our concern today. So tonight I report to you on the matters in controversy and on what I believe the position of the United States must be.

When I talked to you last October, I pointed out that the United States fully realized that military action against Egypt resulted from grave and repeated provocations. But also I said that the use of military force to solve international disputes could not be reconciled with the principles and purposes of the United Nations, to which we had all subscribed. I added that our country could not believe that resort to force and war would for long serve the permanent interests of the attacking nations, which were Britain, France, and Israel.

So I pledged that the United States would seek through the United Nations to end the conflict and to bring about a recall of the forces of invasion, and then make a renewed and earnest effort through that organization to secure justice, under international law, for all of the parties concerned.

Since that time much has been achieved and many of the dangers implicit in the situation have been avoided. The governments of Britain and France have withdrawn their forces from Egypt. Thereby they showed respect for the opinions of mankind as expressed almost unanimously by the eighty-nation members of the United Nations General Assembly.

I want to pay tribute to the wisdom of this action of our friends and allies. They made an immense contribution to world order. Also they put the other nations of the world under a heavy obligation to see to it that those two nations do not suffer by reason of their compliance with the United Nations resolutions. This has special application, I think, to their treaty rights to passage through the Suez Canal, which had been made an international waterway for all by the treaty of 1888.

The prime minister of Israel, in answer to a personal communication, assured me early in November that Israel would willingly withdraw its forces if and when there should be created a United Nations force to move into the Suez Canal area. This force was, in fact, created and has moved into the Canal area. Subsequently, Israeli forces were withdrawn from much of the territory of Egypt which they had occupied. However, Israeli forces still remain outside the armistice lines, notably at the mouth of the Gulf of Aqaba, which is about 100 miles from the nearest Israeli territory, and in the Gaza Strip, which, by the armistice agreement, was to be occupied by Egypt. This fact creates the present crisis.

We are approaching a fateful moment when either we must recognize that the United Nations is unable to restore peace in this area, or the United Nations must renew with increased vigor its efforts to bring about Israeli withdrawal. Repeated, but so far unsuccessful, efforts have been made to bring about a voluntary withdrawal by Israel. These efforts have been made both by the United Nations and by the United States and other member states.

Moreover, equally serious efforts have been made to bring about conditions designed to assure that, if Israel withdraws in response to the repeated requests of the United Nations, there will then be achieved a greater security and tranquillity for that nation. This means that the United Nations would assert a determination to see that in the Middle East there will be a greater degree of justice and compliance with international law than was the case prior to the events of last October-November.

A United Nations Emergency Force, with Egypt's consent, entered that nation's territory in order to help to maintain the cease-fire which the United Nations called for on November 2. The Secretary-General, who ably and devotedly serves the United Nations, has recommended a number of measures which might be taken by the United Nations and by its emergency force to assure for the future the avoidance by either side of belligerent acts.

The United Nations General Assembly on February 2, by an overwhelming vote, adopted a resolution to the effect that, after full withdrawal of Israel from the Gulf of Aqaba and Gaza areas, the United Nations Emergency Force should be placed on the Egyptian-Israeli armistice lines to assure the scrupulous maintenance of the armistice agreement. Also the United Nations General Assembly called for the implementation of other measures proposed by the Secretary-General. These other measures embraced the use of the United Nations Emergency Force at the mouth of the Gulf of Aqaba so as to assure nonbelligerency in this area.

The United States was a cosponsor of this United Nations resolution. Thus the United States sought to assure that Israel would, for the future, enjoy its rights under the armistice and under the international law.

In view of the valued friendly relations which the United States has always had with the State of Israel, I wrote to Prime Minister Ben-Gurion on February 3. I recalled his statement to me on November 8 to the effect that the Israeli forces would be withdrawn under certain conditions, and I urged that, in view of the General Assembly resolutions of February 2, Israel should complete that withdrawal. However, the prime minister, in his reply, took the position that Israel would not evacuate its military forces from the Gaza Strip unless Israel retained the civil administration and police. This would be in contradiction to the armistice agreement. Also, the reply said that Israel would not withdraw from the Straits of Aqaba unless freedom of passage through the straits was assured.

It was a matter of keen disappointment to us that the government of Israel, despite the United Nations action, still felt unwilling to withdraw. However, in a further effort to meet the views of Israel in these respects, Secretary of State Dulles, at my direction, gave to the government of Israel, on February 11, a statement of United States policy. This has now been made public. It was pointed out that neither the United States nor the United Nations had authority to impose upon the parties a substantial modification of the armistice agreement which was freely signed by Israel and Egypt. Nevertheless, the statement said, the United States as a member of the United Nations would seek such disposition of the United Nations emergency force as would assure that the Gaza Strip could no longer be a source of armed infiltration and reprisals.

The secretary of state orally informed the Israeli ambassador that the United States would be glad to urge and support, also, some participation by the United Nations, with the approval of Egypt, in the administration of the Gaza Strip. The principal population of the Strip consists of about 200,000 Arab refugees, who exist largely as a charge upon the benevolence of the United Nations and its members.

With reference to the passage into and through the Gulf of Aqaba, we expressed the conviction that the Gulf constitutes international waters and that no nation has the right to prevent free and innocent passage in the Gulf. We announced that the United States was prepared to exercise this right itself and to join with others to secure general recognition of this right.

The government of Israel has not yet accepted, as adequate insurance of its own safety after withdrawal, the far-reaching United Nations resolution of February 2 plus the important declaration of United States policy made by our secretary of state on February 11.

But Israel seeks something more. It insists on firm guarantees as a condition to withdrawing its forces of invasion.

This raises a basic question of principle: Should a nation which attacks and occupies foreign territory in the face of United Nations disapproval be allowed to impose conditions on its withdrawal?

If we agree that armed attack can properly achieve the purposes of the assailant, then I fear we will have turned back the clock of international order. We will, in effect, have countenanced the use of force as a means of settling international differences and gaining national advantages. I do not myself see how this could be reconciled with the Charter of the United Nations. The basic pledge of all the members of the United Nations is that they will settle their international disputes by peaceful means and will not use force against the territorial integrity of another state. If the United Nations once admits that international disputes can be settled by using force, then we will have destroyed the very foundation of the organization, and our best hope of establishing a real world order. That would be a disaster for us all.

I would, I feel, be untrue to the standards of the high office to which you have chosen me if I were to lend the influence of the United States to the proposition that a nation which invades another should be permitted to exact conditions for withdrawal.

Of course, we and all the members of the United Nations ought to support justice and conformity with international law. The 1st Article of the Charter states the purpose of the United Nations to be "the suppression of acts of aggression or other breaches of the peace and to bring about by peaceful means, and in conformity with justice and international law, adjustment or settlement of international disputes." But it is to be observed that conformity with justice and international law are to be brought about "by peaceful means."

We cannot consider that the armed invasion and occupation of another country are peaceful means or proper means to achieve justice and conformity with international law. We do, however, believe that, upon the suppression of the present act of aggression and breach of the peace, there should be a greater effort by the United Nations and its members to secure justice and conformity with international law. Peace and justice are two sides of the same coin. ...

No one deplores more than I the fact that the Soviet Union ignores the resolutions of the United Nations. Also no nation is more vigorous than is the United States in seeking to exert moral pressure against the Soviet Union, which by reason of its size and power and by reason of its veto in the United Nations Security Council, is relatively impervious to other types of sanction. The United States and other free nations are making clear by every means at their command the evil of Soviet conduct in Hungary. It would indeed be a sad day if the United States ever felt that it had to subject Israel to the same type of moral pressure as is being applied to the Soviet Union.

There can, of course, be no equating of a nation like Israel with that of the Soviet Union. The peoples of Israel, like those of the United States, are imbued with a religious faith and a sense of moral values. We are entitled to expect, and do expect, from such peoples of the free world a contribution to world order which unhappily we cannot expect from a nation controlled by atheistic despots. ...

The present moment is a grave one, but we are hopeful that reason and right will prevail. Since the events of last October and November, solid progress has been made, in conformity with the Charter of the United Nations. There is the cease-fire, the forces of Britain and France have been withdrawn, the forces of Israel have been partially withdrawn, and the clearing of the Canal nears completion. When Israel completes its withdrawal, it will have removed a definite block

to further progress. Once this block is removed, there will be serious and creative tasks for the United Nations to perform. There needs to be respect for the right of Israel to national existence and to internal development. Complicated provisions insuring the effective international use of the Suez Canal will need to be worked out in detail. The Arab refugee problem must be solved. As I said in my special message to Congress on January 5, it must be made certain that all the Middle East is kept free from aggression and infiltration.

Finally, all who cherish freedom, including ourselves, should help the nations of the Middle East achieve their just aspirations for improving the well-being of their peoples.

What I have spoken about tonight is only one step in a long process calling for patience and diligence, but at this moment it is the critical issue on which future progress depends. It is an issue which can be solved if only we will apply the principles of the United Nations. That is why, my fellow Americans, I know you want the United States to continue to use its maximum influence to sustain those principles as the world's best hope for peace.

DWIGHT D. EISENHOWER: FAREWELL ADDRESS (1961)

Source: *Bulletin*, February 6, 1961.

My Fellow Americans:

Three days from now, after half a century in the service of our country, I shall lay down the responsibilities of office as, in traditional and solemn ceremony, the authority of the presidency is vested in my successor.

This evening I come to you with a message of leavetaking and farewell, and to share a few final thoughts with you, my countrymen.

Like every other citizen, I wish the new President and all who will labor with him Godspeed. I pray that the coming years will be blessed with peace and prosperity for all.

Our people expect their President and the Congress to find essential agreement on issues of great moment, the wise resolution of which will better shape the future of the nation.

My own relations with the Congress, which began on a remote and tenuous basis, when long ago a member of the Senate appointed me to West Point, have since ranged to the intimate during the war and immediate postwar period and, finally, to the mutually interdependent during these past eight years.

In this final relationship, the Congress and the administration have, on most vital issues, cooperated well to serve the national good rather than mere partisanship, and so have assured that the business of the nation should go forward. So my official relationship with the Congress ends in a feeling on my part of gratitude that we have been able to do so much together.

We now stand ten years past the midpoint of a century that has witnessed four major wars among great nations.

Three of these involved our own country. Despite these holocausts, America is today the strongest, the most influential, and most productive nation in the world. Understandably proud of this preeminence, we yet realize that America's leadership and prestige depend not merely upon our unmatched material progress, riches, and military strength but on how we use our power in the interests of world peace and human betterment.

Throughout America's adventure in free government our basic purposes have been to keep the peace, to foster progress in human achievement, and to enhance liberty, dignity, and integrity among people and among nations. To strive for less would be unworthy of a free and religious people. Any failure traceable to arrogance or our lack of comprehension or readiness to sacrifice would inflict upon us grievous hurt both at home and abroad.

Progress toward these noble goals is persistently threatened by the conflict now engulfing the world. It commands our whole attention, absorbs our very beings. We face a hostile ideology — global in scope, atheistic in character, ruthless in purpose, and insidious in method. Unhappily, the danger it poses promises to be of indefinite duration. To meet it successfully there is called for not so much the emotional and transitory sacrifices of crisis but rather those which enable us to carry forward steadily, surely, and without complaint the burdens of a prolonged and complex struggle — with liberty the stake. Only thus shall we remain, despite every provocation, on our charted course toward permanent peace and human betterment.

Crises there will continue to be. In meeting them, whether foreign or domestic, great or small, there is a recurring temptation to feel that some spectacular and costly action could become the miraculous solution to all current difficulties. A huge increase in newer elements of our defense, development of unrealistic programs to cure every ill in agriculture, a dramatic expansion in basic and applied research — these and many other possibilities, each possibly promising in itself, may be suggested as the only way to the road we wish to travel.

But each proposal must be weighed in the light of a broader consideration: the need to maintain balance in and among national programs — balance between the private and the public economy, balance between cost and hoped-for advantage, balance between the clearly necessary and the comfortably desirable, balance between our essential requirements as a nation and the duties imposed by the nation upon the individual, balance between actions of the moment and the national welfare of the future. Good judgment seeks balance and progress; lack of it eventually finds imbalance and frustration.

The record of many decades stands as proof that our people and their government have, in the main, understood these truths and have responded to them well in the face of stress and threat. But threats, new in kind or degree, constantly arise. I mention two only.

A vital element in keeping the peace is our military establishment. Our arms must be mighty, ready for instant action, so that no potential aggressor may be tempted to risk his own destruction.

Our military organization today bears little relation to that known by any of my predecessors in peacetime, or indeed by the fighting men of World War II or Korea.

Until the latest of our world conflicts, the United States had no armaments industry. American makers of plowshares could, with time and as required, make swords as well. But now we can no longer risk emergency improvisation of national defense; we have been compelled to create a permanent armaments industry of vast proportions. Added to this, 3.5 million men and women are directly engaged in the defense establishment. We annually spend on military security more than the net income of all United States corporations.

This conjunction of an immense military establishment and a large arms industry is new in the American experience. The total influence — economic, political, even spiritual — is felt in every city, every statehouse, every office of the federal government. We recognize the imperative need for this development. Yet we must not fail to comprehend its grave implications. Our toil, resources, and livelihood are all involved; so is the very structure of our society.

In the councils of government we must guard against the acquisition of unwarranted influence, whether sought or unsought, by the military-industrial complex. The potential for the disastrous rise of misplaced power exists and will persist.

We must never let the weight of this combination endanger our liberties or democratic processes. We should take nothing for granted. Only an alert and knowledgeable citizenry can compel the proper meshing of the huge industrial and military machinery of defense with our peaceful methods and goals so that security and liberty may prosper together.

Akin to, and largely responsible for, the sweeping changes in our industrial-military posture has been the technological revolution during recent decades. In this revolution, research has become central; it also becomes more formalized, complex, and costly. A steadily increasing share is conducted for, by, or at the direction of the federal government.

Today, the solitary inventor, tinkering in his shop, has been overshadowed by task forces of scientists in laboratories and testing fields. In the same fashion, the free university, historically the fountainhead of free ideas and scientific discovery, has experienced a revolution in the conduct of research. Partly because of the huge costs involved, a government contract becomes virtually a substitute for intellectual curiosity. For every old blackboard there are now hundreds of new electronic computers.

The prospect of domination of the nation's scholars by federal employment, project allocations, and the power of money is ever present and is gravely to be regarded. Yet, in holding scientific research and discovery in respect, as we should, we must also be alert to the equal and opposite danger that public policy could itself become the captive of a scientific-technological elite. It is the task of statesmanship to mold, to balance, and to integrate these and other forces, new and old, within the principles of our democratic system — ever aiming toward the supreme goals of our free society.

Another factor in maintaining balance involves the element of time. As we peer into society's future, we — you and I, and our government — must avoid the impulse to live only for today, plundering for our own ease and convenience the precious resources of tomorrow. We cannot mortgage the material assets of our grandchildren without risking the loss also of their political and spiritual heritage. We want democracy to survive for all generations to come, not to become the insolvent phantom of tomorrow.

Down the long lane of the history yet to be written, America knows that this world of ours, ever growing smaller, must avoid becoming a community of dreadful fear and hate, and be, instead, a proud confederation of mutual trust and respect. Such a confederation must be one of equals. The weakest must come to the conference table with the same confidence as do we, protected as we are by our moral, economic, and military strength. That table, though scarred by many past frustrations, cannot be abandoned for the certain agony of the battlefield.

Disarmament, with mutual honor and confidence, is a continuing imperative. Together we must learn how to compose differences, not with arms but with intellect and decent purpose. Because this need is so sharp and apparent, I confess that I lay down my official responsibilities in this field with a definite sense of disappointment. As one who has witnessed the horror and the lingering sadness of war, as one who knows that another war could utterly destroy this civilization which has been so slowly and painfully built over thousands of years, I wish I could say tonight that a lasting peace is in sight.

Happily, I can say that war has been avoided. Steady progress toward our ultimate goal has been made. But so much remains to be done. As a private citizen I shall never cease to do what little I can to help the world advance along that road.

So, in this, my last good night to you as your President, I thank you for the many opportunities you have given me for public service in war and peace. I trust that in that service you find some things worthy; as for the rest of it, I know you will find ways to improve performance in the future.

You and I, my fellow citizens, need to be strong in our faith that all nations, under God, will reach the goal of peace with justice. May we be ever unswerving in devotion to principle, confident but humble with power, diligent in pursuit of the nation's great goals.

To all the peoples of the world, I once more give expression to America's prayerful and continuing aspiration:

We pray that peoples of all faiths, all races, all nations, may have their great human needs satisfied; that those now denied opportunity shall come to enjoy it to the full; that all who yearn for freedom may experience its spiritual blessings; that those who have freedom will understand, also, its heavy responsibilities; that all who are insensitive to the needs of others will learn charity; that the scourges of poverty, disease, and ignorance will be made to disappear from the earth; and that, in the goodness of time, all peoples will come to live together in a peace guaranteed by the binding force of mutual respect and love.

JOHN F. KENNEDY: INAUGURAL ADDRESS (1961)

Source: *Bulletin*, February 6, 1961.

We observe today not a victory of party but a celebration of freedom — symbolizing an end as well as a beginning — signifying renewal as well as change. For I have sworn before you and Almighty God the same solemn oath our forebears prescribed nearly a century and three-quarters ago.

The world is very different now. For man holds in his mortal hands the power to abolish all forms of human poverty and all forms of human life. And yet the same revolutionary beliefs for which our forebears fought are still at issue around the globe — the belief that the rights of man come not from the generosity of the state but from the hand of God.

We dare not forget today that we are the heirs of that first revolution. Let the word go forth from this time and place, to friend and foe alike, that the torch has been passed to a new generation of Americans — born in this century, tempered by war, disciplined by a hard and bitter peace, proud of our ancient heritage — and unwilling to witness or permit the slow undoing of those human rights to which this nation has always been committed, and to which we are committed today at home and around the world.

Let every nation know, whether it wishes us well or ill, that we shall pay any price, bear any burden, meet any hardship, support any friend, oppose any foe to assure the survival and the success of liberty.

This much we pledge — and more.

To those old allies whose cultural and spiritual origins we share, we pledge the loyalty of faithful friends. United, there is little we cannot do in a host of cooperative ventures. Divided, there is little we can do — for we dare not meet a powerful challenge at odds and split asunder.

To those new states whom we welcome to the ranks of the free, we pledge our word that one form of colonial control shall not have passed away merely to be replaced by a far more iron tyranny. We shall not always expect to find them supporting our view. But we shall always hope to find them strongly supporting their own freedom — and to remember that, in the past, those who foolishly sought power by riding the back of the tiger ended up inside.

To those people in the huts and villages of half the globe struggling to break the bonds of mass misery, we pledge our best efforts to help them help themselves, for whatever period is required — not because the Communists may be doing it, not because we seek their votes, but because it is right. If a free society cannot help the many who are poor, it cannot save the few who are rich.

To our sister republics south of our border, we offer a special pledge — to convert our good words into good deeds — in a new alliance for progress — to assist free men and free governments in casting off the chains of poverty. But this peaceful revolution of hope cannot become the prey of hostile powers. Let all our neighbors know that we shall join with them to oppose aggression or subversion anywhere in the Americas. And let every other power know that this hemisphere intends to remain the master of its own house.

To that world assembly of sovereign states, the United Nations, our last best hope in an age where the instruments of war have far outpaced the instruments of peace, we renew our pledge of support — to prevent it from becoming merely a forum for invective — to strengthen its shield of the new and the weak — and to enlarge the area in which its writ may run.

Finally, to those nations who would make themselves our adversary, we offer not a pledge but a request — that both sides begin anew the quest for peace before the dark powers of destruction unleashed by science engulf all humanity in planned or accidental self-destruction. We dare not tempt them with weakness. For only when our arms are sufficient beyond doubt can we be certain beyond doubt that they will never be employed.

But neither can two great and powerful groups of nations take comfort from our present course — both sides overburdened by the cost of modern weapons, both rightly alarmed by the steady spread of the deadly atom, yet both racing to alter that uncertain balance of terror that stays the hand of mankind's final war.

So let us begin anew — remembering on both sides that civility is not a sign of weakness, and sincerity is always subject to proof. Let us never negotiate out of fear. But let us never fear to negotiate.

Let both sides explore what problems unite us instead of belaboring those problems which divide us.

Let both sides, for the first time, formulate serious and precise proposals for the inspection and control of arms — and bring the absolute power to destroy other nations under the absolute control of all nations.

Let both sides seek to invoke the wonders of science instead of its terrors. Together let us explore the stars, conquer the deserts, eradicate disease, tap the ocean depths, and encourage the arts and commerce.

Let both sides unite to heed in all corners of the earth the command of Isaiah — to "undo the heavy burdens ... [and] let the oppressed go free."

And if a beachhead of cooperation may push back the jungle of suspicion, let both sides join in creating a new endeavor, not a new balance of power but a new world of law, where the strong are just and the weak secure and the peace preserved.

All this will not be finished in the first 100 days. Nor will it be finished in the first 1,000 days, nor in the life of this administration, nor even perhaps in our lifetime on this planet. But let us begin.

In your hands, my fellow citizens, more than mine, will rest the final success or failure of our course. Since this country was founded, each generation of Americans has been summoned to give testimony to its national loyalty. The graves of young Americans who answered the call to service surround the globe.

Now the trumpet summons us again — not as a call to bear arms, though arms we need — not as a call to battle, though embattled we are — but a call to bear the burden of a long twilight struggle, year in and year out, "rejoicing in hope, patient in tribulation" — a struggle against the common enemies of man: tyranny, poverty, disease, and war itself.

Can we forge against these enemies a grand and global alliance, North and South, East and West, that can assure a more fruitful life for all mankind? Will you join in that historic effort?

In the long history of the world, only a few generations have been granted the role of defending freedom in its hour of maximum danger. I do not shrink from this responsibility — I welcome it. I do not believe that any of us would exchange places with any other people or any other generation. The energy, the faith, the devotion which we bring to this endeavor will light our country and all who serve it — and the glow from that fire can truly light the world.

And so, my fellow Americans — ask not what your country can do for you — ask what you can do for your country.

My fellow citizens of the world — ask not what America will do for you but what together we can do for the freedom of man.

Finally, whether you are citizens of America or citizens of the world, ask of us here the same high standards of strength and sacrifice which we ask of you. With a good conscience our only sure reward, with history the final judge of our deeds, let us go forth to lead the land we love, asking His blessing and His help, but knowing that here on earth God's work must truly be our own.

JOHN F. KENNEDY: SOVIET MISSILES IN CUBA (1962)

Source: *Bulletin*, November 12, 1962, pp. 715–720.

This government, as promised, has maintained the closest surveillance of the Soviet military buildup on the island of Cuba. Within the past week unmistakable evidence has established the fact that a series of offensive missile sites is now in preparation on that imprisoned island. The purpose of these bases can be none other than to provide a nuclear strike capability against the Western Hemisphere.

Upon receiving the first preliminary hard information of this nature last Tuesday morning [October 16] at 9 a.m., I directed that our surveillance be stepped up. And having now confirmed and completed our evaluation of the evidence and our decision on a course of action, this government feels obliged to report this new crisis to you in fullest detail.

The characteristics of these new missile sites indicate two distinct types of installations. Several of them include medium-srange ballistic missiles capable of carrying a nuclear warhead for a distance of more than 1,000 nautical miles. Each of these missiles, in short, is capable of striking Washington, D.C., the Panama Canal, Cape Canaveral, Mexico City, or any other city in the south-eastern part of the United States, in Central America, or in the Caribbean area. ...

This action also contradicts the repeated assurances of Soviet spokesmen, both publicly and privately delivered, that the arms buildup in Cuba would retain its original defensive character and that the Soviet Union had no need or desire to station strategic missiles on the territory of any other nation.

The size of this undertaking makes clear that it has been planned for some months. Yet only last month, after I had made clear the distinction between any introduction of ground-to-ground missiles and the existence of defensive antiaircraft missiles, the Soviet government publicly stated on September 11 that, and I quote, "The armaments and military equipment sent to Cuba are designed exclusively for defensive purposes," and, and I quote the Soviet government, "There is no need for the Soviet government to shift its weapons for a retaliatory blow to any other country, for instance Cuba," and that, and I quote the government, "The Soviet Union has so powerful rockets to carry these nuclear warheads that there is no need to search for sites for them beyond the boundaries of the Soviet Union." That statement was false.

Only last Thursday, as evidence of this rapid offensive buildup was already in my hand, Soviet Foreign Minister Gromyko told me in my office that he was instructed to make it clear once again, as he said his government had already done, that Soviet assistance to Cuba, and I quote, "pursued solely the purpose of contributing to the defense capabilities of Cuba," that, and I quote him, "training by Soviet specialists of Cuban nationals in handling defensive armaments was by no means offensive," and that "if it were otherwise," Mr. Gromyko went on, "the Soviet government would never become involved in rendering such assistance." That statement also was false.

Neither the United States of America nor the world community of nations can tolerate deliberate deception and offensive threats on the part of any nation, large or small. We no longer live in a world where only the actual firing of weapons represents a sufficient challenge to a nation's security to constitute maximum peril. Nuclear weapons are so destructive and ballistic missiles are so swift that any substantially increased possibility of their use or any sudden change in their deployment may well be regarded as a definite threat to peace. ...

Acting, therefore, in the defense of our own security and of the entire Western Hemisphere, and under the authority entrusted to me by the Constitution as endorsed by the resolution of the Congress, I have directed that the following initial steps be taken immediately:

First, to halt this offensive buildup, a strict quarantine on all offensive military equipment under shipment to Cuba is being initiated. All ships of any kind bound for Cuba from whatever nation or port will, if found to contain cargoes of offensive weapons, be turned back. This quarantine will be extended, if needed, to other types of cargo and carriers. We are not at this time, however, denying the necessities of life as the Soviets attempted to do in their Berlin blockade of 1948.

Second, I have directed the continued and increased close surveillance of Cuba and its military buildup. The Foreign Ministers of the OAS [Organization of American States] in their communiqué of October 3 rejected secrecy on such matters in this hemisphere. Should these offensive military preparations continue, thus increasing the threat to the hemisphere, further action will be justified. I have directed the Armed Forces to prepare for any eventualities; and I trust that, in the interest of both the Cuban people and the Soviet technicians at the sites, the hazards to all concerned of continuing this threat will be recognized.

Third, it shall be the policy of this nation to regard any nuclear missile launched from Cuba against any nation in the Western Hemisphere as an attack by the Soviet Union on the United States, requiring a full retaliatory response upon the Soviet Union.

Fourth, as a necessary military precaution I have reinforced our base at Guantanamo, evacuated today the dependents of our personnel there, and ordered additional military units to be on a standby alert basis.

Fifth, we are calling tonight for an immediate meeting of the Organ of Consultation, under the Organization of American States, to consider this threat to hemisphere security and to invoke Articles 6 and 8 of the Rio Treaty in support of all necessary action. The United Nations Charter allows for regional security arrangements — and the nations of this hemisphere decided long ago against the military presence of outside powers. Our other allies around the world have also been alerted.

Sixth, under the Charter of the United Nations, we are asking tonight that an emergency meeting of the Security Council be convoked without delay to take action against this latest Soviet threat to world peace. Our resolution will call for the prompt dismantling

and withdrawal of all offensive weapons in Cuba, under the supervision of UN observers, before the quarantine can be lifted.

Seventh and finally, I call upon Chairman Khrushchev to halt and eliminate this clandestine, reckless, and provocative threat to world peace and to stable relations between our two nations. I call upon him further to abandon this course of world domination and to join in an historic effort to end the perilous arms race and transform the history of man. He has an opportunity now to move the world back from the abyss of destruction — by returning to his government's own words that it had no need to station missiles outside its own territory, and withdrawing these weapons from Cuba — by refraining from any action which will widen or deepen the present crisis — and then by participating in a search for peaceful and permanent solutions.

This nation is prepared to present its case against the Soviet threat to peace, and our own proposals for a peaceful world, at any time and in any forum — in the OAS, in the United Nations, or in any other meeting that could be useful — without limiting our freedom of action.

We have in the past made strenuous efforts to limit the spread of nuclear weapons. We have proposed the elimination of all arms and military bases in a fair and effective disarmament treaty. We are prepared to discuss new proposals for the removal of tensions on both sides — including the possibilities of a genuinely independent Cuba, free to determine its own destiny. We have no wish to war with the Soviet Union, for we are a peaceful people who desire to live in peace with all other peoples. ...

My fellow citizens, let no one doubt that this is a difficult and dangerous effort on which we have set out. No one can foresee precisely what course it will take or what costs or casualties will be incurred. Many months of sacrifice and self-discipline lie ahead — months in which both our patience and our will will be tested, months in which many threats and denunciations will keep us aware of our dangers. But the greatest danger of all would be to do nothing.

The path we have chosen for the present is full of hazards, as all paths are; but it is the one most consistent with our character and courage as a nation and our commitments around the world. The cost of freedom is always high — but Americans have always paid it. And one path we shall never choose, and that is the path of surrender or submission.

LYNDON B. JOHNSON: THE GREAT SOCIETY (1964)

Source: White House Press Release.

I have come today from the turmoil of your Capitol to the tranquility of your campus to speak about the future of our country. The purpose of protecting the life of our nation and preserving the liberty of our citizens is to pursue the happiness of our people. Our success in that pursuit is the test of our success as a nation. For a century we labored to settle and to subdue a continent. For half a century we called upon unbounded invention and untiring industry to create an order of plenty for all of our people. The challenge of the next half century is whether we have the wisdom to use that wealth to enrich and elevate our national life and to advance the quality of our American civilization.

Your imagination, your initiative, and your indignation will determine whether we build a society where progress is the servant of our needs or a society where old values and new visions are buried under unbridled growth. For, in your time, we have the opportunity to move not only toward the rich society and the powerful society but upward to the Great Society.

The Great Society rests on abundance and liberty for all. It demands an end to poverty and racial injustice, to which we are totally committed in our time. But that is just the beginning. The Great Society is a place where every child can find knowledge to enrich his mind and to enlarge his talents. It is a place where leisure is a welcome chance to build and reflect, not a feared cause of boredom and restlessness. It is a place where the city of man serves not only the needs of the body and the demands of commerce but the desire for beauty and the hunger for community.

It is a place where man can renew contact with nature. It is a place which honors creation for its own sake and for what it adds to the understanding of the race. It is a place where men are more concerned with the quality of their goals than the quantity of their goods. But, most of all, the Great Society is not a safe harbor, a resting place, a final objective, a finished work; it is a challenge constantly renewed, beckoning us toward a destiny where the meaning of our lives matches the marvelous products of our labor.

So I want to talk to you today about three places where we begin to build the Great Society — in our cities, in our countryside, and in our classrooms. Many of you will live to see the day, perhaps fifty years from now, when there will be 400 million Americans, four-fifths of them in urban areas. In the remainder of this century, urban population will double, city land will double, and we will have to build homes, highways, and facilities equal to all those built since this country was first settled. So, in the next forty years, we must rebuild the entire urban United States.

Aristotle said, "Men come together in cities in order to live, but they remain together in order to live the good life." It is harder and harder to live the good life in American cities today. The catalog of ills is long: there is the decay of the centers and the despoiling of the suburbs. There is not enough housing for our people or transportation for our traffic. Open land is vanishing and old landmarks are violated. Worst of all, expansion is eroding the precious and time-honored values of community with neighbors and communion with nature. The loss of these values breeds loneliness and boredom and indifference. Our society will never be great until our cities are great. Today the

frontier of imagination and innovation is inside those cities, and not beyond their borders. New experiments are already going on. It will be the task of your generation to make the American city a place where future generations will come, not only to live but to live the good life.

I understand that if I stay here tonight I would see that Michigan students are really doing their best to live the good life. This is the place where the Peace Corps was started. It is inspiring to see how all of you, while you are in this country, are trying so hard to live at the level of the people.

A second place where we begin to build the Great Society is in our countryside. We have always prided ourselves on being not only America the strong and America the free but America the beautiful. Today that beauty is in danger. The water we drink, the food we eat, the very air that we breathe are threatened with pollution. Our parks are overcrowded. Our seashores overburdened. Green fields and dense forests are disappearing.

A few years ago we were greatly concerned about the Ugly American. Today we must act to prevent an Ugly America. For once the battle is lost, once our natural splendor is destroyed, it can never be recaptured. And once man can no longer walk with beauty or wonder at nature, his spirit will wither and his sustenance be wasted.

A third place to build the Great Society is in the classrooms of America. There your children's lives will be shaped. Our society will not be great until every young mind is set free to scan the farthest reaches of thought and imagination. We are still far from that goal. Today, 8 million adult Americans, more than the entire population of Michigan, have not finished five years of school. Nearly 20 million have not finished eight years of school. Nearly 54 million, more than one-quarter of all America, have not even finished high school.

Each year more than 100,000 high-school graduates, with proved ability, do not enter college because they cannot afford it. And if we cannot educate today's youth, what will we do in 1970 when elementary-school enrollment will be 5 million greater than 1960? And high-school enrollment will rise by 5 million? College enrollment will increase by more than 3 million? In many places, classrooms are overcrowded and curricula are outdated. Most of our qualified teachers are underpaid, and many of our paid teachers are unqualified. So we must give every child a place to sit and a teacher to learn from. Poverty must not be a bar to learning, and learning must offer an escape from poverty.

But more classrooms and more teachers are not enough. We must seek an educational system which grows in excellence as it grows in size. This means better training for our teachers. It means preparing youth to enjoy their hours of leisure as well as their hours of labor. It means exploring new techniques of teaching, to find new ways to stimulate the love of learning and the capacity for creation.

These are three of the central issues of the Great Society. While our government has many programs directed at those issues, I do not pretend that we have the full answer to those problems. But I do promise this: We are going to assemble the best thought and the broadest knowledge from all over the world to find those answers for America. I intend to establish working groups to prepare a series of White House conferences and meetings on the cities, on natural beauty, on the quality of education, and on other emerging challenges. And from these meetings and from this inspiration and from these studies we will begin to set our course toward the Great Society.

The solution to these problems does not rest on a massive program in Washington, nor can it rely solely on the strained resources of local authority. They require us to create new concepts of cooperation, a creative federalism, between the national Capitol and the leaders of local communities.

Woodrow Wilson once wrote: "Every man sent out from his university should be a man of his nation as well as a man of his time." Within your lifetime powerful forces, already loosed, will take us toward a way of life beyond the realm of our experience, almost beyond the bounds of our imagination. For better or for worse, your generation has been appointed by history to deal with those problems and to lead America toward a new age. You have the chance never before afforded to any people in any age. You can help build a society where the demands of morality and the needs of the spirit can be realized in the life of the nation.

So will you join in the battle to give every citizen the full equality which God enjoins and the law requires, whatever his belief, or race, or the color of his skin? Will you join in the battle to give every citizen an escape from the crushing weight of poverty? Will you join in the battle to make it possible for all nations to live in enduring peace as neighbors and not as mortal enemies? Will you join in the battle to build the Great Society, to prove that our material progress is only the foundation on which we will build a richer life of mind and spirit?

There are those timid souls who say this battle cannot be won, that we are condemned to a soulless wealth. I do not agree. We have the power to shape the civilization that we want. But we need your will, your labor, your hearts if we are to build that kind of society.

Those who came to this land sought to build more than just a new country. They sought a free world. So I have come here today to your campus to say that you can make their vision our reality. Let us from this moment begin our work so that in the future men will look back and say: It was then, after a long and weary way, that man turned the exploits of his genius to the full enrichment of his life.

LYNDON B. JOHNSON: WITHDRAWAL SPEECH (1968)

Source: Lyndon Baines Johnson Library and Museum: http://www.lbjlib.utexas. edu/johnson/archives.hom/speeches. hom/680331.asp

Tonight I want to speak to you on peace in Vietnam and Southeast Asia.

No other question so preoccupies our people. No other dream so absorbs the 250 million human beings who live in that part of the world. No other goal motivates American policy in Southeast Asia.

For years, representatives of our government and others have traveled the world — seeking to find a basis for peace talks. Since last September, they have carried the offer I made public at San Antonio.

It was this: that the United States would stop its bombardment of North Vietnam when that would lead promptly to productive discussions — and that we would assume that North Vietnam would not take military advantage of our restraint.

Hanoi denounced this offer, both privately and publicly. Even while the search for peace was going on, North Vietnam rushed their preparations for a savage assault on the people, the government, and the allies of South Vietnam.

Their attack — during the Tet holidays — failed to achieve its principal objectives. It did not collapse the elected government of South Vietnam or shatter its Army — as the Communists had hoped. It did not produce a "general uprising" among the people of the cities. The Communists were unable to maintain control of any city. And they took very heavy casualties.

But they did compel the South Vietnamese and their allies to move certain forces from the countryside, into the cities. They caused widespread disruption and suffering. Their attacks, and the battles that followed, made refugees of half a million human beings.

The Communists may renew their attack. They are, it appears, trying to make 1968 the year of decision in South Vietnam — the year that brings, if not final victory or defeat, at least a turning point in the struggle.

This much is clear: If they do mount another round of heavy attacks, they will not succeed in destroying the fighting power of South Vietnam and its allies. But, tragically, this is also clear: Many men — on both sides of the struggle — will be lost. A nation that has already suffered twenty years of warfare will suffer once again. Armies on both sides will take new casualties. And the war will go on.

There is no need for this to be so. There is no need to delay the talks that could bring an end to this long and bloody war.

Tonight, I renew the offer I made last August — to stop the bombardment of North Vietnam. We ask that talks begin promptly and that they be serious talks on the substance of peace. We assume that during those talks Hanoi would not take advantage of our restraint. We are prepared to move immediately toward peace through negotiations.

Tonight, in the hope that this action will lead to early talks, I am taking the first step to deescalate the conflict. We are reducing — substantially reducing — the present level of hostilities. And we are doing so unilaterally, and at once.

Tonight, I have ordered our aircraft and naval vessels to make no attacks on North Vietnam, except in the area north of the Demilitarized Zone (DMZ) where the continuing enemy build-up directly threatens allied forward positions and where movements of troops and supplies are clearly related to that threat. ...

Now, as in the past, the United States is ready to send its representatives to any forum, at any time, to discuss a means of bringing this war to an end. I am designating one of our most distinguished Americans, Ambassador Averell Harriman, as my personal representative for such talks. In addition, I have asked Ambassador Llewellyn Thompson, who returned from Moscow for consultations, to be available to join Ambassador Harriman at Geneva or any other suitable place just as soon as Hanoi agrees to a conference.

I call upon President Ho Chi Minh to respond positively and favorably to this new step toward peace.

But if peace does not come now through negotiations, it will come when Hanoi understands that our common resolve is unshakable and our common strength is invincible. ...

Every American can take pride in the role we have played in Southeast Asia; we can rightly judge — as responsible Southeast Asians themselves do — that the progress of the past three years would have been far less likely — if not impossible — if America and others had not made the stand in Vietnam.

At Johns Hopkins University, three years ago, I announced that we would take part in the great work of developing Southeast Asia, including the Mekong Valley — for all the people of the region. Our determination to help build a better land — for men on both sides of the present conflict — has not diminished. Indeed, the ravages of war have made it more urgent than ever. I repeat tonight what I said at Johns Hopkins — that North Vietnam could take its place in this common effort just as soon as peace comes.

Over time, a wider framework of peace and security in Southeast Asia may become possible. The new cooperation of the nations of the area could be a foundation stone. Certainly friendship with the nations of such a Southeast Asia is what we seek — and all that we seek.

One day, my fellow citizens, there will be peace in Southeast Asia. It will come because the people of Southeast Asia want it — those whose armies are at war today and those who, though threatened, have thus far been spared. Peace will come because Asians were willing to work for it — to sacrifice for it — to die for it. But let it never be forgotten: Peace will come also because America sent her sons to help secure it. ...

I believe that a peaceful Asia is far nearer to reality, because of what America has done in Vietnam. I believe that the men who endure the dangers of battle there are helping the entire world avoid far greater conflicts than this one.

The peace that will bring them home will come. Tonight I have offered the first in what I hope will be a series of mutual moves toward peace. I pray that it will

not be rejected by the leaders of North Vietnam. I pray that they will accept it as a means by which the sacrifices of their own people may be ended. And I ask your support, my fellow citizens, for this effort to reach across the battlefield toward an early peace. ...

Finally my fellow Americans, let me say this. Those to whom much is given, much is asked. I cannot say — no man could say — that no more will be asked of us. Yet I believe that now — no less than when the decade began — this generation of Americans is willing to "pay any price, bear any burden, meet any hardship, support any friend, oppose any foe, to assure the survival and the success of liberty."

Since those words were spoken by John F. Kennedy, the people of America have kept that compact with mankind's noblest cause. We shall continue to keep it. Yet I believe we must always be mindful of this one thing: Whatever the trials and tests ahead, the ultimate strength of our country and our cause will lie, not in powerful weapons or infinite resources or boundless wealth but in the unity of our people.

This, I believe very deeply.

Throughout my public career, I have followed the personal philosophy that I am a free man, an American, a public servant, and a member of my party — in that order, always and only. For thirty-seven years in the service of our nation — first as congressman, as senator, as Vice-President, and now as your President, I have put the unity of the people first, ahead of any divisive partisanship.

In these times, as in times before, it is true that a house divided against itself — by the spirit of faction, of party, of region, of religion, of race — is a house that cannot stand. There is divisiveness in the American house now. There is divisiveness among us all tonight. Holding the trust that is mine — as President of all the people — I cannot disregard the peril to the progress of the American people and the hope and the prospects of peace for all peoples. I would ask all Americans, whatever their personal interest or concern, to guard against divisiveness and all of its ugly consequences.

Fifty-two months and ten days ago in a moment of tragedy and trauma, the duties of this office fell upon me. I asked then for "your help and God's" that we might continue America on its course, binding up our wounds, healing our history, moving forward in new unity to clear the American agenda and to keep the American commitment for all our people. United, we have kept that commitment, and united, we have enlarged that commitment.

Through all time to come, America will be a stronger nation, a more just society, a land of greater. opportunity and fulfillment because of what we have done together in these years of unparalleled achievement. Our reward will come in the life of freedom and peace and hope that our children will enjoy through ages ahead. What we won when all our people united must not now be lost in suspicion, distrust, and selfishness or politics among any of our people.

Believing this as I do, I have concluded that I should not permit the presidency to become involved in the partisan divisions that are developing in this political year. With America's sons in the field far away, with America's future under challenge here at home, with our hopes and the world's hopes for peace in the balance every day, I do not believe that I should devote an hour or a day of my time to any duties other than the awesome duties of this office, the presidency of your country.

Accordingly, I shall not seek and I will not accept the nomination of my party for another term as your President. But, let men everywhere know, however, that a strong and a confident, a vigilant America stands ready to seek an honorable peace and stands ready tonight to defend an honored cause, whatever the price, whatever the burden, whatever the sacrifice that duty may require.

Thank you for listening. Goodnight, and God bless all of you.

RICHARD M. NIXON: THE MOSCOW SUMMIT (1972)

Source: Department of State Bulletin, June 26, 1972.

Mr. Speaker, Mr. President, Members of the Congress, our distinguished guests, my fellow Americans: Your welcome in this great Chamber tonight has a very special meaning to Mrs. Nixon and to me. We feel very fortunate to have traveled abroad so often representing the United States of America. But we both agree after each journey that the best part of any trip abroad is coming home to America again.

During the past 13 days we have flown more than 16,000 miles and we visited four countries. Everywhere we went—to Austria, the Soviet Union, Iran, Poland—we could feel the quickening pace of change in old international relationships and the people's genuine desire for friendship for the American people. Everywhere new hopes are rising for a world no longer shadowed by fear and want and war, and as Americans we can be proud that we now have an historic opportunity to play a great role in helping to achieve man's oldest dream: a world in which all nations can enjoy the blessings of peace. ...

I have not come here this evening to make new announcements in a dramatic setting. This summit has already made its news. It has barely begun, however, to make its mark on our world, and I ask you to join me tonight—while events are fresh, while the iron is hot—in starting to consider how we can help to make that mark what we want it to be.

The foundation has been laid for a new relationship between the two most powerful nations in the world. Now it is up to us, to all of us here in this Chamber, to all of us across America, to join with other nations in building a new house upon that foundation, one that can be a home for the hopes of mankind and a shelter against the storms of conflict.

As a preliminary, therefore, to requesting your concurrence in some of the agreements we reached and your approval of funds to carry out others, and also as a keynote for the unity in which this government and this Nation must go forward from here, I am rendering this immediate report to the Congress on the results of the Moscow summit. ...

Recognizing the responsibility of the advanced industrial nations to set an example in combating mankind's common enemies, the United States and the Soviet Union have agreed to cooperate in efforts to reduce pollution and enhance environmental quality. We have agreed to work together in the field of medical science and public health, particularly in the conquest of cancer and heart disease.

Recognizing that the quest for useful knowledge transcends differences between ideologies and social systems, we have agreed to expand United States-Soviet cooperation in many areas of science and technology.

We have joined in plans for an exciting new adventure, a new adventure in the cooperative exploration of space, which will begin—subject to congressional approval of funding—with a joint orbital mission of an Apollo vehicle and a Soviet spacecraft in 1975.

By forming habits of cooperation and strengthening institutional ties in areas of peaceful enterprise, these four agreements to which I have referred will create on both sides a steadily growing vested interest in the maintenance of good relations between our two countries.

Expanded United States-Soviet trade will also yield advantages to both of our nations. When the two largest economies in the world start trading with each other on a much larger scale, living standards in both nations will rise and the stake which both have in peace will increase.

Progress in this area is proceeding on schedule. At the summit, we established a Joint Commercial Commission which will complete the negotiations for a comprehensive trade agreement between the United States and the U.S.S.R. And we expect the final terms of such an agreement to be settled, later this year.

Two further accords which were reached last week have a much more direct bearing on the search for peace and security in the world.

One is the agreement between the American and Soviet navies aimed at significantly reducing the chances of dangerous incidents between our ships and aircraft at sea.

And second, and most important, there is the treaty and the related executive agreement which will limit, for the first time, both offensive and defensive strategic nuclear weapons in the arsenals of the United States and the Soviet Union.

Three-fifths of all the people alive in the world today have spent their whole lifetimes under the shadow of a nuclear war which could be touched off by the arms race among the great powers. Last Friday in Moscow we witnessed the beginning of the end of that era which began in 1945. We took the first step toward a new era of mutually agreed restraint and arms limitation between the two principal nuclear powers.

With this step we have enhanced the security of both nations. We have begun to check the wasteful and dangerous spiral of nuclear arms which has dominated relations between our two countries for a generation. We have begun to reduce the level of fear by reducing the causes of fear for our two peoples and for all peoples in the world.

The ABM [antiballistic missile] Treaty will be submitted promptly for the Senate's advice and consent to ratification, and the interim agreement limiting certain offensive weapons will be submitted to both Houses for concurrence—because we can undertake agreements as important as these only on a basis of full partnership between the executive and legislative branches of our government. ...

In addition to the talks which led to the specific agreements I have listed, I also had full, very frank, and extensive discussions with General Secretary [of the Soviet Communist Party Leonid I.] Brezhnev and his colleagues about several parts of the world where Americans and Soviet interests have come in conflict.

With regard to the reduction of tensions in Europe, we recorded our intention of proceeding later this year with multilateral consultations looking toward a Conference on Security and Cooperation in all of Europe. We have also jointly agreed to move forward with negotiations on mutual and balanced force reductions in central Europe.

The problem of ending the Vietnam war, which engages the hopes of all Americans, was one of the most extensively discussed subjects on our agenda. It would only jeopardize the search for peace if I were to review here all that was said on the subject. I will simply say this: Each side obviously has its own point of view and its own approach to this very difficult issue. But at the same time, both the United States and the Soviet Union share an overriding desire to achieve a more stable peace in the world. I emphasize to you once again that this administration has no higher goal, a goal that I know all of you share, than bringing the Vietnam war to an early and honorable end. We are ending the war in Vietnam, but we shall end it in a way which will not betray our friends, risk the lives of the courageous Americans still serving in Vietnam, break faith with those held prisoners by the enemy, or stain the honor of the United States of America.

Another area where we had very full, frank, and extensive discussions was the Middle East. I reiterated the American people's commitment to the survival of the state of Israel and to a settlement just to all the countries in the area. Both sides stated in the communique their intention to support the Jarring peace mission and other appropriate efforts to achieve this objective.

The final achievement of the Moscow conference was the signing of a landmark declaration entitled Basic Principles of Mutual Relations Between the United States and the U.S.S.R. As these 12 basic principles are put into practice, they can provide a solid framework for the future development of better American-Soviet relations.

They begin with the recognition that two nuclear nations, each of which has the power to destroy humanity, have no alternative but to coexist peacefully because in a nuclear war there would be no winners, only losers.

The basic principles commit both sides to avoid direct military confrontation and to exercise constructive leadership and restraint with respect to smaller conflicts in other parts of the world which could drag the major powers into war.

They disavow any intention to create spheres of influence or to conspire against the interests of any other nation—a point I would underscore by saying once again tonight that America values its ties with all nations, from our oldest allies in Europe and Asia, as I emphasized by my visit to Iran, to our good friends in the Third World, and to our new relationship with the People's Republic of China.

The improvement of relations depends not only, of course, on words but far more on actions. The principles to which we agreed in Moscow are like a roadmap. Now that the map has been laid out, it is up to each country to follow it. The United States intends to adhere to these principles. The leaders of the Soviet Union have indicated a similar intention. ...

For decades, America has been locked in hostile confrontation with the two great Communist powers, the Soviet Union and the People's Republic of

China. We were engaged with the one at many points and almost totally isolated from the other, but our relationships with both had reached a deadly impasse. All three countries were victims of the kind of bondage about which George Washington long ago warned in these words: The nation which indulges toward another an habitual hatred is a slave to its own animosity.

But now in the brief space of four months, these journeys to Peking and to Moscow have begun to free us from perpetual confrontation. We have moved toward better understanding, mutual respect, and point-by-point settlement of differences with both the major Communist powers.

This one series of meetings has not rendered an imperfect world suddenly perfect. There still are deep philosophical differences; there still are parts of the world in which age-old hatreds persist. The threat of war has not been eliminated—it has been reduced. We are making progress toward a world in which leaders of nations will settle their differences by negotiation, not by force, and in which they learn to live with their differences so that their sons will not have to die for those differences.

It was particularly fitting that this trip, aimed at building such a world, should have concluded in Poland.

No country in the world has suffered more from war than Poland has, and no country has more to gain from peace. The faces of the people who gave us such a heartwarming welcome in Warsaw yesterday, and again this morning and this afternoon, told an eloquent story of suffering in the past and of hope for peace in the future. One could see it in their faces. It made me more determined than ever that America must do all in its power to help that hope come true for all people.

As we continue that effort, our unity of purpose and action will be all-important.

For the summits of 1972 have not belonged just to one person or one party or to one branch of our government alone. Rather they are part of a great national journey for peace. Every American can claim a share in the credit for success of that journey so far, and every American has a major stake in its success for the future.

RICHARD M. NIXON: RESIGNATION FROM THE PRESIDENCY (1974)

Source: *Weekly Compilation of Presidential Documents*, August 12, 1974.

A. TELEVISION ADDRESS ANNOUNCING THE INTENTION TO RESIGN

Good evening.

This is the 37th time I have spoken to you from this office, where so many decisions have been made that shaped the history of this Nation. Each time I have done so to discuss with you some matter that I believe affected the national interest.

In all the decisions I have made in my public life, I have always tried to do what was best for the Nation. Throughout the long and difficult period of Watergate, I have felt it was my duty to persevere, to make every possible effort to complete the term of office to which you elected me.

In the past few days, however, it has become evident to me that I no longer have a strong enough political base in the Congress to justify continuing that effort. As long as there was such a base, I felt strongly that it was necessary to see the constitutional process through to its conclusion, that to do otherwise would be unfaithful to the spirit of that deliberately difficult process and a dangerously destabilizing precedent for the future.

But with the disappearance of that base, I now believe that the constitutional purpose has been served, and there is no longer a need for the process to be prolonged.

I would have preferred to carry through to the finish whatever the personal agony it would have involved, and my family unanimously urged me to do so. But the interest of the Nation must always come before any personal considerations.

From the discussions I have had with Congressional and other leaders, I have concluded that because of the Watergate matter I might not have the support of the Congress that I would consider necessary to back the very difficult decisions and carry out the duties of this office in the way the interests of the Nation would require.

I have never been a quitter. To leave office before my term is completed is abhorrent to every instinct in my body. But as President, I must put the interest of America first. America needs a full-time President and a full-time Congress, particularly at this time with problems we face at home and abroad.

To continue to fight through the months ahead for my personal vindication would almost totally absorb the time and attention of both the President and the Congress in a period when our entire focus should be on the great issues of peace abroad and prosperity without inflation at home.

Therefore, I shall resign the Presidency effective at noon tomorrow. Vice President Ford will be sworn in as President at that hour in this office.

As I recall the high hopes for America with which we began this second term, I feel a great sadness that I will not be here in this office working on your behalf to achieve those hopes in the next 212 years. But in turning over direction of the Government to Vice President Ford, I know, as I told the Nation when I nominated him for that office 10 months ago, that the leadership of America will be in good hands.

In passing this office to the Vice President, I also do so with the profound sense of the weight of responsibility that will fall on his shoulders tomorrow and, therefore, of the understanding, the patience, the cooperation he will need from all Americans.

As he assumes that responsibility, he will deserve the help and the support of all of us. As we look to the future, the first essential is to begin healing the wounds of this Nation, to put the bitterness and divisions of the recent past behind us, and to rediscover those shared ideals that lie at the heart of our strength and unity as a great and as a free people.

By taking this action, I hope that I will have hastened the start of that process of healing which is so desperately needed in America.

I regret deeply any injuries that may have been done in the course of the events that led to this decision. I would say only that if some of my judgments were wrong, and some were wrong, they were made in what I believed at the time to be the best interest of the Nation.

To those who have stood with me during these past difficult months, to my family, my friends, to many others who joined in supporting my cause because they believed it was right, I will be eternally grateful for your support.

And to those who have not felt able to give me your support, let me say I leave with no bitterness toward those who have opposed me, because all of us, in the final analysis, have been concerned with the good of the country, however our judgments might differ.

So, let us all now join together in affirming that common commitment and in helping our new President succeed for the benefit of all Americans.

I shall leave this office with regret at not completing my term, but with gratitude for the privilege of serving as your President for the past 512 years. These years have been a momentous time in the history of our Nation and the world. They have been a time of achievement in which we can all be proud, achievements that represent the shared efforts of the Administration, the Congress, and the people.

But the challenges ahead are equally great, and they, too, will require the support and the efforts of the Congress and the people working in cooperation with the new Administration.

We have ended America's longest war, but in the work of securing a lasting peace in the world, the goals ahead are even more far-reaching and more difficult. We must complete a structure of peace so that it will be said of this generation, our generation of Americans, by the people of all nations, not only that we ended one war but that we prevented future wars.

We have unlocked the doors that for a quarter of a century stood between the United States and the People's Republic of China.

We must now ensure that the one quarter of the world's people who live in the People's Republic of China will be and remain not our enemies but our friends.

In the Middle East, 100 million people in the Arab countries, many of whom have considered us their enemy for nearly 20 years, now look on us as their friends. We must continue to build on that friendship so that peace can settle at last over the Middle East and so that the cradle of civilization will not become its grave.

Together with the Soviet Union we have made the crucial breakthroughs that have begun the process of limiting nuclear arms. But we must set as our goal not just limiting but reducing and finally destroying these terrible weapons so that they cannot destroy civilization and so that the threat of nuclear war will no longer hang over the world and the people.

We have opened the new relation with the Soviet Union. We must continue to develop and expand that new relationship so that the two strongest nations of the world will live together in cooperation rather than confrontation.

Around the world, in Asia, in Africa, in Latin America, in the Middle East, there are millions of people who live in terrible poverty, even starvation. We must keep as our goal turning away from production for war and expanding production for peace so that people everywhere on this earth can at last look forward in their children's time, if not in our own time, to having the necessities for a decent life.

Here in America, we are fortunate that most of our people have not only the blessings of liberty but also the means to live full and good and, by the world's standards, even abundant lives. We must press on, however, toward a goal of not only more and better jobs but of full opportunity for every American and of what we are striving so hard right now to achieve, prosperity without inflation.

For more than a quarter of a century in public life I have shared in the turbulent history of this era. I have fought for what I believed in. I have tried to the best of my ability to discharge those duties

and meet those responsibilities that were entrusted to me.

Sometimes I have succeeded and sometimes I have failed, but always I have taken heart from what Theodore Roosevelt once said about the man in the arena, "whose face is marred by dust and sweat and blood, who strives valiantly, who errs and comes short again and again because there is not effort without error and shortcoming, but who does actually strive to do the deed, who knows the great enthusiasms, the great devotions, who spends himself in a worthy cause, who at the best knows in the end the triumphs of high achievements and who at the worst, if he fails, at least fails while daring greatly."

I pledge to you tonight that as long as I have a breath of life in my body, I shall continue in that spirit. I shall continue to work for the great causes to which I have been dedicated throughout my years as a Congressman, a Senator, a Vice President, and President, the cause of peace not just for America but among all nations, prosperity, justice, and opportunity for all of our people.

There is one cause above all to which I have been devoted and to which I shall always be devoted for as long as I live.

When I first took the oath of office as President 512 years ago, I made this sacred commitment, to "consecrate my office, my energies, and all the wisdom I can summon to the cause of peace among nations."

I have done my very best in all the days since to be true to that pledge. As a result of these efforts, I am confident that the world is a safer place today, not only for the people of America but for the people of all nations, and that all of our children have a better chance than before of living in peace rather than dying in war.

This, more than anything, is what I hoped to achieve when I sought the Presidency. This, more than anything, is what I hope will be my legacy to you, to our country, as I leave the Presidency.

To have served in this office is to have felt a very personal sense of kinship with each and every American. In leaving it, I do so with this prayer: May God's grace be with you in all the days ahead.

B. FAREWELL TO THE WHITE HOUSE STAFF

Members of the Cabinet, Members of the White House Staff, all of our friends here:

I think the record should show that this is one of those spontaneous things that we always arrange whenever the President comes in to speak, and it will be so reported in the press, and we don't mind because they have to call it as they see it.

But on our part, believe me, it is spontaneous.

You are here to say goodby to us, and we don't have a good word for it in English. The best is au revoir. We will see you again.

I just met with the members of the White House staff, you know, those who serve here in the White House day in and day out, and I asked them to do what I ask all of you to do to the extent that you can and, of course, are requested to do so: to serve our next President as you have served me and previous Presidents— because many of you have been here for many years—with devotion and dedication, because this office, great as it is, can only be as great as the men and women who work for and with the President.

This house, for example, I was thinking of it as we walked down this hall, and I was comparing it to some of the great houses of the world that I have been in. This isn't the biggest house. Many, and most, in even smaller countries are much bigger. This isn't the finest house. Many in Europe, particularly, and in China, Asia, have paintings of great, great value, things that we just don't have here, and probably will never have until we are 1,000 years old or older.

But this is the best house. It is the best house because it has something far more important than numbers of people who serve, far more important than numbers of rooms or how big it is, far more important than numbers of magnificent pieces of art.

This house has a great heart, and that heart comes from those who serve. I was rather sorry they didn't come down. We said goodby to them upstairs. But they are really great. And I recall after so many times I have made speeches, and some of them pretty tough, yet, I always come back, or after a hard day—and my days usually have run rather long—I would always get a lift from them because I might be a little down, but they always smiled.

And so it is with you. I look around here, and I see so many on this staff that, you know, I should have been by your offices and shaken hands, and I would love to have talked to you and found out how to run the world—everybody wants to tell the President what to do, and boy he needs to be told many times—but I just haven't had the time. But I want you to know that each and every one of you, I know, is indispensable to this Government. I am proud of this Cabinet. I am proud of all the members who have served in our Cabinet. I am proud of our sub-Cabinet. I am proud of our White House Staff. As I pointed out last night, sure we have done some things wrong in this Administration, and the top man always takes the responsibility, and I have never ducked it. But I want to say one thing: We can be proud of it—512 years. No man or no woman came into this Administration and left it with more of this world's goods than when he came in. No man or no woman ever profited at the public expense or the public till. That tells something about you.

Mistakes, yes. But for personal gain, never. You did what you believed in. Sometimes right, sometimes wrong. And I only wish that I were a wealthy man— at the present time I have got to find a way to pay my taxes—[laughter]—and if I were, I would like to recompense you for the sacrifices that all of you have made to serve in Government.

But you are getting something in Government—and I want you to tell this to your children, and I hope the Nation's children will hear it, too—something in Government service that is far more important than money. It is a cause bigger than yourself. It is the cause of making this the greatest nation in the world, the leader of the world, because without our leadership the world will know nothing but war, possibly starvation, or worse, in the years ahead. With our leadership it will know peace, it will know plenty.

We have been generous, and we will be more generous in the future as we are able to. But most important, we must be strong here, strong in our hearts, strong in our souls, strong in our belief, and strong in our willingness to sacrifice, as you have been willing to sacrifice, in a pecuniary way, to serve in Government.

There is something else I would like for you to tell your young people. You know, people often come in and say, "What will I tell my kids?" They look at government and say it is sort of a rugged life, and they see the mistakes that are made. They get the impression that everybody is here for the purpose of feathering his nest. That is why I made this earlier point—not in this Administration, not one single man or woman.

And I say to them, "There are many fine careers. This country needs good farmers, good businessmen, good plumbers, good carpenters."

I remembered my old man. I think that they would have called him sort of a little man, common man. He didn't consider himself that way. You know what he was? He was a streetcar motorman first, and then he was a farmer, and then he had a lemon ranch. It was the poorest lemon ranch in California, I can assure you. He sold it before they found oil on it.[Laughter]

And then he was a grocer. But he was a great man because he did his job, and every job counts up to the hilt, regardless of what happens.

Nobody will ever write a book, probably, about my mother. Well, I guess all of you would say this about your mother—my mother was a saint. And I think of her, two boys dying of tuberculosis, nursing four others in order that she could take care of my older brother for 3 years in Arizona, and seeing each of them die, and when they died, it was like one of her own. Yes, she will have no books written about her. But she was a saint.

Now, however, we look to the future. I had a little quote in the speech last night from T.R. As you know, I kind of like to read books. I am not educated, but I do read books—[laughter]—and the T.R. quote was a pretty good one.

Here is another one I found as I was reading, my last night in the White House, and this quote is about a young man. He was a young lawyer in New York. He had married a beautiful girl, and they had a lovely daughter, and then suddenly she died, and this is what he wrote. This was in his diary.

He said: "She was beautiful in face and form and lovelier still in spirit. As a flower she grew and as a fair young flower she died. Her life had been always in the sunshine. There had never come to her a single great sorrow. None ever knew her who did not love and revere her for her bright and sunny temper and her saintly unselfishness. Fair, pure and joyous as a maiden, loving, tender and happy as a young wife. When she had just become a mother, when her life seemed to be just begun and when the years seemed so bright before her, then by a strange and terrible fate death came to her. And when my heart's dearest died, the light went from my life forever."

That was T.R. in his twenties. He thought the light had gone from his life forever—but he went on. And he not only became President but, as an ex-President, he served his country always in the arena, tempestuous, strong, sometimes wrong, sometimes right, but he was a man.

And as I leave, let me say, that is an example I think all of us should remember. We think sometimes when things happen that don't go the right way; we think that when you don't pass the bar exam the first time—I happened to, but I was just lucky; I mean my writing was so poor the bar examiner said, "We have just got to let the guy through." [Laughter] We think that when someone dear to us dies, we think that when we lose an election, we think that when we suffer a defeat, that all is ended. We think, as T.R. said, that the light had left his life forever.

Not true. It is only a beginning always. The young must know it; the old must know it. It must always sustain us because the greatness comes not when things go always good for you, but the greatness comes when you are really tested, when you take some knocks, some disappointments, when sadness comes, because only if you have been in the deepest valley can you ever know how magnificent it is to be on the highest mountain.

And so I say to you on this occasion, as we leave, we leave proud of the people who have stood by us and worked for us and served this country.

We want you to be proud of what you have done. We want you to continue to serve in Government, if that is your wish. Always give your best, never get discouraged, never be petty; always remember others may hate you, but those who hate you don't win unless you hate them, and then you destroy yourself.

And so, we leave with high hopes, in good spirit and with deep humility, and with very much gratefulness in our hearts. I can only say to each and every one of you, we come from many faiths, we pray perhaps to different gods, but really the same God in a sense, but I want to say for each and every one of you, not only will we always remember you, not only will we always be grateful to you but always you will be in our hearts and you will be in our prayers.

Thank you very much.
The President's Letter to the Secretary of State.
August 9, 1974

Dear Mr. Secretary;
I hereby resign the Office of President of the United States.
Sincerely,
Richard Nixon

JIMMY CARTER: A NATIONAL MALAISE (1979)

Source: *Presidential Documents*, week ending July 20, 1979.

I know, of course, being President, that government actions and legislation can be very important. That's why I've worked hard to put my campaign promises into law—and I have to admit, with just mixed success. But after listening to the American people I have been reminded again that all the legislation in the world can't fix what's wrong with America. So, I want to speak to you first tonight about a subject even more serious than energy or inflation. I want to talk to you right now about a fundamental threat to American democracy.

I do not mean our political and civil liberties. They will endure. And I do not refer to the outward strength of America, a nation that is at peace tonight everywhere in the world, with unmatched economic power and military might.

The threat is nearly invisible in ordinary ways. It is a crisis of confidence. It is a crisis that strikes at the very heart and soul and spirit of our national will. We can see this crisis in the growing doubt about the meaning of our own lives and in the loss of a unity of purpose for our Nation.

The erosion of our confidence in the future is threatening to destroy the social and the political fabric of America.

The confidence that we have always had as a people is not simply some romantic dream or a proverb in a dusty book that we read just on the Fourth of July. It is the idea which founded our Nation and has guided our development as a people. Confidence in the future has supported everything else—public institutions and private enterprise, our own families, and the very Constitution of the United States. Confidence has defined our course and has served as a link between generations. We've always believed in something called progress. We've always had a faith that the days of our children would be better than our own.

Our people are losing that faith, not only in government itself but in the ability as citizens to serve as the ultimate rulers and shapers of our democracy. As a people we know our past and we are proud of it. Our progress has been part of the living history of America, even the world. We always believed that we were part of a great movement of humanity itself called democracy, involved in the search for freedom and that belief has always strengthened us in our purpose. But just as we are losing our confidence in the future, we are also beginning to close the door on our past.

In a nation that was proud of hard work, strong families, close-knit communities, and our faith in God, too many of us now tend to worship self-indulgence and consumption. Human identity is no longer defined by what one does, but by what one owns. But we've discovered that owning things and consuming things does not satisfy our longing for meaning. We've learned that piling up material goods cannot fill the emptiness of lives which have no confidence or purpose.

The symptoms of this crisis of the American spirit are all around us. For the first time in the history of our country a majority of our people believe that the next 5 years will be worse than the past 5 years. Two-thirds of our people do not even vote. The productivity of American workers is actually dropping, and the willingness of Americans to save for the future has fallen below that of all other people in the Western world.

As you know, there is a growing disrespect for government and for churches and for schools, the news media, and other institutions. This is not a message of happiness or reassurance, but it is the truth and it is a warning.

These changes did not happen overnight. They've come upon us gradually over the last generation, years that were filled with shocks and tragedy.

We were sure that ours was a nation of the ballot, not the bullet, until the murders of John Kennedy and Robert Kennedy and Martin Luther King, Jr. We were taught that our armies were always invincible and our causes were always just, only to suffer the agony of Vietnam. We respected the Presidency as a place of honor until the shock of Watergate.

We remember when the phrase "sound as a dollar" was an expression of absolute dependability, until 10 years of inflation began to shrink our dollar and our savings. We believed that our Nation's resources were limitless until 1973 when we had to face a growing dependence on foreign oil.

These wounds are still very deep. They have never been healed.

Looking for a way out of this crisis, our people have turned to the Federal Government and found it isolated from the mainstream of our Nation's life. Washington, D.C., has become an island. The gap between our citizens and our Government has never been so wide. The people are looking for honest answers, not easy answers; clear leadership, not false claims and evasiveness and politics as usual.

What you see often in Washington and elsewhere around the country is a system of government that seems incapable of action. You see a Congress twisted and pulled in every direction by hundreds of well-financed and powerful special interests.

You see every extreme position defended to the last vote, almost to the last breath by one unyielding group or another. You often see a balanced and a fair approach that demands sacrifice, a little sacrifice from everyone, abandoned like an orphan without support and without friends.

Often you see paralysis and stagnation and drift. You don't like it, and neither do I. What can we do?

First of all, we must face the truth, and then we can change our course. We simply must have faith in each other, faith in our ability to govern ourselves, and faith in the future of this Nation. Restoring that faith and that confidence to America is now the most important task we face. It is a true challenge of this generation of Americans.

RONALD REAGAN: A TAX SYSTEM THAT IS UNWISE, UNWANTED, AND UNFAIR (1985)

Source: *Presidential Documents*, week ending May 28, 1985.

My fellow citizens, I'd like to speak to you tonight about our future, about a great historic effort to give the words freedom, fairness and hope new meaning and power for every man and woman in America.

Specifically, I want to talk about taxes; about what we must do as a nation this year to transform a system that's become an endless source of confusion and resentment into one that is clear, simple and fair for all; a tax code that no longer runs roughshod over Main Street America, but insures your families and firms incentives and rewards for hard work and risk-taking in an American future of strong economic growth.

No other issue goes so directly to the heart of our economic life; no other issue will have more lasting impact on the well-being of your families and your future.

In 1981 our critics charged that letting you keep more of your earnings would trigger an inflationary explosion, send interest rates soaring and destroy our economy. Well, we cut your tax rates anyway by nearly 25 percent. And what that helped trigger was falling inflation, falling interest rates and the strongest economic expansion in 30 years.

We have made one great dramatic step together. We owe it to ourselves now to take another. For the sake of fairness, simplicity and growth we must radically change the structure of a tax system that still treats our earnings as the personal property of the I.R.S.; radically change a system that still treats people earning similar incomes much differently regarding the tax they pay and, yes, radically change a system that still causes some to invest their money, not to make a better mousetrap but simply to avoid a tax trap.

Over the course of this century our tax system has been modified dozens of times and in hundreds of ways. Yet most of those changes didn't improve the system, they made it more like Washington itself: complicated, unfair, cluttered with gobbledygook and loopholes designed for those with the power and influence to hire high-priced legal and tax advisors.

But there is more to it than that.

Some years ago someone—a historian I believe—said that every time in the past when a Government began taxing above a certain level of the people's earnings trust in Government began to erode. He said it would begin with efforts to avoid paying the full tax. This would become outright cheating, and eventually a distrust and contempt of Government itself

until there would be a breakdown in law and order.

Well, how many times have we heard people brag about clever schemes to avoid paying taxes, or watched luxuries casually written off to be paid for by somebody else—that somebody being you. I believe that in both spirit and substance our tax system has come to be un-American.

Death and taxes may be inevitable, but unjust taxes are not. The first American Revolution was sparked by an unshakable conviction: Taxation without representation is tyranny. Two centuries later a second American Revolution for hope and opportunity is gathering force again, a peaceful revolution but born of popular resentment against a tax system that is unwise, unwanted and unfair.

I've spoken with and received letters from thousands of you, Republicans, Democrats and Independents. I know how hungry you are for change. Make no mistake, we, the sons and daughters of those first brave souls who came to this land to give birth to a new life in liberty, we can change America again; we can change America forever. So let's get started, let's change the tax code to make it fairer, and change tax rates so they are lower.

The proposal I am putting forth tonight for America's future will free us from the grip of special interests and create a binding commitment to the only special interest that counts, you, the people who pay America's bills. It will create millions of new jobs for working people and it will replace the politics of envy with a spirit of partnership, the opportunity for everyone to hitch their wagon to a star and set out to reach the American dream.

I'll start by answering one question on your minds — will our proposal help you? You bet it will. We call it America's tax plan because it will reduce tax burdens on the working people of this country, close loopholes that benefit a privileged few, simplify a code so complex even Albert Einstein reportedly needed help on his 1040 form, and lead us into a future of greater growth and opportunity for all. ...

How would the proposal work? The present tax system has 14 different brackets of tax rates ranging from 11 to 50 percent. We would take a giant step toward an ideal system by replacing all that with a simple three-bracket system, with tax rates of 15, 25 and 35 percent. ... By lowering everyone's tax rates all the way up the income scale, each of us will have a greater incentive to climb higher, to excel, to help America grow.

I believe the worth of any economic policy must be measured by the strength of its commitment to American families, the bedrock of our society. There is no instrument of hard work, savings and job creation as effective as the family. There is no cultural institution as ennobling as family life. And there is no superior, indeed, no equal means to rear the young, protect the weak or attend the elderly. None.

Yet past Government policies betrayed families and family values.

They permitted inflation to push families relentlessly into higher and higher tax brackets. And not only did the personal exemption fail to keep pace with inflation, in real dollars its actual value dropped dramatically over the last 30 years.

The power to tax is the power to destroy. For three decades, families have paid the freight for the special interests. Now families are in trouble. As one man from Memphis, Tennessee, recently wrote: "The taxes that are taken out of my check, is money that I need, not extra play money. Please do all that you can to make the tax system more equitable toward the family."

Well, sir, that's just what we intend to do, to pass the strongest profamily initiative in postwar history. In addition to lowering your tax rates further we will virtually double the personal exemption, raising it by next year to $2,000 for every taxpayer and every dependent. And that $2,000 exemption will be indexed to protect against inflation.

Further, we propose to increase the standard deduction, raising it to $4,000 for joint returns.

Beyond this we intend to strengthen families' incentives to save through individual retirement accounts, I.R.A.'s, by nearly doubling—to $4,000—the amount all couples can deduct from their taxable income. From now on each spouse could put up to $2,000 a year into his or her I.R.A. and invest the money however they want. And the value of the I.R.A. would not be taxable until they approach retirement.

Some families could save more, others less, but whether it's $400 or $4,000, every dollar saved up to $4,000 each year would be fully deductible from taxable earnings. Let me add that we would also raise, by nearly a full third, the special tax credit for low-income working Americans. That special incentive, a credit to reduce the tax they owe, would be raised from the present $550 to a maximum level of over $700. ...

The power of these incentives would send one simple, straightforward message to an entire nation: America, go for it.

We are reducing tax rates by simplifying the complex system of special provisions that favor some at the expense of others. Restoring confidence in our tax system means restoring, and respecting, the principle of fairness for all. This means curtailing some business deductions now being written off; it means ending several personal deductions, including the state and local tax deduction, which actually provides a special subsidy for high-income individuals, especially in a few high-tax states.

Two-thirds of Americans don't even itemize, so they receive no benefit from the state and local tax deduction. But they're being forced to subsidize the high-tax policies of a handful of states. This is truly taxation without representation.

But other deductions widely used, deductions central to American values, will be maintained. The mortgage interest deduction on your home would be fully retained. And on top of that no less than $5,000 in other interest expenses would still be deductible. The itemized deductions for your charitable contributions will remain intact. The deductions for your medical expenses will be protected and preserved. Deductions for casualty losses would be continued; so too would the current preferential treatment of Social Security. Military allowances will not be taxed. And veteran's disability payments will remain totally exempt from Federal taxation. These American veterans have already paid their dues.

The number of taxpayers who need to itemize would be reduced to one in four. We envision a system where more than half of us would not even have to fill out a return. We call it the return-free system and it would be totally voluntary. If you decided to participate you would automatically receive your refund or a letter explaining any additional tax you owe. Should you disagree with this figure you would be free to fill out your taxes using the regular form. We believe most Americans would go from the long form or the short form to no form. Comparing the distance between the present system and our proposal is like comparing the distance between a Model T and the space shuttle. I should know; I've seen both.

I have spoken of our proposed changes to help individuals and families. Let me explain how we would complement them with proposals for business, proposals to ensure fairness by eliminating or modifying special privileges that are economically unjustifiable, and to strengthen growth by preserving incentives for investment, research and development.

We begin with a basic recognition: The greatest innovations for new jobs, technologies, and economic vigor today come from a small but growing circle of heroes, the small-business people, American entrepreneurs, the men and women of faith, intellect, and daring who take great risks to invest in and invent our future. The majority of the 8 million new jobs created over the last two and a half years were created by small enterprises, enterprises often born in the dream of one human heart.

To young Americans wondering tonight, where will I go, what will I do with my future, I have a suggestion: Why not set out with your friends on the path of adventure and try to start up your own business. Follow in the footsteps of those two college students who launched one of America's great computer firms from the garage behind their house. You, too, can help us unlock the doors to a golden future. You, too, can become leaders in this great new era of progress, the age of the entrepreneur.

My goal is an America bursting with opportunity, an America that celebrates freedom every day by giving every citizen an equal chance, an America that is once again the youngest nation on earth, her spirit unleashed and breaking free. For starters, lowering personal tax rates will give a hefty boost to the nearly 15 million small businesses which are individual proprietorships or partnerships.

To further promote business formation we propose to reduce the maximum corporate tax rate, now 46 percent, to 33 percent. And most small corporations would pay even lower rates. So with lower rates small business can lead the way in creating jobs for all who want to work.

To these incentives we would add another, a reduction in the tax on capital gains. Since the capital gains tax rates were cut in 1978 and 1981, capital raised for new ventures has increased by over one-hundredfold. That old, tired economy wheezing from neglect in the 1970's has been swept aside by a young, powerful locomotive of progress carrying a trainload of new jobs, higher incomes and opportunities for more and more Americans of average means.

So to marshal more venture capital for more new industries, the kind of efforts that begin with a couple of partners setting out to create and develop a new product, we intend to lower the maximum capital gains tax rate to 1712 percent.

Under our new tax proposal, the oil and gas industry will be asked to pick up a larger share of the national tax burden. The old oil depletion allowance will be dropped from the tax code, except for wells producing less than 10 barrels a day. By eliminating this special preference we will go a long way toward insuring that those who earn their wealth in the oil industry will be subject to the same taxes as the rest of us. This is only fair. To continue our drive for energy independence, the current treatment of the costs of exploring and drilling for new oil will be maintained.

We are determined to cut back on special preferences that have too long favored some industries at the expense of others. We would repeal the investment tax credit and reform the depreciation system. Incentives for research and experimentation, however, would be preserved.

There is one group of losers in our tax plan, those individuals and corporations who are not paying their fair share or, for that matter, any share. These abuses cannot be tolerated. From now on they shall pay a minimum tax. The free rides are over.

This, then, is our plan, America's plan: a revolutionary first for fairness in our future; a long-overdue commitment to help working Americans and their families, and a challenge to our entire nation to excel, a challenge to give the U.S.A. the lowest overall marginal rates of taxation of any major industrial democracy. And, yes, a challenge to lift us into a future of unlimited promise, an endless horizon lit by the star of freedom guiding America to supremacy in jobs, productivity, growth and human progress.

The tax system is crucial not just to our personal, material well-being and our nation's economic well being, it must also reflect and support our deeper values and highest aspirations. It must promote opportunity, lift up the weak, strengthen the family and, perhaps most importantly, it must be rooted in that unique American quality, our special commitment to fairness. It must be an expression of both America's eternal frontier spirit, and all the virtues from the heart and soul of a good and decent people—those virtues held high by the Statue of Liberty standing proudly in New York Harbor.

A great national debate now begins. It should not be a partisan debate, for the authors of tax reform come from both parties and all of us want greater fairness, incentives and simplicity in taxation. I am heartened by the cooperation and serious interest already shown by key Congressional leaders, including the chairman of the Senate Finance Committee, Republican Bob Packwood, and the chairman of the House Ways and Means Committee, Democrat Dan Rostenkowski.

The pessimists will give a hundred reasons why this historic proposal won't pass and can't work. Well, they've been opposing progress and predicting disaster for four years now. Yet here we are tonight, a stronger, more united, more confident nation than at any time in recent memory.

Remember, there are no limits to growth and human progress when men and women are free to follow their dreams. The American dream belongs to you; it lives in millions of different hearts; it can be fulfilled in millions of different ways: And with you by our side we're not going to stop moving and shaking this town until that dream is real, for every American, from the sidewalks of Harlem to the mountaintops of Hawaii.

My fellow citizens, let's not let this magnificent moment slip away. Tax relief is in sight. Let's make it a reality. Let's not let prisoners of mediocrity wear us down. Let's not let the special interest raids of the few rob us all of our dreams.

In these last years we've made a fresh start together. In these next four we can begin a new chapter in our history, freedom's finest hour. We can do it. If you help we will do it this year.

RONALD REAGAN: REMARKS AT THE BRANDENBURG GATE IN WEST BERLIN (1987)

Source: *Public Papers of the Presidents of the United States*, June 12, 1987.

Thank you very much. Chancellor Kohl, Governing Mayor Diepgen, ladies and gentlemen: Twenty four years ago, President John F. Kennedy visited Berlin, speaking to the people of this city and the world at the city hall. Well, since then two other presidents have come, each in his turn, to Berlin. And today, I, myself, make my second visit to your city.

We come to Berlin, we American Presidents, because it's our duty to speak, in this place, of freedom. But I must confess, we're drawn here by other things as well: by the feeling of history in this city, more than 500 years older than our own nation; by the beauty of the Grunewald and the Tiergarten; most of all, by your courage and determination. Perhaps the composer, Paul Lincke, understood something about American Presidents.

You see, like so many Presidents before me, I come here today because wherever I go, whatever I do: "Ich hab noch einen koffer in Berlin." [I still have a suitcase in Berlin.]

Our gathering today is being broadcast throughout Western Europe and North America. I understand that it is being seen and heard as well in the East. To those listening throughout Eastern Europe, I extend my warmest greetings and the good will of the American people. To those listening in East Berlin, a special word: Although I cannot be with you, I address my remarks to you just as surely as to those standing here before me. For I join you, as I join your fellow countrymen in the West, in this firm, this unalterable belief: Es gibt nur ein Berlin. [There is only one Berlin.]

Behind me stands a wall that encircles the free sectors of this city, part of a vast system of barriers that divides the entire continent of Europe. From the Baltic, south, those barriers cut across Germany in a gash of barbed wire, concrete, dog runs, and guardtowers. Farther south, there may be no visible, no obvious wall. But there remain armed guards and checkpoints all the same—still a restriction on the right to travel, still an instrument to impose upon ordinary men and women the will of a totalitarian state. Yet it is here in Berlin where the wall emerges most clearly; here, cutting across your city, where the news photo and the television screen have imprinted this brutal division of a continent upon the mind of the world. Standing before the Brandenburg Gate, every man is a German, separated from his fellow men. Every man is a Berliner, forced to look upon a scar....

We hear much from Moscow about a new policy of reform and openness. Some political prisoners have been released. Certain foreign news broadcasts are no longer being jammed. Some economic enterprises have been permitted to operate with greater freedom from state control. Are these the beginnings of profound changes in the Soviet state? Or are they token gestures, intended to raise false hopes in the West, or to strengthen the Soviet system without changing it? We welcome change and openness; for we believe that freedom and security go together, that the advance of human liberty can only strengthen the cause of world peace.

There is one sign the Soviets can make that would be unmistakable, that would advance dramatically the cause of freedom and peace. General Secretary Gorbachev, if you seek peace, if you seek prosperity for the Soviet Union and Eastern Europe, if you seek liberalization: Come here to this gate! Mr. Gorbachev, open this gate! Mr. Gorbachev, tear down this wall!...

In Europe, only one nation and those it controls refuse to join the community of freedom. Yet in this age of redoubled economic growth, of information and innovation, the Soviet Union faces a choice: It must make fundamental changes, or it will become obsolete. Today thus represents a moment of hope.

We in the West stand ready to cooperate with the East to promote true openness, to break down barriers that separate people, to create a safer, freer world.

And surely there is no better place than Berlin, the meeting place of East and West, to make a start. Free people of Berlin: Today, as in the past, the United States stands for the strict observance and full implementation of all parts of the Four Power Agreement of 1971. Let us use this occasion, the 750th anniversary of this city, to usher in a new era, to seek a still fuller, richer life for the Berlin of the future. Together, let us maintain and develop the ties between the Federal Republic and the Western sectors of Berlin, which is permitted by the 1971 agreement.

And I invite Mr. Gorbachev: Let us work to bring the Eastern and Western parts of the city closer together, so that all the inhabitants of all Berlin can enjoy the benefits that come with life in one of the great cities of the world. To open Berlin still further to all Europe, East and West, let us expand the vital air access to this city, finding ways of making commercial air service to Berlin more convenient, more comfortable, and more economical. We look to the day when West Berlin can become one of the chief aviation hubs in all central Europe....

In these four decades, as I have said, you Berliners have built a great city. You've done so in spite of threats—the Soviet attempts to impose the East-mark, the blockade. Today the city thrives in spite of the challenges implicit in the very presence of this wall. What keeps you here? Certainly there's a great deal to be said for your fortitude, for your defiant courage. But I believe there's something deeper, something that involves Berlin's whole look and feel and way of life—not mere sentiment. No one could live long in Berlin without being completely disabused of illusions. Something instead, that has seen the difficulties of life in Berlin but chose to accept them, that continues to build this good and proud city in contrast to a surrounding totalitarian presence that refuses to release human energies or aspirations. Something that speaks with a powerful voice of affirmation, that says yes to this city, yes to the future, yes to freedom. In a word, I would submit that what keeps you in Berlin is love—love both profound and abiding.

Perhaps this gets to the root of the matter, to the most fundamental distinction of all between East and West. The totalitarian world produces backwardness because it does such violence to the spirit, thwarting the human impulse to create, to enjoy, to worship. The totalitarian world finds even symbols of love and of worship an affront. Years ago, before the East Germans began rebuilding their churches, they erected a secular structure: the television tower at Alexander Platz. Virtually ever since, the authorities have been working to correct what they view as the tower's one major flaw, treating the glass sphere at the top with paints and chemicals of every kind. Yet even today when the Sun strikes that sphere—that sphere that towers over all

Berlin—the light makes the sign of the cross. There in Berlin, like the city itself, symbols of love, symbols of worship, cannot be suppressed.

As I looked out a moment ago from the Reichstag, that embodiment of German unity, I noticed words crudely spray-painted upon the wall, perhaps by a young Berliner, "This wall will fall. Beliefs become reality." Yes, across Europe, this wall will fall. For it cannot withstand faith; it cannot withstand truth. The wall cannot withstand freedom.

GEORGE BUSH: OPERATION DESERT STORM (1991)

Source: *Public Papers of the Presidents of the United States*, January 16, 1991.

Just 2 hours ago, allied air forces began an attack on military targets in Iraq and Kuwait. These attacks continue as I speak. Ground forces are not engaged.

This conflict started August 2d when the dictator of Iraq invaded a small and helpless neighbor. Kuwait—a member of the Arab League and a member of the United Nations—was crushed; its people, brutalized. Five months ago, Saddam Hussein started this cruel war against Kuwait. Tonight, the battle has been joined....

As I report to you, air attacks are underway against military targets in Iraq. We are determined to knock out Saddam Hussein's nuclear bomb potential. We will also destroy his chemical weapons facilities. Much of Saddam's artillery and tanks will be destroyed. Our operations are designed to best protect the lives of all the coalition forces by targeting Saddam's vast military arsenal. Initial reports from General Schwarzkopf are that our operations are proceeding according to plan.

Our objectives are clear: Saddam Hussein's forces will leave Kuwait. The legitimate government of Kuwait will be restored to its rightful place, and Kuwait will once again be free. Iraq will eventually comply with all relevant United Nations resolutions, and then, when peace is restored, it is our hope that Iraq will live as a peaceful and cooperative member of the family of nations, thus enhancing the security and stability of the Gulf.

Some may ask: Why act now? Why not wait? The answer is clear: The world could wait no longer. Sanctions, though having some effect, showed no signs of accomplishing their objective. Sanctions were tried for well over 5 months, and we and our allies concluded that sanctions alone would not force Saddam from Kuwait.

While the world waited, Saddam Hussein systematically raped, pillaged, and plundered a tiny nation, no threat to his own. He subjected the people of Kuwait to unspeakable atrocities—and among those maimed and murdered, innocent children.

While the world waited, Saddam sought to add to the chemical weapons arsenal he now possesses, an infinitely more dangerous weapon of mass destruction—a nuclear weapon.

And while the world waited, while the world talked peace and withdrawal, Saddam Hussein dug in and moved massive forces into Kuwait.

While the world waited, while Saddam stalled, more damage was being done to the fragile economies of the Third World, emerging democracies of Eastern Europe, to the entire world, including to our own economy.

The United States, together with the United Nations, exhausted every means at our disposal to bring this crisis to a peaceful end. However, Saddam clearly felt that by stalling and threatening and defying the United Nations, he could weaken the forces arrayed against him.

While the world waited, Saddam Hussein met every overture of peace with open contempt. While the world prayed for peace, Saddam prepared for war.

I had hoped that when the United States Congress, in historic debate, took its resolute action, Saddam would realize he could not prevail and would move out of Kuwait in accord with the United Nations resolutions. He did not do that. Instead, he remained intransigent, certain that time was on his side.

Saddam was warned over and over again to comply with the will of the United Nations: Leave Kuwait, or be driven out. Saddam has arrogantly rejected all warnings. Instead, he tried to make this a dispute between Iraq and the United States of America.

Well, he failed. Tonight, 28 nations—countries from 5 continents, Europe and Asia, Africa, and the Arab League—have forces in the Gulf area standing shoulder to shoulder against Saddam Hussein. These countries had hoped the use of force could be avoided. Regrettably, we now believe that only force will make him leave.

Prior to ordering our forces into battle, I instructed our military commanders to take every necessary step to prevail as quickly as possible, and with the greatest degree of protection possible for American and allied service men and women. I've told the American people before that this will not be another Vietnam, and I repeat this here tonight. Our troops will have the best possible support in the entire world, and they will not be asked to fight with one hand tied behind their back. I'm hopeful that this fighting will not go on for long and that casualties will be held to an absolute minimum.

This is an historic moment. We have in this past year made great progress in ending the long era of conflict and cold war. We have before us the opportunity to forge for ourselves and for future generations a new world order—a world where the rule of law, not the law of the jungle, governs the conduct of nations. When we are successful—and we will be—we have a real chance at this new world order, an order in which a credible United Nations can use its peacekeeping role to fulfill the promise and vision of the U.N.'s founders.

We have no argument with the people of Iraq. Indeed, for the innocents caught in this conflict, I pray for their safety. Our goal is not the conquest of Iraq. It is the liberation

of Kuwait. It is my hope that somehow the Iraqi people can, even now, convince their dictator that he must lay down his arms, leave Kuwait, and let Iraq itself rejoin the family of peace-loving nations.

Thomas Paine wrote many years ago: "These are the times that try men's souls." Those well-known words are so very true today. But even as planes of the multinational forces attack Iraq, I prefer to think of peace, not war. I am convinced not only that we will prevail but that out of the horror of combat will come the recognition that no nation can stand against a world united, no nation will be permitted to brutally assault its neighbor.

No President can easily commit our sons and daughters to war. They are the Nation's finest. Ours is an all-volunteer force, magnificently trained, highly motivated. The troops know why they're there....

And let me say to everyone listening or watching tonight: When the troops we've sent in finish their work, I am determined to bring them home as soon as possible.

Tonight, as our forces fight, they and their families are in our prayers. May God bless each and every one of them, and the coalition forces at our side in the Gulf, and may He continue to bless our nation, the United States of America.

HILLARY CLINTON: ATTEMPTS AT HEALTH CARE REFORM (1993)

Source: *Vital Speeches of the Day*, July 15, 1993.

All of us respond to children. We want to nurture them so they can dream the dreams that free and healthy children should have. This is our primary responsibility as adults. And it is our primary responsibility as a government. We should stand behind families, teachers and others who work with the young, so that we can enable them to meet their own needs by becoming self-sufficient and responsible so that they, in turn, will be able to meet their families and their own children's needs.

When I was growing up, not far from where we are today, this seemed an easier task. There seemed to be more strong families. There seemed to be safer neighborhoods. There seemed to be an outlook for caring and cooperation among adults that stood for and behind children. I remember so well my father saying to me that if you get in trouble at school, you get in trouble at home—no questions asked—because there was this sense among the adult community that all of them, from my child's perspective, were involved in helping their own and others' children.

Much has changed since those days. We have lost some of the hope and optimism of that earlier time. Today, we too often meet our greatest challenges, whether it is the raising of children or reforming the health care system, with a sense that our problems have grown too large and unmanageable. And I don't need to tell you that kind of attitude begins to undermine one's sense of hope, optimism, and even competence.

We know now—and you know better than I—that over the last decade our health care system has been under extraordinary stress. It is one of the many institutions in our society that has experienced such stress. That stress has begun to break down many of the relationships that should stand at the core of the health care system. That breakdown has, in turn, undermined your profession in many ways, changing the nature of and the rewards of practicing medicine.

Most doctors and other health care professionals choose careers in health and medicine because they want to help people. But too often because our system isn't working and we haven't taken full responsibility for fixing it, that motive is clouded by perceptions that doctors aren't the same as they used to be. They're not really doing what they used to do. They don't really care like they once did. . . .

As you know, the President is in the process of finalizing his proposal for health care reform, and I am grateful to speak with you about the process and where it is today and where it is going. I had originally hoped to join you at your meeting in March in Washington, D.C. And I, again, want to apologize for my absence. I very much appreciated Vice President Gore attending for me, and I also appreciated the kind words from your executive officials on behalf of the entire association because of my absence.

My father was ill and I spent several weeks with him in the hospital before he died. During his hospitalization at

St. Vincent's Hospital in Little Rock, Arkansas, I witnessed firsthand the courage and commitment of health care professionals, both directly and indirectly. I will always appreciate the sensitivity and the skills they showed, not just in caring for my father, not just in caring for his family—which, as you know, often needs as much care as the patient, but in caring for the many others whose names I will never know. I know that some of you worry about what the impact of health care reform will be on your profession and on your practice. Let me say from the start, if I read only what the newspapers have said about what we are doing in our plan, I'd probably be a little afraid myself, too, because it is very difficult to get out what is going on in such a complex process.

But the simple fact is this: The President has asked all of us, representatives of the AMA, of every other element of the health care system, as well as the administration, to work on making changes where they are needed, to keeping and improving those things that work, and to preserving and conserving the best parts of our system as we try to improve and change those that are not.

This system is not working as well as it did, or as well as it could—for you, for the private sector, for the public or for the nation. The one area that is so important to be understood on a macronational level is how our failure to deal with the health care system and its financial demands is at the center of our problems financially in Washington. Because we cannot control health care costs and become further and further behind in our efforts to do so, we find our economy, and particularly the federal budget, under increasing pressure.

Just as it would be irresponsible, therefore, to change what is working in the health care system, it is equally irresponsible for us not to fix what we know is no longer working. So let us start with some basic principles that are remarkably like the ones that you have adopted in your statements, and in particularly in Health Assess America. We must guarantee all Americans access to a comprehensive package of benefits, no matter where they work, where they live, or whether they have ever been sick before. If we do not reach universal access, we cannot deal with our other problems.

And that is a point that you understand that you have to help the rest of the country understand—that until we do provide security for every American when it comes to health care, we cannot fix what is wrong with the health care system. Secondly, we do have to control costs. How we do that is one of the great challenges in this system, but one thing we can all agree on is that we have to cut down on the paperwork and reduce the bureaucracy in both the public and private sectors.

We also have to be sure that when we look at costs, we look at it not just from a financial perspective, but also from a human perspective. I remember sitting in the family waiting area of St. Vincent's, talking to a number of my physician friends who stopped by to see how we were doing. And one day, one of my friends told me that, every day, he discharges patients who need medication to stabilize a condition. And at least once a day, he knows there is a patient who will not be able to afford the prescription drugs he has prescribed, with the result that that patient may decide not to fill the prescription when the hospital supply runs out. Or that patient may decide that even though the doctor told him to take three pills a day, he'll just take one a day so it can be stretched further.

And even though St. Vincent's has created a fund to try to help support the needs of patients who cannot afford prescriptions, there's not enough to go around, and so every day there is someone who my friend knows and you know will be back in the hospital because of their inability either to afford the care that is required after they leave, or because they try to cut the corners on it, with the net result that then you and I will pay more for that person who is back in the hospital than we would have if we had taken a sensible approach toward what the real costs in the medical system are. That is why we will try, for example, to include prescription drugs in the comprehensive benefit package for all Americans, including those over 65, through Medicare.

We believe that if we help control costs up front, we will save costs on the back end. That is a principle that runs through our proposal and which each of you knows from firsthand experience is more likely to be efficient in both human and financial terms. We will also preserve what is best in the American health care system today.

We have looked at every other system in the world. We have tried to talk to every expert whom we can find to describe how any other country tries to provide health care. And we have concluded that what is needed is an American solution for an American problem by creating an American health care system that works for America. And two of the principles that underlie that American solution are quality and choice.

We want to ensure and enhance quality. And in order to do that, we're going to have to make some changes, and you know that. We cannot, for example, promise to really achieve universal access if we do not expand our supply of primary care physicians, and we must do that. And you will have to help us determine the best way to go about achieving that goal. . . .

I know that many of you feel that as doctors you are under siege in the current system. And I think there is cause for you to believe that, because we are witnessing a disturbing assault on the doctor/patient relationship. More and more employers are buying into managed care plans that force employees to choose from a specific pool of doctors. And too often, even when a doctor is willing to join a new plan to maintain his relationship with patients, he, or she I should say, is frozen out.

What we want to see is a system in which the employer does not make the choice as to what plan is available for the employee, the employee makes that choice for him or herself. But if we do not change and if the present pattern continues, as it will if we do not act quickly, the art of practicing medicine will be forever transformed. Gone will be the patients treasured privilege to choose his or her doctor. Gone will be the close trusting bonds built up between physicians and patients over the years. Gone will be the security of knowing you can switch jobs and still visit your longtime internist or pediatrician or OB/GYN.

We cannot afford to let that happen. But the erosion of the doctor/patient relationship is only one piece of the problem. Another piece is the role that insurance companies have come to play and the role that the government has come to play along with them in second-guessing medical decisions.

I can understand how many of you must feel. When instead of being trusted for your expertise, you're expected to call an 800 number and get approval for even basic medical procedures from a total stranger.

Frankly, despite my best efforts of the last month to understand every aspect of the health care system, it is and remains a mystery to me how a person sitting at a computer in some air-conditioned office thousands of miles away can make a judgment about what should or shouldn't happen at a patient's bedside in Illinois or Georgia or California. The result of this excessive oversight, this peering over all of your shoulder's is a system of backward incentives. It rewards providers for over prescribing, overtesting, and

generally overdoing. And worse, it punishes doctors who show proper restraint and exercise their professional judgment in ways that those sitting at the computers disagree with. . . .

Now, adding to these difficulties doctors and hospitals and nurses, particularly, are being buried under an avalanche of paperwork. There are mountains of forms, mountains of rules, mountains of hours spent on administrative minutiae instead of caring for the sick. Where, you might ask yourself, did all this bureaucracy come from? And the short answer is, basically, everywhere.

There are forms to ensure appropriate care for the sick and the dying; forms to guard against unnecessary tests and procedures. And from each insurance company and government agency there are forms to record the decisions of doctors and nurses. I remember going to Boston and having a physician bring into a hearing I held there a stack of forms his office is required to fill out. And he held up a Medicare form and next to it he held up an insurance company form. And he said that they are the same forms that ask the same questions, but the insurance company form will not be accepted by the government, and the government form will not be accepted by the insurance company. And the insurance company basically took the government form, changed the title to call it by its own name and required them to have it filled out. That was the tip of the iceberg.

One nurse told me that she entered the profession because she wanted to care for people. She said that if she had wanted to be an accountant, she would have gone to work for an accounting company instead. But she, like many other nurses, and as you know so well, many of the people in your offices now, are required to be book-keepers and accountants, not clinicians, not caregivers.

The latest statistic I have seen is that for every doctor a hospital hires, four new administrative staff are hired. And that in the average doctor's office 80 hours a month is now spent on administration. That is not time spent with a patient recovering from bypass surgery or with a child or teenager who needs a checkup and maybe a little extra TLC time of listening and counseling, and certainly not spent with a patient who has to run in quickly for some kind of an emergency.

Blanketing an entire profession with rules aimed at catching those who are not living up to their professional standards does not improve quality. What we need is a new bargain. We need to remove from the vast majority of physicians these unnecessary, repetitive, often even unread forms and instead substitute for what they were attempting to do—more discipline, more peer review, more careful scrutiny of your colleagues. You are the ones who can tell better than I or better than some bureaucrat whether the quality of medicine that is being practiced in your clinic, in your hospital, is what you would want for yourself and your family.

Let us remove the kind of micromanagement and regulation that has not improved quality and has wasted billions of dollars, but then you have to help us substitute for it, a system that the patients of this country, the public of this country, the decision-makers of this country can have confidence in. Now, I know there are legal obstacles for your being able to do that, and we are looking very closely at how we can remove those so that you can be part of creating a new solution in which everyone, including yourself, can believe in.

In every private conversation I've had with a physician, whether it's someone I knew from St. Vincent's or someone I had just met, I have asked: Tell me, have you ever practiced with or around someone you did not think was living up to your standards? And, invariably, the answer is, well, yes, I remember in my training; well, yes, I remember this emergency room work I used to do; yes, I remember in the hospital when so-and-so had that problem. And I've said, do you believe enough was done by the profession to deal with that problem and to eliminate it? And, invariably, no matter who the doctor is, I've been told, no, I don't.

We want you to have the chance so that in the future you can say, yes, I do believe we've been dealing with our problems. It is not something we should leave for the government, and, certainly, we cannot leave it to the patient. That is the new kind of relationship I think that we need to have.

Finally, if we do not, as I said earlier, provide universal coverage, we cannot do any of what I have just been speaking about because we cannot fulfill our basic commitment, you as physicians, us as a society, that we will care for one another. It should no longer be left to the individual doctor to decide to probe his conscience before determining whether to treat a needy patient. I cannot tell you what it is like for me to travel around to hear stories from doctors and patients that are right on point.

But the most poignant [story] that I tell because it struck me so personally was of the woman with no insurance; working for a company in New Orleans; had worked there for a number of years; tried to take good care of herself; went for the annual physical every year; and I sat with her on a folding chair in the loading dock of her company along with others— all of whom were uninsured; all of whom had worked numbers of years—while she told me at her last physical her doctor had found a lump in her breast and referred her to a surgeon. And the surgeon told her that if she had insurance, he would have biopsied it but because she did not he would watch it.

I don't think you have to be a woman to feel what I felt when the woman told me that story. And I don't think you have to be a physician to feel what you felt when you heard that story. We need to create a system in which no one ever has to say that for good cause or bad, and no one has to hear it ever again.

If we move toward universal coverage, so therefore everyone has a payment stream behind them to be able to come into your office, to be able to come into the hospital, and you will again be able to make decisions that should be made with clinical autonomy, with professional judgment. And we intend to try to give you the time and free you up from other conditions to be able to do that. . . .

Time and again, groups, individuals, and particularly the government, has walked up to trying to reform health care and then walked away.

There's enough blame to go around, every kind of political stripes can be included, but the point now is that we could have done something about health care reform 20 years ago and solved our problems for millions of dollars, and we walked away. Later we could have done something and solved our problems for hundreds of millions, and we walked away.

After 20 years with rate of medical inflation going up and with all of the problems you know so well, it is a harder and more difficult solution that confronts us. But I believe that if one looks at what is at stake, we are not talking just about reforming the way we finance health care, we are not talking just about the particulars of how we deliver health care, we are talking about creating a new sense of community and caring in this country in which we once again value your contribution, value the dignity of all people.

How many more meetings do we need? How many alerts? How many more plans? How many more brochures? The time has come for all of us, not just with respect to health care, but with respect to all of the difficulties our country faces to stop walking away and to start stepping up and taking responsibility. We are supposed to be the ones to lead for our children and our grandchildren. And the way we have behaved in the last years, we have run away and abdicated that responsibility. And at the core of the human experience is responsibility for children to leave them a better world than the one we found.

We can do that with health care. We can make a difference now that will be a legacy for all of you. We can once again give you the confidence to say to your grandsons and granddaughters, yes, do go into medicine; yes, it is the most rewarding profession there is.

So let's celebrate your profession by improving health care. Let's celebrate our children by reforming this system. Let's come together not as liberals or conservatives or Republicans or Democrats, but as Americans who want the best for their country and know we can no longer wait to get about the business of providing it.

Thank you all very much.

CONTRACT WITH AMERICA (1994)

Source: http://www.house.gov

As Republican Members of the House of Representatives and as citizens seeking to join that body we propose not just to change its policies, but even more important, to restore the bonds of trust between the people and their elected representatives. That is why, in this era of official evasion and posturing, we offer instead a detailed agenda for national renewal, a written commitment with no fine print.

This year's election offers the chance, after four decades of one-party control, to bring to the House a new majority that will transform the way Congress works. That historic change would be the end of government that is too big, too intrusive, and too easy with the public's money. It can be the beginning of a Congress that respects the values and shares the faith of the American family. Like Lincoln, our first Republican president, we intend to act "with firmness in the right, as God gives us to see the right." To restore accountability to Congress. To end its cycle of scandal and disgrace. To make us all proud again of the way free people govern themselves.

On the first day of the 104th Congress, the new Republican majority will immediately pass the following major reforms, aimed at restoring the faith and trust of the American people in their government:

- FIRST, require all laws that apply to the rest of the country also apply equally to the Congress;
- SECOND, select a major, independent auditing firm to conduct a comprehensive audit of Congress for waste, fraud or abuse;
- THIRD, cut the number of House committees, and cut committee staff by one-third;
- FOURTH, limit the terms of all committee chairs;
- FIFTH, ban the casting of proxy votes in committee;

- SIXTH, require committee meetings to be open to the public;
- SEVENTH, require a three-fifths majority vote to pass a tax increase;
- EIGHTH, guarantee an honest accounting of our Federal Budget by implementing zero base-line budgeting.

Thereafter, within the first 100 days of the 104th Congress, we shall bring to the House Floor the following bills, each to be given full and open debate, each to be given a clear and fair vote and each to be immediately available this day for public inspection and scrutiny.

1. THE FISCAL RESPONSIBILITY ACT: A balanced budget/tax limitation amendment and a legislative line-item veto to restore fiscal responsibility to an out-of-control Congress, requiring them to live under the same budget constraints as families and businesses.

2. THE TAKING BACK OUR STREETS ACT: An anti-crime package including stronger truth-in-sentencing, "good faith" exclusionary rule exemptions, effective death penalty provisions, and cuts in social spending from this summer's "crime" bill to fund prison construction and additional law enforcement to keep people secure in their neighborhoods and kids safe in their schools.

3. THE PERSONAL RESPONSIBILITY ACT: Discourage illegitimacy and teen pregnancy by prohibiting welfare to minor mothers and denying increased AFDC for additional children while on welfare, cut spending for welfare programs, and enact a tough two-years-and-out provision with work requirements to promote individual responsibility.

4. THE FAMILY REINFORCEMENT ACT: Child support enforcement, tax incentives for adoption, strengthening rights of parents in their children's education, stronger child pornography laws, and an elderly dependent care tax credit to reinforce the central role of families in American society.

5. THE AMERICAN DREAM RESTORATION ACT: A $500 per child tax credit, begin repeal of the marriage tax penalty, and creation of American Dream Savings Accounts to provide middle class tax relief.

6. THE NATIONAL SECURITY RESTORATION ACT: No U.S. troops under U.N. command and restoration of the essential parts of our national security funding to strengthen our national defense and maintain our credibility around the world.

7. THE SENIOR CITIZENS FAIRNESS ACT: Raise the Social Security earnings limit which currently forces seniors out of the work force, repeal the 1993 tax hikes on Social Security benefits and provide tax incentives for private long-term care insurance to let Older Americans keep more of what they have earned over the years.

8. THE JOB CREATION AND WAGE ENHANCEMENT ACT: Small business incentives, capital gains cut and indexation, neutral cost recovery, risk assessment/cost-benefit analysis,

strengthening the Regulatory Flexibility Act and unfunded mandate reform to create jobs and raise worker wages.

9. THE COMMON SENSE LEGAL REFORM ACT: "Loser pays" laws, reasonable limits on punitive damages and reform of product liability laws to stem the endless tide of litigation.

10. THE CITIZEN LEGISLATURE ACT: A first-ever vote on term limits to replace career politicians with citizen legislators.

Further, we will instruct the House Budget Committee to report to the floor and we will work to enact additional budget savings, beyond the budget cuts specifically included in the legislation described above, to ensure that the Federal budget deficit will be less than it would have been without the enactment of these bills.

Respecting the judgment of our fellow citizens as we seek their mandate for reform, we hereby pledge our names to this Contract with America.

KENNETH W. STARR: THE STARR REPORT (1998)

Source: http://www.house.gov

INTRODUCTION

As required by Section 595(c) of Title 28 of the United States Code, the Office of the Independent Counsel ("OIC" or "Office") hereby submits substantial and credible information that President William Jefferson Clinton committed acts that may constitute grounds for an impeachment.

The information reveals that President Clinton:

- lied under oath at a civil deposition while he was a defendant in a sexual harassment lawsuit;
- lied under oath to a grand jury;
- attempted to influence the testimony of a potential witness who had direct knowledge of facts that would reveal the falsity of his deposition testimony;
- attempted to obstruct justice by facilitating a witness's plan to refuse to comply with a subpoena;
- attempted to obstruct justice by encouraging a witness to file an affidavit that the President knew would be false, and then by making use of that false affidavit at his own deposition;
- lied to potential grand jury witnesses, knowing that they would repeat those lies before the grand jury; and
- engaged in a pattern of conduct that was inconsistent with his constitutional duty to faithfully execute the laws.

The evidence shows that these acts, and others, were part of a pattern that began as an effort to prevent the disclosure of information about the President's relationship with a former White House intern and employee, Monica S. Lewinsky, and continued as an effort to prevent the information from being disclosed in an ongoing criminal investigation.

FACTUAL BACKGROUND

In May 1994, Paula Corbin Jones filed a lawsuit against William Jefferson Clinton in the United States District Court for the Eastern District of Arkansas. Ms. Jones alleged that while he was the Governor of Arkansas, President Clinton sexually harassed her during an incident in a Little Rock hotel room. President Clinton denied the allegations. He also challenged the ability of a private litigant to pursue a lawsuit against a sitting President. In May 1997, the Supreme Court unanimously rejected the President's legal argument. The Court concluded that Ms. Jones, "[l]ike every other citizen who properly invokes [the District Court's] jurisdiction...has a right to an orderly disposition of her claims," and that therefore Ms. Jones was entitled to pursue her claims while the President was in office. A few months later, the pre-trial discovery process began. . . .

On January 17, 1998, President Clinton was questioned under oath about his relationships with other women in the workplace, this time at a deposition. Judge Wright presided over the deposition. The President was asked numerous questions about his relationship with Monica Lewinsky, by then a 24-year-old former White House intern, White House employee, and Pentagon employee. Under oath and in the presence of Judge Wright, the President denied that he had engaged in a "sexual affair," a "sexual relationship," or "sexual relations" with Ms. Lewinsky. The President also stated that he had no specific memory of having been alone with Ms. Lewinsky, that he remembered few details of any gifts they might have exchanged, and indicated that no one except his attorneys had kept him informed of Ms. Lewinsky's status as a potential witness in the Jones case.

THE INVESTIGATION

On January 12, 1998, this Office received information that Monica Lewinsky was attempting to influence the testimony of one of the witnesses in the Jones litigation, and that Ms. Lewinsky herself was prepared to provide false information under oath in that lawsuit. The OIC was also informed that Ms. Lewinsky had spoken to the President and the President's close friend Vernon Jordan about being subpoenaed to testify in the Jones suit, and that Vernon Jordan and others were helping her find a job. The allegations with respect to Mr. Jordan and the job search were similar to ones already under review in the ongoing Whitewater investigation.

After gathering preliminary evidence to test the information's reliability, the OIC presented the evidence to Attorney General Janet Reno. Based on her review of the information, the Attorney General determined that a further investigation by the Independent Counsel was required.

On the following day, Attorney General Reno petitioned the Special Division of the United States Court of Appeals for the District of Columbia Circuit, on an expedited basis, to expand the jurisdiction of Independent Counsel Kenneth W. Starr. On January 16, 1998, in response to the Attorney General's request, the Special Division issued an order that provides in pertinent part:

The Independent Counsel shall have jurisdiction and authority to investigate to the maximum extent authorized by the Independent Counsel Reauthorization Act of 1994 whether Monica Lewinsky or others suborned perjury, obstructed justice, intimidated witnesses, or otherwise violated federal law other than a Class B or C misdemeanor or infraction in dealing with witnesses, potential witnesses, attorneys, or others concerning the civil case Jones v. Clinton. . . .

THE SIGNIFICANCE OF THE EVIDENCE OF WRONGDOING

It is not the role of this Office to determine whether the President's actions warrant impeachment by the House and removal by the Senate; those judgments are, of course, constitutionally entrusted to the legislative branch. This Office is authorized, rather, to conduct criminal investigations and to seek criminal prosecutions for matters within its jurisdiction. In carrying out its investigation, however, this Office also has a statutory duty to disclose to Congress information that "may constitute grounds for an impeachment," a task that inevitably requires judgment about the seriousness of the acts revealed by the evidence.

From the beginning, this phase of the OIC's investigation has been criticized as an improper inquiry into the President's personal behavior; indeed, the President himself suggested that specific inquiries into his conduct were part of an effort to "criminalize my private life." The regrettable fact that the investigation has often required witnesses to discuss sensitive personal matters has fueled this perception.

All Americans, including the President, are entitled to enjoy a private family life, free from public or governmental scrutiny. But the privacy concerns raised in this case are subject to limits, three of which we briefly set forth here.

First. The first limit was imposed when the President was sued in federal court for alleged sexual harassment. The evidence in such litigation is often personal. At times, that evidence is highly embarrassing for both plaintiff and defendant. As Judge Wright noted at the President's January 1998 deposition, "I have never had a sexual harassment case where there was not some embarrassment." Nevertheless, Congress and the Supreme Court have concluded that embarrassment-related concerns must give way to the greater interest in allowing aggrieved parties to pursue their claims. Courts have long recognized the difficulties of proving sexual harassment in the workplace, inasmuch as improper or unlawful behavior often takes place in private. To excuse a party who lied or concealed evidence on the ground that the evidence covered only "personal" or "private" behavior would frustrate the goals that Congress and the courts have sought to achieve in enacting and interpreting the Nation's sexual harassment laws. That is particularly true when the conduct that is being concealed—sexual relations in the workplace between a high official and a young subordinate employee—itself conflicts with those goals.

Second. The second limit was imposed when Judge Wright required disclosure of the precise information that is in part the subject of this Referral. A federal judge specifically ordered the President, on more than one occasion, to provide the requested information about relationships with other women, including Monica Lewinsky. The fact that Judge Wright later determined that the evidence would not be admissible at trial, and still later granted judgment in the President's favor, does not change the President's legal duty at the time he testified. Like every litigant, the President was entitled to object to the discovery questions, and to seek guidance from the court if he thought those questions were improper. But having failed to convince the court that his objections were well founded, the President was duty bound to testify truthfully and fully. Perjury and attempts to obstruct the gathering of evidence can never be an acceptable response to a court order, regardless of the eventual course or outcome of the litigation.

The Supreme Court has spoken forcefully about perjury and other forms of obstruction of justice: In this constitutional process of securing a witness'[s]

testimony, perjury simply has no place whatever. Perjured testimony is an obvious and flagrant affront to the basic concepts of judicial proceedings. Effective restraints against this type of egregious offense are therefore imperative. The insidious effects of perjury occur whether the case is civil or criminal. Only a few years ago, the Supreme Court considered a false statement made in a civil administrative proceeding: "False testimony in a formal proceeding is intolerable. We must neither reward nor condone such a 'flagrant affront' to the truth-seeking function of adversary proceedings. . . . Perjury should be severely sanctioned in appropriate cases." Stated more simply, "[p]erjury is an obstruction of justice."

Third. The third limit is unique to the President. "The Presidency is more than an executive responsibility. It is the inspiring symbol of all that is highest in American purpose and ideals." When he took the Oath of Office in 1993 and again in 1997, President Clinton swore that he would "faithfully execute the Office of President." As the head of the Executive Branch, the President has the constitutional duty to "take Care that the Laws be faithfully executed." The President gave his testimony in the Jones case under oath and in the presence of a federal judge, a member of a co-equal branch of government; he then testified before a federal grand jury, a body of citizens who had themselves taken an oath to seek the truth. In view of the enormous trust and responsibility attendant to his high Office, the President has a manifest duty to ensure that his conduct at all times complies with the law of the land.

In sum, perjury and acts that obstruct justice by any citizen—whether in a criminal case, a grand jury investigation, a congressional hearing, a civil trial, or civil discovery—are profoundly serious matters. When such acts are committed by the President of the United States, we believe those acts "may constitute grounds for an impeachment."

GEORGE W. BUSH: DECLARATION OF WAR ON TERRORISM (2001)

Source: "Address to a Joint Session of Congress and the American People," September 20, 2001, http://www.whitehouse.gov

On the morning of September 11, 2001, nineteen Middle Eastern terrorists hijacked four American passenger jets and used the planes as guided missiles to attack symbolic targets on the eastern seaboard of the United States. Two planes slammed into the World Trade Center Towers in New York City, causing both towers to collapse. A third plane crashed into the Pentagon, near Washington, D.C., and a fourth went down in the Pennsylvania countryside when passengers resisted the hijackers. The devastating series of attacks killed some 3,000 Americans, more than had died in the Japanese attack at Pearl Harbor, Hawaii, 60 years previously. In the hours and days following September 11, American and foreign intelligence services identified Osama bin Laden, a Saudi millionaire living in exile in Afghanistan, as the mastermind behind the attacks. On September 20, President George W. Bush spoke before a Joint Session of Congress and outlined America's response to the events of September 11. In the speech, televised live around the nation and the world and excerpted here, Bush announced that "Our war on terror begins with al-Qaeda (the terrorist network associated with bin Laden), but it does not end there. It will not end until every terrorist group of global reach has been found, stopped, and defeated." Less than three weeks after Bush's speech, American forces launched a military campaign in Afghanistan to capture bin Laden and overthrow Afghanistan's Taliban government, which had long aided and abetted bin Laden and other terrorists. Although bin Laden's whereabouts and fate were unknown at the end of 2001, the American campaign in Afghanistan succeeded in toppling the Taliban from power and inflicting major damage on bin Laden's terrorist network. With American support, a new pro-Western government was installed in Afghanistan in early 2002.

Source: "Address to a Joint Session of Congress and the American People," September 20, 2001, http://www.whitehouse.gov

Mr. Speaker, Mr. President Pro Tempore, members of Congress, and fellow Americans: In the normal course of events, Presidents come to this chamber to report on the state of the Union.

Tonight, no such report is needed. It has already been delivered by the American people.

We have seen it in the courage of passengers, who rushed terrorists to save others on the ground—passengers like an exceptional man named Todd Beamer. And would you please help me to welcome his wife, Lisa Beamer, here tonight. We have seen the state of our Union in the endurance of rescuers, working past exhaustion. We have seen the unfurling of flags, the lighting of candles, the giving of blood, the saying of prayers—in English, Hebrew, and Arabic. We have seen the decency of a loving and giving people who have made the grief of strangers their own. My fellow citizens, for the last nine days, the entire world has seen for itself the state of our Union—and it is strong. Tonight we are a country awakened to danger and called to defend freedom. Our grief has turned to anger, and anger to resolution. Whether we bring our enemies to justice, or bring justice to our enemies, justice will be done.

I thank the Congress for its leadership at such an important time. All of America was touched on the evening of the tragedy to see Republicans and Democrats joined together on the steps of this Capitol, singing "God Bless America." And you did more than sing; you acted, by delivering $40 billion to rebuild our communities and meet the needs of our military. Speaker Hastert, Minority Leader Gephardt, Majority Leader Daschle and Senator Lott, I thank you for your friendship, for your leadership and for your service to our country.

And on behalf of the American people, I thank the world for its outpouring of support. America will never forget the sounds of our National Anthem playing at Buckingham Palace, on the streets of Paris, and at Berlin's Brandenburg Gate. We will not forget South Korean children gathering to pray outside our embassy in Seoul, or the prayers of sympathy offered at a mosque in Cairo. We will not forget moments of silence and days of mourning in Australia and Africa and Latin America. Nor will we forget the citizens of 80 other nations who died with our own: dozens of Pakistanis; more than 130 Israelis; more than 250 citizens of India; men and women from El Salvador, Iran, Mexico and Japan; and hundreds of British citizens. America has no truer friend than Great Britain. Once again, we are joined together in a great cause—so honored the British Prime Minister has crossed an ocean to show his unity of purpose with America. Thank you for coming, friend.

On September the 11th, enemies of freedom committed an act of war against our country. Americans have known wars—but for the past 136 years, they have been wars on foreign soil, except for one Sunday in 1941. Americans have known the casualties of war—but not at the center of a great city on a peaceful morning. Americans have known surprise attacks—but never before on thousands of civilians. All of this was brought upon us in a single day—and night fell on a different world, a world where freedom itself is under attack.

Americans have many questions tonight. Americans are asking: Who attacked our country? The evidence we have gathered all points to a collection of loosely affiliated terrorist organizations known as al Qaeda. They are the same murderers indicted for bombing American embassies in Tanzania and Kenya, and responsible for bombing the USS Cole. Al Qaeda is to terror what the mafia is to crime. But its goal is not making money; its goal is remaking the world—and imposing its radical beliefs on people everywhere. The terrorists practice a fringe form of Islamic extremism that has been rejected by Muslim scholars and the vast majority of Muslim clerics—a fringe movement that perverts the peaceful teachings of Islam. The terrorists' directive commands them to kill Christians and Jews, to kill all Americans, and make no distinction among military and civilians, including women and children.

This group and its leader—a person named Osama bin Laden—are linked to many other organizations in different countries, including the Egyptian Islamic Jihad and the Islamic Movement of Uzbekistan. There are thousands of these terrorists in more than 60 countries. They are recruited from their own nations and neighborhoods and brought to camps in places like Afghanistan, where they are trained in the tactics of terror. They are sent back to their homes or sent to hide in countries around the world to plot evil and destruction. The leadership of al Qaeda has great influence in Afghanistan and supports the Taliban regime in controlling most of that country. In Afghanistan, we see al Qaeda's vision for the world.

Afghanistan's people have been brutalized—many are starving and many have fled. Women are not allowed to attend school. You can be jailed for owning a television. Religion can be practiced only as their leaders dictate. A man can be jailed in Afghanistan if his beard is not long enough. The United States respects the people of Afghanistan—after all, we are currently its largest source of humanitarian aid—but we condemn the Taliban regime. It is not only repressing its own people, it is threatening people everywhere by sponsoring and sheltering and supplying terrorists. By aiding and abetting murder, the Taliban regime is committing murder.

And tonight, the United States of America makes the following demands on the Taliban: Deliver to United States authorities all the leaders of al Qaeda who hide in your land. Release all foreign nationals, including American citizens, you have unjustly imprisoned. Protect foreign journalists, diplomats and aid workers in your country. Close immediately and permanently every terrorist training camp in Afghanistan, and hand over every terrorist, and every person in their support structure, to appropriate authorities. Give the United States full access to terrorist training camps, so we can make sure they are no longer operating. These demands are not open to negotiation or discussion. The Taliban must act, and act immediately. They will hand over the terrorists, or they will share in their fate.

I also want to speak tonight directly to Muslims throughout the world. We respect your faith. It's practiced freely by many millions of Americans, and by millions more in countries that America counts as friends. Its teachings are good and peaceful, and those who commit evil in the name of Allah blaspheme the name of Allah. The terrorists are traitors to their own faith, trying, in effect, to hijack Islam itself. The enemy of America is not our many Muslim friends; it is not our many Arab friends. Our enemy is a radical network of terrorists, and every government that supports them. Our war on terror begins with al Qaeda, but it does not end there. It will not end until every terrorist group of global reach has been found, stopped and defeated.

Americans are asking, why do they hate us? They hate what we see right here in this chamber—a democratically elected government. Their leaders are self-appointed. They hate our freedoms— our freedom of religion, our freedom of speech, our freedom to vote and assemble and disagree with each other. They want to overthrow existing governments in many Muslim countries, such as Egypt, Saudi Arabia, and Jordan. They want to drive Israel out of the Middle East. They want to drive Christians and Jews out of vast regions of Asia and Africa. These terrorists kill not merely to end lives, but to disrupt and end a way of life. With every atrocity, they hope that America grows fearful, retreating from the world and forsaking our friends. They stand against us, because we stand in their way.

We are not deceived by their pretenses to piety. We have seen their kind before. They are the heirs of all the murderous ideologies of the 20th century. By sacrificing human life to serve their radical visions—by abandoning every value except the will to power—they follow in the path of fascism, and Nazism, and totalitarianism. And they will follow that path all the way, to where it ends: in history's unmarked grave of discarded lies.

Americans are asking: How will we fight and win this war? We will direct every resource at our command—every means of diplomacy, every tool of intelligence, every instrument of law enforcement, every financial influence, and every necessary weapon of war—to the disruption and to the defeat of the global terror network. . . . Our response involves far more than instant retaliation and isolated strikes. Americans should not expect one battle, but a lengthy campaign, unlike any other we have ever seen. It may include dramatic strikes, visible on TV, and covert operations, secret even in success. We will starve terrorists of funding, turn them one against another, drive them from place to place, until there is no refuge or no rest. And we will pursue nations that provide aid or safe haven to terrorism. Every nation, in every region, now has a decision to make. Either you are with us, or you are with the terrorists.

From this day forward, any nation that continues to harbor or support terrorism will be regarded by the United States as a hostile regime.

Our nation has been put on notice: We are not immune from attack. We will take defensive measures against terrorism to protect Americans. Today, dozens of federal departments and agencies, as well as state and local governments, have responsibilities affecting homeland security. These efforts must be coordinated at the highest level. So tonight I announce the creation of a Cabinet-level position reporting directly to me—the Office of Homeland Security. And tonight I also announce a distinguished American to lead this effort, to strengthen American security: a military veteran, an effective governor, a true patriot, a trusted friend— Pennsylvania's Tom Ridge. He will lead, oversee and coordinate a comprehensive national strategy to safeguard our country against terrorism, and respond to any attacks that may come.

These measures are essential. But the only way to defeat terrorism as a threat to our way of life is to stop it, eliminate it, and destroy it where it grows. Many will be involved in this effort, from FBI agents to intelligence operatives to the reservists we have called to active duty. All deserve our thanks, and all have our prayers. And tonight, a few miles from the damaged Pentagon, I have a message for our military: Be ready. I've called the Armed Forces to alert, and there is a reason. The hour is coming when America will act, and you will make us proud.

This is not, however, just America's fight. And what is at stake is not just America's freedom. This is the world's fight. This is civilization's fight. This is the fight of all who believe in progress and pluralism, tolerance and freedom. We ask every nation to join us. We will ask, and we will need, the help of police forces, intelligence services, and banking systems around the world. The United States is grateful that many nations and many international organizations have already responded—with sympathy and with support. Nations from Latin America, to Asia, to Africa, to Europe, to the Islamic world. Perhaps the NATO Charter reflects best the attitude of the world: An attack on one is an attack on all. . . .

Americans are asking: What is expected of us? I ask you to live your lives, and hug your children. I know many citizens have fears tonight, and I ask you to be calm and resolute, even in the face of a continuing threat.

I ask you to uphold the values of America, and remember why so many have come here. We are in a fight for our principles, and our first responsibility is to live by them. No one should be singled out for unfair treatment or unkind words because of their ethnic background or religious faith. . . .

We will come together to give law enforcement the additional tools it needs to track down terror here at home. We will come together to strengthen our intelligence capabilities to know the plans of terrorists before they act, and find them before they strike. We will come together to take active steps that strengthen America's economy, and put our people back to work. Tonight we welcome two leaders who embody the extraordinary spirit of all New Yorkers: Governor George Pataki, and Mayor Rudolph Giuliani. As a symbol of America's resolve, my administration will work with Congress, and these two leaders, to show the world that we will rebuild New York City.

After all that has just passed—all the lives taken, and all the possibilities and hopes that died with them—it is natural to wonder if America's future is one of fear. Some speak of an age of terror. I know there are struggles ahead, and dangers to face. But this country will define our times, not be defined by them. As long as the United States of America is determined and strong, this will not be an age of terror; this will be an age of liberty, here and across the world.

Great harm has been done to us. We have suffered great loss. And in our grief and anger we have found our mission and our moment. Freedom and fear are at war. The advance of human freedom—the great achievement of our time, and the great hope of every time—now depends on us. Our nation—this generation—will lift a dark threat of violence from our people and our future. We will rally the world to this cause by our efforts, by our courage. We will not tire, we will not falter, and we will not fail.

It is my hope that in the months and years ahead, life will return almost to normal. We'll go back to our lives and routines, and that is good. Even grief recedes with time and grace. But our resolve must not pass. Each of us will remember what happened that day, and to whom it happened. We'll remember the moment the news came—where we were and what we were doing. Some will remember an image of a fire, or a story of rescue. Some will carry memories of a face and a voice gone forever.

And I will carry this: It is the police shield of a man named George Howard, who died at the World Trade Center trying to save others. It was given to me by his mom, Arlene, as a proud memorial to her son. This is my reminder of lives that ended, and a task that does not end.

I will not forget this wound to our country or those who inflicted it. I will not yield; I will not rest; I will not relent in waging this struggle for freedom and security for the American people. The course of this conflict is not known, yet its outcome is certain. Freedom and fear, justice and cruelty, have always been at war, and we know that God is not neutral between them.

Fellow citizens, we'll meet violence with patient justice—assured of the rightness of our cause, and confident of the victories to come. In all that lies before us, may God grant us wisdom, and may He watch over the United States of America.

JOHN P. MURTHA: WAR IN IRAQ (2005)

Source: Address delivered from Washington, D.C., Nov. 17, 2005, http://

www.house.gov/apps/list/press/pa12_murtha/pr051117iraq.html

The war in Iraq is not going as advertised. It is a flawed policy wrapped in illusion. The American public is way ahead of us. The United States and coalition troops have done all they can in Iraq, but it is time for a change in direction. Our military is suffering. The future of our country is at risk. We can not continue on the present course. It is evident that continued military action in Iraq is not in the best interest of the United States of America, the Iraqi people or the Persian Gulf Region.

General Casey said in a September 2005 Hearing, "the perception of occupation in Iraq is a major driving force behind the insurgency." General Abizaid said on the same date, "Reducing the size and visibility of the coalition forces in Iraq is a part of our counterinsurgency strategy."

For 2 years I have been concerned about the U.S. policy and the plan in Iraq. I have addressed my concerns with the Administration and the Pentagon and have spoken out in public about my concerns. The main reason for going to war has been discredited. A few days before the start of the war I was in Kuwait—the military drew a red line around Baghdad and said when U.S. forces cross that line they will be attacked by the Iraqis with Weapons of Mass Destruction—but the US forces said they were prepared. They had well trained forces with the appropriate protective gear.

We spend more money on Intelligence than all the countries in the world together, and more on Intelligence than most countries GDP. But the intelligence concerning Iraq was wrong. It is not a world intelligence failure. It is a U.S. intelligence failure and the way that intelligence was misused.

I have been visiting our wounded troops at Bethesda and Walter Reed hospitals almost every week since the beginning of the War. And what demoralizes them is going to war with not enough troops and equipment to make the transition to peace; the devastation caused by IEDs; being deployed to Iraq when their homes have been ravaged by hurricanes; being on their second or third deployment and leaving their families behind without a network of support.

The threat posed by terrorism is real, but we have other threats that cannot be ignored. We must be prepared to face all threats. The future of our military is at risk. Our military and their families are stretched thin. Many say that the Army is broken. Some of our troops are on their third deployment. Recruitment is down, even as our military has lowered its standards. Defense budgets are being cut. Personnel costs are skyrocketing, particularly in health care. Choices will have to be made. We can not allow promises we have made to our military families in terms of service benefits, in terms of their health care, to be negotiated away. Procurement programs that ensure our military dominance cannot be negotiated away. We must be prepared. The war in Iraq has caused huge shortfalls at our bases in the U.S.

Much of our ground equipment is worn out and in need of either serious overhaul or replacement. George Washington said, "To be prepared for war is one of the most effective means of preserving peace." We must rebuild our Army. Our deficit is growing out of control. The Director of the Congressional Budget Office recently admitted to being "terrified" about the budget deficit in the coming decades. This is the first prolonged war we have fought with three years of tax cuts, without full mobilization of American industry and without a draft. The burden of this war has not been shared equally; the military and their families are shouldering this burden.

Our military has been fighting a war in Iraq for over two and a half years. Our military has accomplished its mission and done its duty. Our military captured Saddam Hussein, and captured or killed his closest associates. But the war continues to intensify. Deaths and injuries are growing, with over 2,079 confirmed American deaths. Over 15,500 have been seriously injured and it is estimated that over 50,000 will suffer from battle fatigue. There have been reports of at least 30,000 Iraqi civilian deaths.

I just recently visited Anbar Province Iraq in order to assess the conditions on the ground. Last May 2005, as part of the Emergency Supplemental Spending Bill, the House included the Moran Amendment, which was accepted in Conference, and which required the Secretary of Defense to submit quarterly reports to Congress in order to more accurately measure stability and security in Iraq. We have now received two reports. I am disturbed by the findings in key indicator areas. Oil production and energy production are below pre-war levels. Our reconstruction efforts have been crippled by the security situation. Only $9 billion of the $18 billion appropriated for reconstruction has been spent. Unemployment remains at about 60 percent. Clean water is scarce. Only $500 million of the $2.2 billion appropriated for water projects has been spent. And most importantly, insurgent incidents have increased from about 150 per week to over 700 in the last year. Instead of attacks going down over time and with the addition of more troops, attacks have grown dramatically. Since the revelations at Abu Ghraib, American casualties have doubled. An annual State Department report in 2004 indicated a sharp increase in global terrorism.

I said over a year ago, and now the military and the Administration agrees, Iraq can not be won "militarily." I said two years ago, the key to progress in Iraq is to Iraqitize, Internationalize and Energize. I believe the same today. But I have concluded that the presence of U.S. troops in Iraq is impeding this progress.

Our troops have become the primary target of the insurgency. They are united against U.S. forces and we have become a catalyst for violence. U.S. troops are the common enemy of the Sunnis, Saddamists and foreign jihadists. I believe with a U.S. troop redeployment, the Iraqi security forces will be incentivized to take control.

A poll recently conducted shows that over 80% of Iraqis are strongly opposed to the presence of coalition troops, and about 45% of the Iraqi population believe attacks against American troops are justified. I believe we need to turn Iraq over to the Iraqis.

I believe before the Iraqi elections, scheduled for mid December, the Iraqi people and the emerging government must be put on notice that the United States will immediately redeploy. All of Iraq must know that Iraq is free. Free from United States occupation. I believe this will send a signal to the Sunnis to join the political process for the good of a "free" Iraq.

My plan calls:

- To immediately redeploy U.S. troops consistent with the safety of U.S. forces.
- To create a quick reaction force in the region.
- To create an over-the-horizon presence of Marines.
- To diplomatically pursue security and stability in Iraq.

This war needs to be personalized. As I said before I have visited with the severely wounded of this war. They are suffering.

Because we in Congress are charged with sending our sons and daughters into battle, it is our responsibility, our OBLIGATION to speak out for them. That's why I am speaking out.

Our military has done everything that has been asked of them, the U.S. can not accomplish anything further in Iraq militarily. IT IS TIME TO BRING THEM HOME.

BARACK OBAMA: INAUGURAL ADDRESS (2009)

Source: Inaugural Address, delivered by U.S. President Barack Obama, Washington, D.C., Jan. 20, 2009, http://www.whitehouse.gov

My fellow citizens:

I stand here today humbled by the task before us, grateful for the trust you have bestowed, mindful of the sacrifices borne by our ancestors. I thank President Bush for his service to our nation, as well as [for] the generosity and cooperation he has shown throughout this transition.

Forty-four Americans have now taken the presidential oath. The words have been spoken during rising tides of prosperity and the still waters of peace. Yet, every so often the oath is taken amidst gathering clouds and raging storms. At these moments, America has carried on not simply because of the skill or vision of those in high office, but because we the people have remained faithful to the ideals of our forebears, and true to our founding documents.

So it has been. So it must be with this generation of Americans.

That we are in the midst of crisis is now well understood. Our nation is at war, against a far-reaching network of violence and hatred. Our economy is badly weakened, a consequence of greed and irresponsibility on the part of some, but also our collective failure to make hard choices and prepare the nation for a new age. Homes have been lost; jobs shed; businesses shuttered. Our health care is too costly; our schools fail too many; and each day brings further evidence that the ways we use energy strengthen our adversaries and threaten our planet.

These are the indicators of crisis, subject to data and statistics. Less measurable but no less profound is a sapping of confidence across our land—a nagging fear that America's decline is inevitable, that the next generation must lower its sights.

Today I say to you that the challenges we face are real. They are serious and they are many. They will not be met easily or in a short span of time. But know this, America—they will be met.

On this day, we gather because we have chosen hope over fear, unity of purpose over conflict and discord.

On this day, we come to proclaim an end to the petty grievances and false promises, the recriminations and worn-out dogmas, that for far too long have strangled our politics.

We remain a young nation, but in the words of Scripture, the time has come to set aside childish things. The time has come to reaffirm our enduring spirit; to choose our better history; to carry forward that precious gift, that noble idea, passed on from generation to generation: the God-given promise that all are equal, all are free, and all deserve a chance to pursue their full measure of happiness.

In reaffirming the greatness of our nation, we understand that greatness is never a given. It must be earned. Our journey has never been one of shortcuts or settling for less. It has not been the path for the fainthearted—for those who prefer leisure over work, or seek only the pleasures of riches and fame. Rather, it has been the risk takers, the doers, the makers of things—some celebrated but more often men and women obscure in their labor, who have carried us up the long, rugged path towards prosperity and freedom.

For us, they packed up their few worldly possessions and traveled across oceans in search of a new life.

For us, they toiled in sweatshops and settled the West; endured the lash of the whip and plowed the hard earth.

For us, they fought and died, in places like Concord and Gettysburg; Normandy and Khe Sanh.

Time and again these men and women struggled and sacrificed and worked till their hands were raw so that we might live a better life. They saw America as bigger than the sum of our individual ambitions; greater than all the differences of birth or wealth or faction.

This is the journey we continue today. We remain the most prosperous, powerful nation on Earth. Our workers are no less productive than when this crisis began. Our minds are no less inventive, our goods and services no less needed than they were last week or last month or last year. Our capacity remains undiminished. But our time of standing pat, of protecting narrow interests and putting off unpleasant decisions—that time has surely passed. Starting today, we must pick ourselves up, dust ourselves off, and begin again the work of remaking America.

For everywhere we look, there is work to be done. The state of our economy calls for action, bold and swift, and we will act—not only to create new jobs, but to lay a new foundation for growth. We will build the roads and bridges, the electric grids and digital lines that feed our commerce and bind us together. We will restore science to its rightful place, and wield technology's wonders to raise health care's quality and lower its cost. We will harness the sun and the winds and the soil to fuel our cars and run our factories. And we will transform our schools and colleges and universities to meet the demands of a new age. All this we can do. All this we will do.

Now, there are some who question the scale of our ambitions—who suggest that our system cannot tolerate too many big plans. Their memories are short. For they have forgotten what this country has already done; what free men and women can achieve when imagination is joined to common purpose, and necessity to courage.

What the cynics fail to understand is that the ground has shifted beneath them—that the stale political arguments that have consumed us for so long no longer apply. The question we ask today is not whether our government is too big or too small, but whether it works—whether it helps families find jobs at a decent wage, care they can afford, a retirement that is dignified. Where the answer is yes, we intend to move forward. Where the answer is no, programs will end. And those of us who manage the public's dollars will be held to account—to spend wisely, reform bad habits, and do our business in the light of day—because only then can we restore the vital trust between a people and their government.

Nor is the question before us whether the market is a force for good or ill. Its power to generate wealth and expand freedom is unmatched, but this crisis has reminded us that without a watchful eye, the market can spin out of control. The nation cannot prosper long when it favors only the prosperous. The success of our economy has always depended not just on the size of our gross domestic product, but on the reach of our prosperity; on the ability to extend opportunity to every willing heart—not out of charity, but because it is the surest route to our common good.

As for our common defense, we reject as false the choice between our safety and our ideals. Our Founding Fathers, faced with perils we can scarcely imagine, drafted a charter to assure the rule of law and the rights of man, a charter expanded by the blood of generations. Those ideals still light the world, and we will not give them up for expedience's sake. And so to all the other peoples and governments who are watching today, from the grandest capitals to the small village where my father was born: know that America is a friend of each nation and every man, woman, and child who seeks a future of peace and dignity, and we are ready to lead once more.

Recall that earlier generations faced down fascism and communism not just with missiles and tanks, but with the [sic] sturdy alliances and enduring convictions. They understood that our power alone cannot protect us, nor does it entitle us to do as we please. Instead, they knew that our power grows through its prudent use; our security emanates from the justness of our cause, the force of our example, the tempering qualities of humility and restraint.

We are the keepers of this legacy. Guided by these principles once more, we can meet those new threats that demand even greater effort— even greater cooperation and understanding between nations. We will begin to responsibly leave Iraq to its people, and forge a hard-earned peace in Afghanistan. With old friends and former foes, we'll work tirelessly to lessen the nuclear threat, and roll back the specter of a warming planet. We will not apologize for our way of life, nor will we waver in its defense, and for those who seek to advance their aims by inducing terror and slaughtering innocents, we say to you now that

our spirit is stronger and cannot be broken; you cannot outlast us, and we will defeat you.

For we know that our patchwork heritage is a strength, not a weakness. We are a nation of Christians and Muslims, Jews and Hindus— and nonbelievers. We are shaped by every language and culture, drawn from every end of this Earth; and because we have tasted the bitter swill of civil war and segregation, and emerged from that dark chapter stronger and more united, we cannot help but believe that the old hatreds shall someday pass; that the lines of tribe shall soon dissolve; that as the world grows smaller, our common humanity shall reveal itself; and that America must play its role in ushering in a new era of peace.

To the Muslim world, we seek a new way forward, based on mutual interest and mutual respect. To those leaders around the globe who seek to sow conflict, or blame their society's ills on the West—know that your people will judge you on what you can build, not what you destroy. To those who cling to power through corruption and deceit and the silencing of dissent, know that you are on the wrong side of history; but that we will extend a hand if you are willing to unclench your fist.

To the people of poor nations, we pledge to work alongside you to make your farms flourish and let clean waters flow; to nourish starved bodies and feed hungry minds. And to those nations like ours that enjoy relative plenty, we say we can no longer afford indifference to the suffering outside our borders; nor can we consume the world's resources without regard to effect. For the world has changed, and we must change with it.

As we consider the road that unfolds before us, we remember with humble gratitude those brave Americans who, at this very hour, patrol far-off deserts and distant mountains. They have something to tell us, just as the fallen heroes who lie in Arlington whisper through the ages. We honor them not only because they are guardians of our liberty, but because they embody the spirit of service; a willingness to find meaning in something greater than themselves. And yet, at this moment—a moment that will define a generation—it is precisely this spirit that must inhabit us all.

For as much as government can do and must do, it is ultimately the faith and determination of the American people upon which this nation relies. It is the kindness to take in a stranger when the levees break, the selflessness of workers who would rather cut their hours than see a friend lose their job which sees us through our darkest hours. It is the firefighter's courage to storm a stairway filled with smoke, but also a parent's willingness to nurture a child, that finally decides our fate.

Our challenges may be new. The instruments with which we meet them may be new. But those values upon which our success depends— honesty and hard work, courage and fair play, tolerance and curiosity, loyalty and patriotism— these things are old. These things are true. They have been the quiet force of progress throughout our history. What is demanded then is a return to these truths. What is required of us now is a new era of responsibility—a recognition, on the part of every American, that we have duties to ourselves, our nation, and the world, duties that we do not grudgingly accept but rather seize gladly, firm in the knowledge that there is nothing so satisfying to the spirit, so defining of our character, than giving our all to a difficult task.

This is the price and the promise of citizenship.

This is the source of our confidence— the knowledge that God calls on us to shape an uncertain destiny.

This is the meaning of our liberty and our creed—why men and women and children of every race and every faith can join in celebration across this magnificent Mall, and why a man whose father less than sixty years ago might not have been served in a local restaurant can now stand before you to take a most sacred oath.

So let us mark this day with remembrance, of who we are and how far we have traveled. In the year of America's birth, in the coldest of months, a small band of patriots huddled by dying campfires on the shores of an icy river. The capital was abandoned. The enemy was advancing. The snow was stained with blood. At the moment when the outcome of our revolution was most in doubt, the father of our nation ordered these words be read to the people:

"Let it be told to the future world... that in the depth of winter, when nothing but hope and virtue could survive...that the city and the country, alarmed at one common danger, came forth to meet (it)."

America: in the face of our common dangers, in this winter of our hardship, let us remember these timeless words. With hope and virtue, let us brave once more the icy currents, and endure what storms may come. Let it be said by our children's children that when we were tested we refused to let this journey end, that we did not turn back nor did we falter; and with eyes fixed on the horizon and God's grace upon us, we carried forth that great gift of freedom and delivered it safely to future generations.

Thank you. God bless you. And God bless the United States of America.

accord A formal reaching of agreement.

adjustable rate mortgage A mortgage having an interest rate which is usually initially lower than that of a mortgage with a fixed rate but is adjusted periodically according to the cost of funds to the lender.

amnesty The act of an authority (as a government) by which pardon is granted to a large group of individuals.

campaign finance Funds that are contributed to a political campaign to promote a candidate, group, or cause.

Cold War The ideological conflict between the United States and the Soviet Union during the second half of the 20th century carried on by methods short of sustained overt military action.

containment The policy, process, or result of preventing the expansion of a hostile power or ideology.

counterculture A culture with values and mores that run counter to those of established society.

détente Period of the easing of Cold War tensions between the United States and the Soviet Union from 1967 to 1979 and the policy promoting this.

draft Compulsory enrollment for service in a country's armed forces; conscription.

embargo A legal prohibition on commerce.

filibuster The parliamentary tactic used in the United States Senate by a minority of the senators—sometimes even a single senator—to delay or prevent parliamentary action by talking so long that the majority either grants concessions or withdraws the bill.

foreclosure Legal proceeding by which a mortgagor's rights to a mortgaged property may be extinguished if the mortgagor (borrower) fails to live up to the obligations agreed to in the mortgage.

glasnost Soviet policy permitting open discussion of political and social issues and freer dissemination of news and information that was instituted by Mikhail Gorbachev in the late 1980s.

impeach To charge a public official before a competent tribunal with misconduct in office.

inflation A continuing rise in the general price level usually attributed to an increase in the volume of money and credit relative to available goods and services.

lame-duck Of or pertaining to an elected official or group continuing to hold political office during the period between the election and the inauguration of a successor.

malaise A vague sense of mental or moral ill-being.

military-industrial complex An informal alliance of the military and related government departments with defense industries that is held to influence government policy.

pardon A release from the legal penalties of an offense.

perestroika Program instituted in the Soviet Union by Mikhail Gorbachev in the mid-1980s to restructure Soviet economic and political policy.

perjury The voluntary violation of an oath or vow either by swearing to what is untrue or by omission to do what has been promised under oath.

recession A downward trend in the business cycle characterized by a decline in production and employment, which in turn causes the incomes and spending of households to decline.

stagflation Persistent inflation combined with stagnant consumer demand and relatively high unemployment.

subprime mortgage A mortgage having an interest rate that is higher than a prime rate and is extended especially to low-income borrowers.

supply-side economics Theory that focuses on influencing the supply of labour and goods, using tax cuts to encourage earnings, savings, and investments, thereby expanding economic activity.

Supreme Soviet The highest legislative body of the former Soviet Union.

voucher A coupon issued by government to a parent or guardian to be used to fund a child's education in either a public or private school.

General discussions of U.S. history since 1945 include Michael Schaller, Virginia Scharff, and Robert D. Schulzinger, *Present Tense: The United States Since 1945*, 2nd ed. (1996); Paul S. Boyer, *Promises to Keep: The United States Since World War II* (2005); and William H. Chafe, Harvard Sitkoff, and Beth Bailey (eds.), *A History of Our Time: Readings on Postwar America*, 7th ed. (2008). A critical perspective is Melvyn Dubofsky and Athan Theoharis, *Imperial Democracy: The United States Since 1945*, 2nd ed. (1988). An overview of the early postwar years is John Patrick Diggins, *The Proud Decades: America in War and in Peace, 1941–1960* (1988). Sean Wilentz, *The Age of Reagan: A History, 1974–2008* (2008); and James Gilbert, *Another Chance: Postwar America, 1945–1985*, 2nd ed., edited by R. Jackson Wilson (1986), are useful surveys. The McCarthy era is considered in Ellen Schrecker, *The Age of McCarthyism: A Brief History with Documents*, 2nd. ed. (2002). David Halberstam, *The Fifties* (1993), is comprehensive and engaging. Coverage of the Cold War is provided by Ralph B. Levering, *The Cold War, 1945–1987*, 2nd ed. (1988); John Lewis Gaddis, *Strategies of Containment* (1982), and The Long Peace: Inquiries into the History of the Cold War (1988); and Alice L. George, *Awaiting Armageddon: How Americans Faced the Cuban Missile Crisis* (2003). Burton I. Kaufman, *The Korean War* (1986), is a reliable overview. Taylor Branch, *Parting the Waters: America in the King Years, 1954–63* (1988), *Pillar of Fire: America in the King Years, 1963–65* (1998), and *At Canaan's Edge: America in the King Years, 1965–68* (2006), offer fascinating portraits of Martin Luther King, Jr., and other key figures in the American civil rights movement. Joanne Meyerowitz (ed.), *Not June Cleaver: Women and Gender in Postwar America, 1945–1960* (1994); and David Carter, *Stonewall: The Riots That Sparked the Gay Revolution* (2004), are very informative. Christian Appy, *Patriots: The Vietnam War Remembered from All Sides* (2003); and George C. Herring, *America's Longest War: The United States and Vietnam, 1950–1975*, 2nd ed. (1986), examine the Vietnam War. William L. O'Neill, *Coming Apart: An Informal History of America in the 1960's*, with a new introduction from the author (2005), is a study of the quality of American life under the impact of changing social values. The era is also studied in Todd Gitlin, *The Sixties: Years of Hope, Days of Rage*, rev. ed. (1993). Frederick F. Siegel, *Troubled Journey: From Pearl Harbor to Ronald Reagan* (1984), analyzes the relationship between American social and cultural life and government policy. Lyndon Johnson is the subject of Robert Dallek, *Lyndon Johnson and His Times*, 2 vol. (1991–98). Rick Perlstein, *Nixonland: The Rise of a President and the Fracturing of America* (2008), considers Richard Nixon's place in American history.

INDEX